CHINA
SINGS TO ME

CHINA
SINGS TO ME

A JOURNEY INTO THE
MIDDLE KINGDOM AND MYSELF

For Deedee —

Enjoy the journey my

Vassar friend.

Best,

Andrew August 2018

ANDREW SINGER

STATION
SQUARE
≡ MEDIA ≡
NEW YORK, NEW YORK

CHINA SINGS TO ME: A Journey into the Middle Kingdom and Myself
Copyright © 2018 by Andrew Singer
Published by Station Square Media
1204 Broadway, 4th Floor
New York, NY 10001

Editorial Production: Diane O'Connell, Write to Sell Your Book, LLC
Cover and Layout Design: Steve Plummer/SPBookDesign
Production Management: Janet Spencer King, Book Development Group

Printed in the United States of America for Worldwide Distribution

ISBN: 978-0-9993727-0-8
Electronic editions:
Mobi ISBN: 978-0-9993727-1-5
Epub ISBN: 978-0-9993727-2-2

This is a work of nonfiction. As such, places, people, and events are real. Except where permission has been granted, names have been changed and biographical backgrounds may have been altered or omitted. In addition, while many of the conversations are real, others have been recreated. The latter, however, are in all instances faithful to the contexts of the original settings. At the end of the day, what transpires in this memoir is my sole recollection of those places, people, and events, how I experienced them at the time, and recall them in the present. Any errors or mischaracterizations are mine and mine alone. I have enjoyed writing this book, and I hope readers will enjoy reading it.

TABLE OF CONTENTS

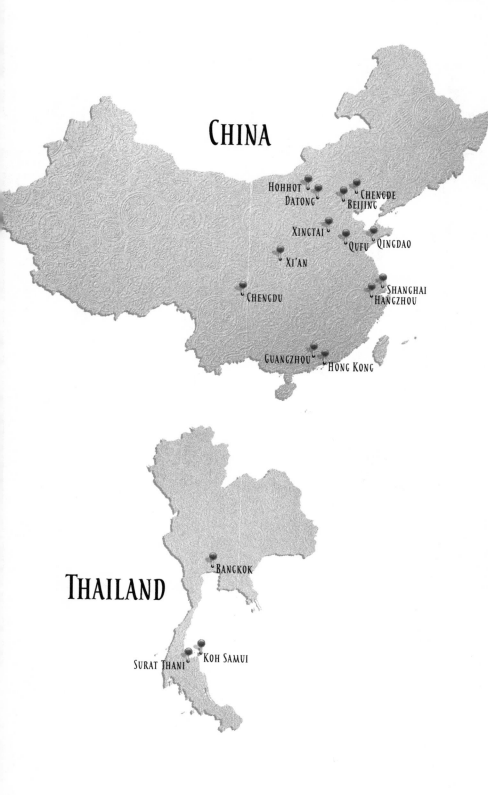

CHINA

Hohhot
Datong
Chengde
Beijing
Xingtai
Qufu
Qingdao
Xi'an
Chengdu
Shanghai
Hangzhou
Guangzhou
Hong Kong

THAILAND

Bangkok

Surat Thani
Koh Samui

The Silhouette upon my breast,
The warm, deep breath of sleeping Dream.
I lay awake and Marvel such,
The quiet Bliss of Memories.
                                    —ANDREW SINGER

见者易，学者难。*Jian zhe yi, xue zhe nan.*
Seeing is easy, learning is difficult.
                                    —CHINESE PROVERB

生有涯，知无涯。 *Sheng you ya, zhi wuya.*
Life has limits, knowledge has no bounds.
                                    —CHINESE PROVERB

INTRODUCTION

T HERE IS NOTHING Asian in my known history. Yet from before I can
remember I have been fixated with China and all things Chinese.

I grew up on Cape Cod, a sandy flexed arm of American soil jut-
ting into the North Atlantic. Cape Cod is on the other side of the planet
from the Middle Kingdom. My mother and father transplanted to this
corner of Massachusetts from the Boston area in 1965, a year before I was
born. My parents' parents' parents all came from Eastern Europe. I was
raised Jewish in an area lacking in significant ethnic, cultural, and religious diversity, with limited exposure to Asia.

I am often asked, "Why China?" I could say it is because mom and
dad planted a seed when they told a little me that if I dig deep enough in
our backyard sandbox, I would reach China. I could say it is because my
mother also has a fascination with the East (which I did not know then).
The joke at home is that I must have been Chinese in an earlier life. This
last possibility may be closest to the mark.

We visited my grandparents' cottage on Sebago Lake in Maine for
Labor Day weekend before school started each summer. I was drawn to
a small Chinese curio sitting on a shelf in the cozy living room near the
sofa. It was an ornate ivory bridge, about five inches long, spanning a
stream. A little, bent-over man made of wood pulled a cart with delicate

wheels. There might have been animals too. Two decades later, my dad told me that when I left for college, his mother told him that she always knew China would be a part of my life because I gave her that Chinese curio when I was a young boy.

Whatever the reason, the young me had a mission: to study Chinese and go to China. When I graduated high school in 1984, neither was easy. However, thanks to the prior persistence of a Chinese professor at Vassar College in Poughkeepsie, New York, two years later I found my way to China to live, study, and learn. In a time of no cell phones, no world wide web, and the absence of the constant contact we now take for granted, the world was a larger place.

China then was a cauldron, an ancient civilization struggling to emerge from a 150-year-long nightmare. The shadow of Mao Zedong and the Cultural Revolution clung thickly on China's landscape. Fewer than three years before Chinese students took over Tiananmen Square and raised the Goddess of Democracy, I had a front-row seat at an intramural ping-pong game between a suffocating past and an uncertain future. The Communist Party's all-encompassing grip on society repeatedly clashed with the Communist Party's baby steps toward expanding the economy and improving the lives of the people. It was a time of opening and closing; two steps forward, one step back.

At the same time, life in China was a trial I was often ill prepared to weather, a journey inside myself that was not for the faint of heart. I was a nervous nerd, self-conscious and easily excitable. I was halfway around the globe, alone. There were no safety nets. I was reminded daily that the cloistered classroom and the outside world are distinct realities. I faced a personal Tower of Babel in attempting to communicate, to understand, and to function in this real world, particularly one as alien as China. This was the first time I was truly on my own and in charge of me. I had to learn to be comfortable in my own skin, to chart my way forward, or to crash for the effort.

FIRST SEMESTER

学期一

CHAPTER 1

FOLLOWING THE PATH TO CHINA

August 1986

"I LOVE YOU, MOM."

I am not a hugger and do not often share my emotions with my family. I cannot recall the last time I said this to her, if ever. The moment is not lost on mom.

Why does he have to say this now? flashes across her moist eyes.

"United Flight 285 to Tokyo now boarding."

With that, her composure crumbles. The first leg of my flight to China is about to begin.

My father and I share a hearty handshake. This is it.

I am numb.

The swirl of the departure area at JFK International Airport in New York City is so much white noise.

Thank you Professor Chin. I headed to Vassar College and the Hudson Valley in the first place after meeting Yin-lien C. Chin and learning of the opportunity she had forged to send her students to China. We had an early chemistry that blossomed in Beginning Mandarin my freshman year.

This is a step I have wanted to take—have planned to take—for so long. My insides are a jumble of intense desire coupled with near-paralyzing fear.

I will my heart to slow down and my feet to move.

"Mom, I promise to call when I get there."

I float down the jetway in a haze.

My parents begin their 250-mile drive home, minus their eldest child.

—⁂—

About nineteen hours later, after a refueling stopover in Alaska, my nerves awaken with a jolt over the Sea of Japan. The friendly missionary on my left from Brigham Young University is speaking, but his words are lost in a rush of silent emotions.

What am I doing here? Am I nuts? I can't do this. I can't handle this. HELP!

The People's Republic of China re-opened to the West a brief seven years ago when Deng Xiaoping re-asserted control after Mao's death. I have studied Mandarin for a grand total of twenty-four months. I am voluntarily moving to a communist country during the Cold War. I must be crazy.

The throbbing in my chest becomes greater and greater. Can only I hear it?

I try to remember my Chinese lessons.

Chinese is a pictographic language, and I have a good memory for facts and pictures. I'm not so good with names and faces, but I can memorize. When I was in elementary school, I won a state capitals contest in class by memorizing and reciting all fifty the quickest. I was proud of myself for being first and ecstatic that I won a big Charleston Chew candy bar. I do not have a photographic memory, but if I study hard enough I can visualize the Chinese characters in my mind as I try to recall the individual strokes that make up each character, the correct order of each stroke, and how all these lines come together to form a meaning, a language.

4

But reading and writing are not the same as speaking and listening. Mandarin is a tonal language. Each character is articulated with one of four separate tones, and each character with its respective tone has a different meaning. The rising tone is different than the falling tone. The elevated tone is different than the dipping tone. The word *ma* can mean mother, numb, horse, or scold, depending on how it comes out of my mouth. There is even a fifth neutral tone for *ma*, which is used at the end of questions. Thus, it is easy to scold your mother as a numb horse, and then make it a question! There are also multiple characters that have the same sound and the same tone, but different meanings. Further still, when Chinese characters are combined as they often are with one, two, or three other characters (and their corresponding tones), these make up additional words, phrases, expressions of ideas, and concepts. The possibilities of meaning in such a scenario multiply exponentially and the ability to distinguish among the tones is essential. This is not my strength.

Comfortable as I am sitting in business class (thanks for splurging, mom and dad), at this moment I cannot for the life of me recall such basic phrases as, "I need a taxi"; "Do you have a room for the night?"; "How do I make a collect phone call?"

—⚭—

My sheltered, middle-class existence appears to have left me rootless. I have had all that I need, much of what I want. It leads to comfort, complacency. I get good grades and rarely get into trouble. I'm not a party boy. A weekend playing Cosmic Encounter with childhood friends is more my speed. I was a trumpet player in my high school marching band. The word "nerd" oozes from my frequently clogged pores and unhip jeans and button-down shirts. I am self-conscious, particularly among girls, yet also a cynic—a skeptical soul who is quick to judge. I study the world in college, and think I know it.

Here I am. I wanted to do this thing, and I am doing this thing. Then why is there this primal disquiet coursing through my body? If I had a teddy bear, I would close my eyes and hug it tight. I feel this overpowering urge to crawl into my bed and hide. But I cannot. I am well past the point of no return.

—◊◊—

As we taxi towards the terminal, the stewardess announces, "Ladies and gentlemen, welcome to Narita Airport. Local Tokyo time is *blah, blah, blah.*"

Ding. The red seatbelt light goes dark. Stretching my cramped shoulders, I reach up to get my garment bag.

The stewardess gets back on the PA system with the same steady intonation. "Attention, please leave everything and everyone exit the plane." Several hundred weary passengers stare at each other with blank expressions. No one moves. An awkward silence settles over the compartment. "NOW!"

Jump-started by her sudden emotion, we hustle off the plane. *What the hell is going on?*

Welcome to Asia, Andrew. Practically pushed off a jumbo jet. Looking out the terminal window at the airplane sitting in the growing dark, I hold my carry-on bag tight (OK, I grabbed it anyway on my way off) and think, *Oh no, my luggage!*

It turns out to be a false alarm. A fire warning light went off in the luggage hold and they ordered the evacuation.

—◊◊—

After the scare in Tokyo, an extra adrenalin rush that I did not need in my state, the last leg of my trip to Beijing continues.

We land at Capital Airport.

I am in China.

I am alone.

I am on my own.

The sun has long since set and the eerie concourse echoes with shadows around the empty luggage carousels, the closed ticket counters, the locked restaurants and shops.

First, I need Chinese money. The money-exchange office is still open. I have heard that airport exchange rates are horrible so I change only a small amount and exit the building.

Second, I need to get to Beijing University. I manage to hail a taxi, a Toyota sedan, for a nearly one-hour drive across Beijing's northern suburbs. We race west toward what I hope is where I want to be. The taxicab driver is not chatty, and I have no words. I sit silently listening to the blood pump through my veins.

It is a pitch-black night some seven thousand miles from home. My driver does not bother with lights nor lanes, preferring instead to straddle the center line of the road, hurtling around bicycles and carts, buses, and trucks, flicking his lights as he speeds into intersections with his foot glued to the accelerator.

Fists clenched on the worn fabric of the back seat, my eyes stare out the front window into nothingness. I am well beyond nervous. Scared was left back in Japan; I am petrified. Closing my eyes—not that it is any less dark with them open—I think back to Professor Chin's advice before I left:

> *"Xin Ande."*
> *"Yes, Chin Laoshi?"*
> *"Andrew, you are leaving for China."*
> *"Yes, Professor Chin."*
> *"Don't expect anything and you'll be pleasantly surprised."*

Well that's easy for her to say now, isn't it? This is the beginning of my journey. I am where I set out to be. Yet all I can think about is, *What have I gotten myself into?*

My stomach is doing somersaults. As the taxi flies through the ghostly darkness and I recall her words of wisdom, I realize in a moment of sudden clarity that the phrase "sink or swim" has become for me a very tangible and incredibly serious reality.

CHAPTER 2

GETTING SETTLED

THE CAB PULLS up in front of a boxy, U-shaped building. The five stories are dark and quiet. The front courtyard is deserted. It is after 11:00 p.m., an unheard-of hour in a country where most everything still closes with the sun.

I haul my large frame pack, suitcase, and garment bag, the sum total of my belongings for the next year, out of the taxi and walk up the steps. Shao Yuan Lou, the Spoon Garden Building, is the home away from home for foreigners on the Beijing University campus.

Most *liuxuesheng*, foreign-exchange students, enter China via Hong Kong as part of a group. I don't go with the flow. I am a self-pay student and make my own way here. New York to Anchorage to Tokyo to Beijing.

I am ready to collapse.

Trembling with anxiety and exhaustion, and boasting what to me sounds like a child's-level speaking ability, I pace the silent lobby while a sleepy night clerk finds someone who speaks English. I have no confidence in my Chinese. I have no idea whether the sounds coming out of my mouth, be they in Mandarin or English, are coherent. All semblance of rational thought and control has pretty much escaped me at this point.

The new clerk, who speaks a smattering of heavily accented English, may not understand that I am under the impression that I am expected, but she does get that I am desperately seeking a bed for the night. She charges me separately for the room and the key. Before I left for China, it was drilled into me that I should avoid water unless it is boiled. Problem. The thermos in my room is empty. There is no way I'm going to use the tap water. I brush camper style with my finger and Crest and fall into bed. I have never been so happy to lay my head on a pillow and close my eyes. Quickly, this alien environment fades from immediate concern.

Several hours later, I stir and roll over. My body does not want to move. My hip aches miserably. I strain to sit up and throw my legs onto the floor. Sleeping on a towel-thin mat laid over a piece of plywood re-aggravates an injury I suffered earlier this summer while visiting my girl-friend, Jill, in Montana. The trip was fantastic up until that afternoon. We were riding bicycles and came up to a metal cattle guard placed in the road. I did not notice that the grate was set parallel within the pavement. As my front tire sank between the steel bars and I began my flight over the handlebars, it gave a whole new meaning to the Big Sky Experience.

This is not an auspicious beginning to my first day in China.

My nerves are frayed. I am not sure what to do. I have never felt so rudderless, so unsure of my next step. I have never faced nor feared the possibility of failing with such ferocity.

As I wander in the little corner of campus that is my dorm complex, a tightness grips my chest. I fight the urge to cry.

Thus far, albeit in limited circumstances, I have been able to get across what I want to say in simple Mandarin. Understanding the responses is another matter. When I am speaking, I know what I am trying to say. When others are speaking, I have to concentrate in an attempt to figure out what they know they are trying to tell me. The tones are a beast. Mix in strong local accents, which seem to vary from person to person, and an intrinsically fast pace of speech, and I more often than not feel like I am drowning. The sounds blur, and I cannot distinguish a thing. The ability to process all of this in real time is the key to communication. Anything else is illusion. The frustration at not being able to communicate, not to be understood, even more so not to understand, is staggering. It is elemental. It does nothing to soothe my state of being.

During lunch on the second full day in China, the urge to speak in English overcomes my innate shyness and I approach a Caucasian guy sitting in the cafeteria.

"Hi. Do you mind company?"

Looking up from behind full, round glasses, the bearded stranger smiles and welcomes me to sit. There is something open and relaxed about him that is comforting. We exchange basic information, and I learn that George is an American here on a law program exchange and has been in Beijing for several months. He does not speak Chinese.

After discussing baseball, China, and anything and everything that comes to mind, George's face lights up. He has an idea. "You speak Chinese. Let's be adventurous and head out into the city." He also has a destination in mind. "How about the Beijing Zoo? It's not too far away, and I've wanted to see it before I head home."

I agree, but hope I know what I am getting myself into. George has no idea what I think of my Chinese. We leave Shao Yuan together and head towards the southerly main campus gate on Haidian Lu, Shallow Sea Road. The monolithic library stands sturdy behind a large statue of Mao on the front lawn. School buildings with flared red and green roofs and boxier student dorms spread out on either side of the campus road as we walk. It is dusty. Approaching the main gate, I leave campus for the first time.

George and I board a double accordion bus connected by ungainly poles to overhead electricity wires. Traffic on the roads consists mostly of buses, taxis, and bicycles. In my best Mandarin, I ask for two tickets to *dongwuyuan*, the animal garden. I enunciate each syllable. My tones are impeccable. The ticket taker looks at me blankly. The line is not moving. More and more people are bunching up behind me. I begin to feel the weight of the situation. What am I doing wrong?

I recall something Professor Chin mentioned, and I improvise with the Beijing tradition of changing the ends of words to *rrr*. I now ask for two tickets to the guttural *dongwuyuarrr*. I slur the sounds so that it sounds gibberish to my ears. She immediately hands us the tickets. Wow. I think I've learned something. For three cents we crawl the short distance to the zoo, and I am elated to be traveling like a native.

We enter the zoo for two cents. Steps beyond the entrance gate, a Chinese student from Shanghai comes up to us. Cheng is wearing the ubiquitous white T-shirt of Chinese men and a white cotton bucket hat. He gathers himself and tentatively asks, "Are you both Americans?" His face glows with anticipation.

We spend the next hour with Cheng. His English is good. While speaking with him, a large group of Chinese surrounds us. They look. They stare. I do not like being the center of attention. The silent screaming of sixty-plus eyeballs becomes too much. In my mind I hear them calling, *Dabi*, Big Nose, *Meigui*, American Ghost, *Yangguizi*, Foreign Devil— all common, not-so-flattering Chinese nicknames for Americans. Sweat starts to dampen my shirt, my heart races, my legs get skittish. George is in his element, having a grand old time. I am too focused on trying not to freak out.

The Chinese seem genuinely curious about the *waiguoren*, foreigners—literally, "people from outside China"—discovered in their zoo. While I am relatively tall for China at five feet, eleven inches, George towers at several inches taller than me. I am clean shaven; George's thick-bearded face is unique. I, however, have hairy arms, legs, and chest. I am taken aback when some of the Chinese start touching, rubbing, and pulling the chest hair peeking out of my jersey top and the hair on my arms. They are not shy. In stunned silence, I become an interactive zoo exhibit this sunny afternoon. I feel sudden kinship with the nearby polar bears boiling in the ninety-degree late-August heat.

When we return to campus, I head for my permanent room at Shao Yuan Lou, Building 2, Room 323. Our foreigners-only complex is located at the western edge of campus. We live and study here, segregated from the Chinese dorms and classroom buildings. My dorm building is spartan, but clean. *Fuwuyuan*, service people, clean the halls and bathrooms several times a day. There are transoms over each door, but little light comes from this direction because the hallway is so dark. The men's bathroom is eclectic—three floor-length urinals, one western-style toilet, and two eastern-style squat toilets. The sinks and basins to brush teeth and wash hands, clothes, pots, pans, and food are across the hall. Three shower stalls occupy a third room. Our co-ed Vassar floors and bathrooms are not an option. The girls are housed on the other end of the building.

Room 323 is a high-ceilinged, narrow room with two beds, two desks, three bookcases, and two small closets with storage nooks above. It is a symmetrical rectangle with a large double window facing east. And the room is disgusting. Dust threatens to lift my bed from the floor. Food crumbs lie scattered in small piles. Pots and pans overflow my roommate's side of the room. The biggest problem is that there are cockroaches on the floor, on and under the desk, and, worst of all, on my bed. I kill more of them tonight than I can count, and they are still crawling around.

Dripping in the humid air, pulse racing, and grossed out, I realize my task this first night is to try and tame this disaster. I fret meeting my Japanese roommate, who looks like a lifer. I cannot believe how much crap he has crammed in here.

After too many hours of trying to clean up, I crash down on my bed, close my eyes to the presence of roaches, and dream of Jill. I long to hold her in my arms, to feel her body pressed against mine. Jill is a vivacious and voluptuous blonde (a first for me) who captured my heart and my body last year. We were inseparable, so much so that my Vassar floor mates on the Josselyn Fourth-Floor Alley were tired of seeing her in the bathroom we all shared. I fall asleep wondering how she is and what she is doing at this very moment.

The room is not much better the next morning. My request for a room change is met with an official "wait a week until your roommate returns." I am not so sure that I will make it that long.

At the same time, room situation aside, my frayed nerves are slightly, and I mean slightly, coming back into balance. Learning to walk on a high wire without a net is daunting. Now, however, I've met a few people, settled in more, and my Chinese is showing signs of life. Nothing stimulates learning as well as having no other alternative.

CHAPTER 3

MOBILE IN BEIJING

A T 7:45 A.M. Monday, I call my parents at 6:45 p.m. Sunday. This takes getting used to. I am half a day ahead of them. Their present is my past; their future, my present. I head to the Beida Foreign Telephone and Telegraph Office and ask the operator to place a collect call. She does. I sit. I wait. And wait. As the call finally connects, I am directed to one of the phone booths set along the wall.

"Mom, I arrived safely and am not dead."

After five days of silence, I fulfill my promise to my mother. I can see her tightened jaw muscles as she takes in my nonchalant delivery. She has no sense of humor where my flip attitude comes into play, but I am who I am. My father rolls with it, and even shares a similar dryness, but not my mother. She is so serious. Maybe it's a maternal thing. The line is patchy and keeps dropping.

For the first time, I am missing our traditional Labor Day family weekend with my grandparents in Maine. As I sit far, far away, straining to catch pieces of conversation, images of normalcy dance in my mind: The crunch of rocks under our station wagon as we pass through the bright white birch trees on the aptly named Birch Hill Road; the anticipation of the low-slung cottage around the next curve; Grandma and

Grandpa Singer standing at the front screen door. I picture the graceful Chinese curio sitting on the living room shelf. I hear Sebago Lake lapping onto the small beach and waves caused by a water skier smacking against the concrete patio. I feel the neighbor's seaplane coming and going with an echoing roar. The late afternoon sun sets over the bridge separating Little Basin from the main lake.

—⁓—

Last summer (when I wasn't crashing a bicycle in rural Montana) I interned at the National Committee on US-China Relations in New York City. I sublet a room in a Columbia University apartment in gritty Spanish Harlem. My roommates included a Chinese couple on an exchange program at Columbia. The Chinese government required their little boy to remain behind as a parental, non-defection insurance policy. He is staying with his uncle's family here in Beijing. I briefly meet Uncle Wang Ping outside the Beida front gate and give him the toy bear and candy my roommates asked me to deliver to their infant son. Our conversation is stilted. I so hope I am making sense. He is the first local Chinese I have met one-on-one. I am probably the first American he has met. Hesitant and quiet, Wang invites me to visit his home and family, and then he is gone.

Standing on Shallow Sea Road, I realize that I need to prepare for living as a local. Beijing is now my home. A nearby bike shop beckons and before long, I am riding my very own top-of-the-line Flying Pigeon bicycle north through the village of Zhongguancun. Dusty, paved streets lined with predominantly one- and two-story buildings peter out until I am in the countryside. The day is sunny. The air is clean. This China is more remote. My destination is the nearby ruins of Yuanmingyuan, the Old Summer Palace. On the way, I take a series of wrong turns. At one of them, an armed guard steps out and brusquely blocks the road. He does not seem like one who would be happy to give me directions.

Yuanmingyuan is a former imperial palace of the Qing Dynasty. To call it a summer palace is a misnomer because it became the principal residence, place of work, and expansive pleasure garden for five Qing Emperors—from Kangxi the founder through his great-great grandson, Xianfeng, and their Courts. For 150 years, they preferred it to the formal Forbidden City in the center of Beijing, some ten kilometers (six miles) to the southeast. Hundreds of wooden halls, pavilions, and temples; numerous interconnected lakes, canals, and waterways; recreated landscapes of hills, paths, and famous natural scenes; and myriad acres of wonder dotted the enormous enclave into which Yuanmingyuan eventually grew. The greatest treasures of the empire, of China's long history, the collected written and visual wisdom of centuries—all of this and more resided within the garden walls. The cosmopolitan Emperor Qianlong, grandson of Kangxi, went so far as to commission European artisans to create a western section of gardens and stone palaces for his delight. Alas, the beauty and history are no more. At the end of the Second Opium War in 1860, French and British troops captured Yuanmingyuan, looted its valuables, and torched the place.

Although there is an extant Summer Palace, expanded in the late 1800s, about five kilometers (three miles) west, the remains of Yuanmingyuan seduce me. Today, while much of the former garden grounds lie either overgrown or taken over by twentieth-century development, portions of the palace have been reclaimed as a park with meandering paths that are spectacularly quiet and isolated. I love roaming the section of stone ruins, aware that I am walking in the footsteps of history. It is similar to when I recently rode a bus past the north wall of the *Gugong*, the Forbidden City, for the first time. My breath caught, and I actually felt it: a physical presence emanating from its imposing red wall, calling me. The same sense envelops me here. The ground speaks. The long-ago spirits of those who lived, loved, and died here inhabit the soil. On this site there was peace and refinement and imperial luxury. There was also war, fire, and death. Now, more than 125 years after Yuanmingyuan was sacked, the grounds are becoming a tourist attraction with souvenir and food stands springing up along the roadways.

Having ridden my new bicycle (without much incident) a short distance north into the countryside, I turn my sights south toward downtown. The eight-kilometer (five-mile) bike ride to the heart of Beijing takes about one and a half hours, same as on the bus. I head out with Linda, an American acupuncturist I met when she was holding court at the roof-top beer garden at the Youyi Bingguan, the Friendship Hotel, near Beida. Linda, the antithesis of the gregarious George, is a spitfire who radiates compressed energy and likes to be in charge. As with George, though, her time in China is approaching its conclusion. I consider what it means that the first two Western people I meet are about to leave the country. No matter. We are on a hunt for the so-called Underground City.

Riding a bicycle in China is being Chinese. There are a billion Chinese, many millions of bicycles, and thousands of motor vehicles all vying for the same space. When mobile, the Chinese don't look, don't stop, and don't try to avoid anything. It is a free-for-all. If you get hit, it is your fault. And it may be the last mistake you will ever make.

Linda and I pedal into Tiananmen Square, the center of Beijing. Located south of the Forbidden City and named for its southerly gate, the Gate of Heavenly Peace, Tiananmen Square is humbling. We are two, puny individuals in the midst of acres upon acres upon acres of stone openness bordered by mammoth, out-sized buildings: the Great Hall of the People, the Chinese History and Revolution Museums, Mao's Mausoleum, and the preserved and restored Qianmen Gate. One million people can fit into this space.

This is the heart of modern China. It was the site of governmental offices and ministries and other life, but not a public square, during the Ming and Qing Dynasties. The public square first came into being after the destruction caused by the Boxer Rebellion at the beginning of the twentieth century. Mao Zedong subsequently tore down gates, offices, streets, and alleys, and moved the Chinese away to create the vast plaza it is today.

Parking our bicycles in the designated corral, we walk over to the line for Mao's Mausoleum. The queue is six abreast and half a mile long, but it moves. We cross the great distance to the entrance in minutes. My hands are in my pockets as we shuffle along with the crowd closer and closer towards the front of the line. As we near the door, a guard barrels towards us without warning. Startled, Linda and I freeze. This representative of the communist government, dressed proper in a starched uniform and racing in earnest in our direction, extends his arms at me. Time stops. I am a statue as he reaches out and physically rips my hands out of my pockets. Task complete, he silently turns around and struts back to his post. Linda and I exchange a glance, and I have to mentally make sure my heart is still beating.

I am still a little in shock as we soon enter and pass the transparent coffin and Mao's waxy-looking, mummified body. "Do not stop. Do not slow down. Keep moving," the guards intone repeatedly. It is a surreal experience, over in seconds. There is no time to contemplate, to even try to begin to process what we are looking at or what it means. I have heard that poor preservation techniques in 1976 led to significant decay. It is rumored that they had to re-stitch one of Mao's ears back on because it was about to fall off his dead head.

Back outside, the looming front wall of the Forbidden City and the Gate of Heavenly Peace rise to the north. Staring up at Tiananmen Gate and its immense portrait of Mao Zedong, I spin 360 degrees watching the throngs mill about in the late summer sun, gathering my perspective on the moment. I recall with a smile what two Chinese computer students told me recently when I was walking up Wangfujing Street, Beijing's main drag. They told me that Wangfujing is like *"Belloway"* in New York. Surveying the teeming Chinese masses around me now, I realize that the fast New York City weave to which I am partial won't work in China. It is so crowded that the only choice is to lay back and shuffle along Beijing's Broadway.

Linda and I are filthy. Our clothes, our hair, and our faces are caked with dirt after close to six hours of bike riding in China's capital. My eyes will not stop watering. I now appreciate why the government is planting a "Green Great Wall" around parts of the dusty city in an attempt to keep the expanding Gobi Desert at bay. Humans cut down the forests, the soil erodes from the denuded land, desertification intensifies, and the humans plant a new forest to reclaim that which they destroyed in the first instance. What a vicious cycle.

Pedaling back into Beida, I cannot recall how many near collisions I avoided today. Bike riding in China's capital is a thrillingly native and excitedly terrifying experience. At the end of the day, we never did find the Underground City.

Looking up at Shao Yuan as we arrive exhausted and grungy, I notice a light on in my room. My roommate has returned. This ought to be interesting.

A short, thirty-one-year-old student of Ming Dynasty philosophy, Toshiro looks the part of an Asian thinker all prim and proper with a tight beard and mustache. How much Buddhism or Daoism or Confucianism, maybe a combination of all three, flows through this quiet and reserved man? He doesn't strike me as a slob, nor the type of person who loses his temper easily. If the latter is so, then this is one attribute he and I do not share. His spoken English, like my spoken Chinese, is not so good, but he reads and writes English well. We manage to communicate to an extent, relying on the liberal use of pad, paper, and dictionaries.

Toshiro must have returned several hours ago because he has already cleaned up his half of the room and deposited a serious pile of stuff in the gloomy hall. He tells me that while the clutter is his, the food (and cockroach) problem was caused by his previous roommate, an Indian guy who Toshiro appears glad has moved on. I regret that I panicked and asked the school officials for a room change, both because Toshiro seems like a decent guy and also because they told him. Toshiro relates this to me unemotionally, and I shrink with embarrassment at being caught in my impetuousness. I feel terrible. After talking, we agree to go to the housing office tomorrow and tell them we are all set. At least, I think this is what we have agreed to do.

CHAPTER 4

ADVENTURING BEYOND THE GREAT WALL

THE SLIGHT, MIDDLE-AGED Chinese man pedals his three-wheeled bicycle through the dusky Beijing streets. Ted and I perch on the swaying plywood bed in back, clenching the thin board to keep from flying off. Compartmentalizing my moral qualms about being human cargo, I stare out at the Chinese capital. Eerily quiet, the normal background din is muted. Men and women walk and bike ride around us. They sit on sidewalks resting and chatting with neighbors. They look up to watch us and the occasional truck rumble past. I see all of this, but I hear nothing. We are cocooned in a Cone of Silence. Ghost-like, we bounce, swerve, and coast through the city as if on a magic carpet.

We have combative Linda to thank for this experience. If she had not been arguing with the Beida officials over her final rent, we would have been on tonight's train to Inner Mongolia. I would normally be upset by such a turn of events, by plans being thrown awry. Tonight, I am faced with the odd sensation of not flipping out. Quite strange. When it became clear that tonight was not going to happen, Ted and I, the remaining two of our trio, went to the train station and switched our tickets to the following night. Linda will not be joining us.

Ted is another adventurous American who I bumped into in Beijing.

He is a filmmaker from New York heading to the hinterlands to scout a potential project. Ted has a sense of maturity and depth in his eyes that tells me he has got to have ten years or so on me (though I am horrible at estimating ages). Self-assured, intrepid, and intellectual, he is not me. Our traveling together is yet another example of this environment facilitating strangers meeting, bonding, and deciding to go off on an adventure. If we had run into each other in Manhattan, I would have avoided the opportunity of getting to know him, keeping instead to my safe self.

We would never have found ourselves walking the mile or so from the Beijing train station to the 103 Bus stop near the Beijing Hotel. We would never have sought refuge in a little hole-in-the-wall restaurant when the heavens unleased. I would never have ordered a beer while waiting. Oh, my friends back home would be amused. Drinking is one of the main pastimes at Vassar, and I was a token teetotaler. The beer flows there. It didn't matter that New York State raised the drinking age from eighteen to twenty-one after our freshman year, although it did make the largest keg parties a bit more challenging to pull off. I find beer bitter, unsatisfying. Give me a carbonated soda any day. In China, however, one thing you can count on with beer is that it is pasteurized, prevalent, and safe to drink. I drink up with Ted, scrunching my nose as I swallow the acrid liquid. By the time we finally arrive at the bus stop at the zoo, we have missed the last connection to campus and there are no cabs. The freight bicycle is it.

Arriving at Shao Yuan wet, cold, and exhausted, we thank our driver, but do not tip him for his efforts. Tipping is prohibited. In an officially egalitarian society, tipping manifests a difference in classes and is seen as a form of corruption. Giving gifts is another matter. China runs on *guanxi*, best translated as relationships, a deeply embedded cultural concept by which who you know is much more relevant than what you know. Bringing gifts, a token or two, to someone helping you out is not only acceptable, but expected. It helps cement the relationship and begin or continue a mutually beneficial connection. It is the key way to survive and thrive in Chinese society. *Guanxi* is something we have not yet cultivated. We do not give our driver a gift either.

—ⵡ—

I squish into my room and say hello to Toshiro. I am such a heel. Toshiro is kind and generous. Over the last several days, he helped me fill out my student ID form when the written Chinese confounded me, picked up my photos for my ID cards at the off-campus store because I was not supposed to be here, and even offered to submit my student ID form to the office because it takes a week to process, and he did not want me to have to wait until I return from Hohhot to apply. Not only that, he continues to clean. The hallway outside our room narrows as ever more boxes are stacked higher and wider in the dim passageway in what appears to be a Japanese thing here at Shao Yuan. He removed his open food, and in the most appreciated gesture of all, he agreed to smoke outside.

I regret my earlier pre-meeting impressions of Toshiro. I wish my default reaction to situations was not so often frustration and anger. This is nothing new, but that does not make it easier to accept. When things do not go my way, when faced with bumps, when I clash with my parents and brother and sister, I blow. I am the oldest child and am bossy with my younger siblings; you know, the way younger kids just won't listen when I tell them what is right. My mother and I in particular have a rocky relationship. She tells me that this is because we are more similar in personality than I am willing to acknowledge. Is she right? She has this need to be so involved and is definitely opinionated. OK, there might be something there. In any event, I wish I could, no, I wish I *would* take a couple deep breathes before reacting. Like when our travel plans hiccupped earlier today. With Toshiro, I lucked out with my roommate.

We are three hours outside of Hohhot (*Huhehaote* in Mandarin), the capital of Chinese Inner Mongolia. It is mid-morning on September 6, and the train is bouncing. Ted and I share a cozy soft-sleeper compartment with two visiting French professors. I sit back and watch my demonstrative companion take the lead in discussing modern China with our learned companions. Feet folded yoga-like, arms gesticulating, Ted is an animated conversationalist. We are here, in the most expensive class of seats, because the ticket lady in Beijing claimed that all other classes were sold out. No *guanxi* for us. This is no Western first-class, but the compartment is fairly comfortable and private. We are, however, next to the bathroom at the end of the car. The squat-style toilets open directly to the track below, and the wafting stench of urine stings.

We've left the mountainous region and entered the plain. We pass some of the fabled Mongolian grasslands, but it is generally dry, dusty and drab. The river we parallel is not much more than a dirt trickle. Cornfields which should be tall and proud in September are stubby stalks barely one foot in height. We pass tiny, tawny villages, the houses and outer walls made of mud and hay. These are Han Chinese villages in Inner Mongolia beyond the Great Wall. The people appear to be all Han Chinese. The Han ethnic group makes up more than ninety percent of China's population. The rest is spread among fifty-six minority nationality groups. The Mongolians, descendants of Genghis Khan and one of the fifty-six, tend to live deeper in the region. We pass two army convoys unsuccessfully trying to camouflage their big guns.

Upon arriving in Hohhot, the two French guys split, and Ted and I catch a cab to the guesthouse recommended by *Lonely Planet. Buxing.* No good. The guesthouse no longer takes foreigners. Our driver and the other cabbies out front rally to our cause and join us in pleading with the clerk to take us in. Animated argument, cajoling, badgering. We make a spirited case, but alas to no avail. We are turned away. Lack of *guanxi* is one thing. This is different. This is my first true introduction to an important aspect of modern Chinese society, a part of life symbolized by the two characters 麻, *ma,* and 烦, *fan.* 麻烦, *mafan.* Literally translated, it means inconvenience, hassle. Such a simple word, but then not. It embodies so much more. *Mafan* is a weighty expression of deep angst, nay resignation, in the face of that which, whether logical or illogical, cannot be surmounted. It carries with it a commentary, a fundamental futile frustration that cannot be understated. *Mafan* is interwoven into all facets of Chinese existence.

Where does this all leave Ted and me this soggy early afternoon? I do not need confirmation that winging it makes me skittish, but here it is. We come up on one-way tickets because the Chinese do not do round trip. We come up with no reservations. I have the travel bug, the call to venture to the unknown, but the uncertainty of the unknown is unnerving. My heart races. I sweat. My scalp itches. The dreaded sensation of losing control, of having no control, sweeps over me, and it is so hard to stay composed. My comfort zone has been blown to pieces. I am a little over a week in China and find myself in Inner Mongolia with no train tickets out and no place to stay. Ted takes it all in stride. I think he is having fun. He is so not me.

Eventually we find shared dorm accommodations at a nearby hotel that are comfortable, clean, and cheap, only a buck and change per bed. I calm down. The weather stinks. It is chilly, windy, and rainy. We dump our bags and set out. In drab Hohhot, I am blazing in a bright-red rain poncho, while Ted rocks a thin blue, plastic poncho he buys on the street. The smile on his face as he takes in his surroundings is one of simple joy. Passing a mound of cabbage, a flowing pile of scallions, and a river of fruit along the muddy cement sidewalk, our first stop is the Museum of Inner Mongolia. It's supposed to be good. Alas, I will never know. It is closed for renovations.

We enter a bookstore to get out of the rain. A Chinese gentleman looks up and comes over. He studied at Beida and lived in Shao Yuan as well. Quick bonding over shared experience. Our new friend is a Chinese professor at Qing Shan University here in Hohhot. He offers to take us on a bike tour of the city Sunday morning. We eagerly accept.

—m—

Ted and I head back out then to catch a bus to the advance train ticket office to purchase my return ticket. The lady in the ticket office sits behind a wall and I can hardly see her, let alone hear her. My listening comprehension being what it is, or rather is not, it might not have mattered if I could hear her. She is speaking Mandarin with a heavy accent, and all my ears pick up are sounds that wrap themselves around me without semblance of meaning or comprehension. I have to be back in Beijing on Monday morning and do not know what this woman is saying to me. Here it comes. The anxiety. I feel it bubbling up as my tenuous sense of calm fractures.

I am saved by the bilingual Chinese man we met on the bus over to the station who offers to accompany us. The late Sunday afternoon train I want is sold out—soft seat (first class, short distances), soft sleeper (first class, long distances), hard sleeper (second class), and hard seat (third class). I will take anything, and do. The 8:24 a.m. Sunday train is the only one that will have me in Beijing in time. I will thus be in Hohhot a grand total of twenty hours. I buy the ticket, say goodbye with tremendous thanks to my Chinese savior, and settle down to try and enjoy the remaining few hours of Saturday with Ted.

As we walk the streets, little kids hit their siblings and gaze at us with wide eyes. We attract a crowd wherever we go. Western people, Western ideas, and Western influence are growing steadily in China eight years after US-China relations were normalized, but they are still far from the norm, particularly outside the main cities. We are looking for the Minority Handicrafts Factory. We don't know its Chinese name, and our guidebook is of little use. It takes effort—a bus ride, a mile or so walk, asking six people for directions, but we make it. The Minority Handicrafts Factory turns out to be a small shop with little inventory. I buy a simple metal snuff bottle, my first. It is dark brown with unadorned front and back sides leading up to a long tapered neck. It has animal mask designs on the sloping shoulders and a milky green stopper that is likely glass, all sitting on a pronounced raised foot. I like the cool feel of it nestled in the palm of my hand.

After dinner at our hotel, we are not ready to turn in. The Inner Mongolia Hotel behind our place is supposed to have Mongolian post-cards. The back gate between the two hotels is locked. We scale the ten-foot wall only to find the gift shop closed. Walking back the long way, Ted and I stop into a little store with a light on and spend an hour chatting with four laid-back young Chinese clerks. They welcome us in and offer us tea and sunflower seeds and cigarettes.

When they learn that Ted is a filmmaker, all four perk up and erupt in quick succession. It's as if an electric current passed through each of them simultaneously.

"Did you see Rambo? They showed it here recently," said the talkative guy with eyes that are dancing. "We all loved it."

"John Rambo is so cool. He wastes those Vietnamese," adds another with gusto as he makes a yanking motion with his arm.

The third hops to his feet and excitedly chimes in, "We like it when an oppressed person fights back."

Not to be left out, the last clerk states simply, "If you are hit, retaliate." His statement contains a finality that brooks no challenge.

Wow, are these guys animated. China and Vietnam are historical adversaries. They fought their most recent border war in 1979. The Vietnamese kicked butt. It is evidently a raw wound.

About my age, the guys are curious and ask questions about life in America. Ted tells them that he earns fifteen dollars per hour and pays $380 per month in rent in New York City. I can see in their faces that they have a hard time processing such numbers. They work six days a week, eight hours a day for sixteen dollars per month. Their main task is to sit and talk.

Like many Chinese youth, they are down on their country and see America as a shining star. They want more out of life, can't find it here, and look outwards for inspiration. Their understanding of what America is may not be nuanced, but America worship is all the rage in today's China.

"You're so rich. America is such a land of wealth," says Mr. Gusto.

"That is so much money. I will never see that much," adds Mr. Talkative.

"America." They each give the thumbs up sign. "China." The thumbs turn down.

I realize that these four young men are just like any young person, just like me. They are struggling to make their way, to figure out what they can do with their lives in the here and now. I look over at Ted, who is earnestly soaking it all in.

—⁂—

When I wake at 6:35 a.m. Sunday, the weather is ferocious: lightning, thunder, pouring rain, high winds. It is the kind of morning where you want nothing more than to hunker down under warm sheets and listen to the storm. But I don't; I can't. I have somewhere to be.

Getting up quietly so as not to disturb Ted, I pull on my fatigues and heavy sweater. I haven't shaved or showered in two days. Bracing for the thirty-minute walk to the train station, I slip my backpack and me under my rain poncho and head out. The rain stops. Hohhot is flooded. I slog along roads covered with at least six inches of water. A little ways from the hotel I flag down an auto rickshaw, a motorcycle with a hard-covered front and a soft-covered, open back. I am the fourth person to hop in and before I know it, we are driving away from the train station. This is OK, I tell myself. After all, the others were first, and it is only 7:15 a.m.

A short distance away we stall in the middle of Inner Mongolia's newest lake. Five minutes tick by. The driver restarts the rickshaw, and we move on down the flooded street. The first person gets dropped off and we head for the next person's stop. The second hand on my watch keeps ticking, and my anxiety begins ratcheting up as we are still not heading towards the train station. The second person and then the third reach their destinations. I am now riding solo. We start back to the train station. It is only a smidge past 7:35 a.m., but I am nervous.

What happens next is inevitable. It isn't my morning. The valiant auto rickshaw dies for good in the middle of Inner Mongolia's next newest lake. We are stuck. My anxiety reaches its breaking point. My nerves shred. I am on my own, trapped in a situation that is beyond my control, far outside the Great Wall. My calm demeanor of taking life in stride flows out of me as surely as the water in the street does not. I am one part nervous, one part furious. As the clock strikes 8:00 a.m., it is no longer a question of changing trains, which had been my original idea on the advice of our friends from last night, but of even making the scheduled train. Will I be stuck here and miss registration? This is not happening!

I hail random cars from the back of the rickshaw. No one will stop. I have now officially lost it. In my best colloquial English—OK, I am swearing my American head off—I tell each vehicle as it passes exactly what the driver can do with himself. I am out of control. The rickshaw driver soon joins in the act. I am now his problem. Problems lead to the dreaded *mafan*, trouble. The last thing he wants is the authorities to be summoned to deal with a raving *dabizi*, a Big Nose Foreigner. By helping me, he helps himself. He flags down a car.

The driver of the car backs up so that his side door is next to the back of the auto rickshaw. I swing over the water, full pack on covered by my flaming red poncho, and fall into the back seat of this stranger's car. I never stop to consider, *Who this is that has a private car out on an early Sunday morning drive in Inner Mongolia? Did the rickshaw driver*

31

contact somebody? Is it a public security person following a foreigner? Is it what it appears to be, a lucky break? Coincidence or not, in my state of mind—pure survival mode—it does not matter. My only goal is to get out. Although time crawls in my frightened, flipped-out state, I enter the train station as the clocks ticks 8:06 a.m.

I head straight for the track, enter the car, and fold into a hard seat booth for six to decompress. I am on the train, a Friendly's restaurant on wheels. A worker comes by periodically and sweeps the floor. Other workers provide hot water and sell candy. I sit with a Mongolian family of three heading home and two guys from Hailar way up north near the border with Outer Mongolia heading south for work. All Chinese speak their native tongue, and most have had to learn the government-mandated *Putonghua*, the common language. This family speaks Mongolian. The guys, one who appears to be Mongolian and the other Han Chinese, translate as the train leaves the station and begins the long journey back.

When they learn I haven't eaten, the guys immediately give me a *yuebing*, a moon cake, and hot water. A mooncake is round like a hockey puck, but denser. The soft outer crust conceals a filling that is often ground bean curd. This one is tasty and quickly fills my stomach. Before I can stop them, they also open a small can of meat and present it to me. I feel horrible. I cannot eat another bite. To not accept this gift is an insult. To waste it, even more so. I leave the can on the top of the table in the hope that it will magically disappear (or keep for several hours until I am hungry again). I offer a chocolate bar I bought in Hohhot to the family's adorable three-year-old little girl, but she jumps back into her mother's arms and won't accept it. Large, unshaven and unkempt foreign man mumbling in a strange tongue offers candy. I probably wouldn't have accepted it either.

We are on a different track than the one we came up on. Rolling mountains and plains, grasslands, and valleys produce an exquisite panorama of contrasts. There must be irrigation because this panorama is green and alive. The Mongolian family gets off. A new crowd sits down. I haven't been talking much because I'm beat and carrying on a conversation in Chinese requires more effort than I am able or, more honestly, willing to make at this time. I'm the solitary foreigner in this car and am warily beginning to accept people staring at me.

CHAPTER 5

TRAVELING WITH NEW FRIENDS

Monday, September 8, 1986. I bust my hump to get back to campus in time to register, and when I go in this morning, I hear, "There has been a change. Classes will now begin next week."

I stare at the registration lady. *Excuse me? I missed a bike tour of Hohhot and maybe a trip to the grasslands for this!*

"You must first take a placement test, and then we will assign you a class and level."

"When is the placement test?" I ask, hopefully not in a huff.

"Next week."

Of course it is. Tomorrow, I have to see someone else to get a test time. I've been here a mere ten days, and I am quickly learning that the left hand doesn't know what the right is doing, the right hand doesn't know what the left is doing, and the left and the right hands themselves don't even know what they are each doing respectively.

I have another week to kill.

I leave campus to go dictionary shopping with Billy and Peter, two American students from New York State who also live in Shao Yuan. I am so far outside my comfort zone that I am pushing (or being dragged) past my natural social awkwardness to reach out to others for friendship and grounding. With Billy and Peter, I might have finally met people who will be at Beida awhile. They came here together to study Chinese and are closer to me in age. Billy sports a dense, dark beard and thick glasses, and seems to be the more serious of the two. Peter is a clean-shaven blond and more happy-go-lucky, quick to smile and laugh. The three of us want to explore. This is a defining characteristic of Americans in China, based on my unscientific survey.

Pedaling downtown, we get separated from Billy. There are mobile masses of bicyclists, cabs, busses. One minute, we are together. The next, he is gone. Peter and I soldier on without stopping to consider what might have happened to Billy. Nice friends, aren't we? Peter and I stumble into the Underground City. It actually does exist. Built decades ago in case of enemy attack, this so-called city is now a warren of little restaurants and shops. We are both excited as we park our bikes, pay the attendant, and head into a dark doorway.

Descending three flights of stairs beneath Beijing, we enter a maze of air-raid shelter passageways and weave our way to one of several different holes in the same dilapidated wall. The air in this grimy section of tunnel is thick. The smell of bubbling oil and sweat is fierce. Dime-store chairs at cheap tables with grease-splattered plastic covers greet us. Flimsy paper napkins and a container with two dozen chopsticks sit on top. We order a couple of plates to start. The *jiaozi*, boiled dumplings with pork filling, arrive steaming hot and glistening. Cleaning the chopsticks as well as we can with hot tea, Peter and I dip this dumpling into the small saucer of soy sauce and that dumpling into a saucer of vinegar. Soon, the plates are empty. We order more. Between savory mouthfuls, I learn that Pete is engaged. His fiancée is a Chinese woman who taught Peter and Billy Chinese as an exchange student at their college in New York. We keep ordering additional plates. When neither of us can squeeze in one more dumpling, we sit back and digest for a few long minutes.

Shuffling our way back to the city above, our bellies full, Peter and I retrieve our bicycles and set a blistering pace back to Beida. The traffic is heavy. Bells blazing, near misses too numerous to worry about, we make the hour-long ride in forty minutes. Billy is waiting for us. He made his way back to campus on his own. He is not sure what happened either. He was with us, and then he was not. If he is disappointed that he missed our discovery, he hides it well.

The three of us fast friends decide that we should not waste this free time. More traveling it is. We qualify for the cheaper local prices now with our new student ID cards and foreign resident cards. We have to wait in longer native lines, but we pay Chinese prices. My foreign resident card is my visa in China. I can stay until next August.

The guys and I make plans to visit Datong, a monastery town an overnight train ride northwest of Beijing in Shanxi Province. It is the home of Yungang Shikou, the Yungang Grottoes. Toshiro, who is focusing on Buddhism in his philosophy studies, has been there three times to view the ancient Buddhist cave art that was carved directly into the southern face of Wuzhongshan, the Wuzhong Mountain, 1,500 years ago during the Northern Wei Dynasty. Situated about sixteen kilometers (nine miles) southwest of Datong, the fifty-three caves and cliff-face grottoes are the largest collection of Buddhist cave carvings in China.

Toshiro relaxes a bit when reminiscing about the grottoes. His excitement for our destination is contagious. He and I have been getting along well, and our room is shaping up. We're decorating with wall hangings and we have hung a tie-dyed half tapestry across the door entrance to give the place character and a bit of privacy. Toshiro helps me out constantly. Today, he brought my pants down to the cleaners in Shao Yuan because I was away the few hours they are open. We are able to communicate increasingly in Chinese. He is leaving in March. I wish he was staying longer.

Peter, Billy, and I discover upon boarding the train to Datong that they've given two of our beds to Belgian tourists. The female conductor tells us to wait until the train leaves the station. Billy and Peter, like Ted, take bumps in stride. What do I do? Naturally, I kvetch and get agitated. I stew in my corner of the train car. Also to pattern, once my default, blood-racing reaction to aggravating reality vents, I begin to calm down. My mind clears. It is then that I can process the situation. What keeps me from processing first? Is it simple lack of self-control? Is it something hardwired into me? I have no ready answer (or is it that I do not want to answer?), but we all ultimately get a rolling place to sleep for the night.

We're in hard sleeper, six bunks in an open compartment (three vertical on each side), which is more comfortable than my bed at Shao Yuan. I like this hard sleeper much better than the soft sleeper I rode to Inner Mongolia. In soft sleeper, you're segregated and closeted away. Here, there's room to breathe and move about. You mingle with others, especially the Chinese. It's cheaper, and the food's better. In the foreigners-only areas, they give you what they think you want, which is usually a poor knockoff of something that is supposed to be western. On my last trip, the pseudo fried egg was drowned in grease, and the so-called toast could be used as a hammer. Here, it is Chinese faire of noodles and lightly sautéed cabbage.

—◊◊◊—

A solitary pavilion encircled by a rock garden sits on a hill at the east edge of Datong. The golden-yellow flared roof and red poles of this traditional open structure are set against a cloudy backdrop. This is simpler than the Huaiyuan Temple complex we visited earlier with its detailed architecture and sophisticated Buddhas and Bodhisattvas. Here, two little boys and a girl are playing a game, running around and yelling, having fun, oblivious to us. We sit down and watch. These children are the stage, framed by Old Town Datong and distant mountains. A couple of Chinese teenagers work up the courage to come over and talk with us. Each of these interactions is like a first date. Who are you? Where are you from? Why are you here? It has quickly become a repetitive dance and arrives with the anticipation of watching a B-rated movie to which you have memorized all of the scenes. Yet, again and again and again we dance.

On the walk back to the main drag, Datong's famous *Jiulong Bi*, Nine-Dragon Screen, pulls us in. This screen, the largest of three such screens in China, was originally the screening wall facing an imperial prince's mansion during the early Ming Dynasty. Made from glazed tiles, it is enormous at twenty-six feet (eight meters) tall and more than 147 feet (forty-five meters) long. Six hard centuries have taken a toll, but the nine, intricate, yellow-gold dragons leap out of the blue glazed background. This is the China that speaks to me. I see it in the back streets of the old section of the city, in the temples and pavilions, and right here in this colorful screen. No pretenses, just culture.

We stroll into a park surrounding the Nine-Dragon Screen and enter the adjacent market. I am looking for a blue padded Mao jacket for the fall. They have green, but not my size. As one jacket goes on, then off, and then another goes on, then off, a group of almost two dozen locals collect to watch and laugh. I feel my heart begin beating louder. The memory of being a human attraction at the Beijing Zoo comes roaring back. My scalp tickles with the beginnings of the dreaded prickliness. I lose track of Billy and Peter and have no idea if they witness the scene. I am focused on my inner turmoil. I have to force myself to calmly remember Professor Chin's advice each time this happens. Her sage words notwithstanding, this is not easy.

Professor Chin drilled into us that we must understand the cultural tendencies reflected in language and actions if we want to ultimately speak and understand the language like a native. Language is reflective of culture. It is a window into thinking and feeling. If a Chinese person says you speak well, you should respond, "No, I do not." Self-deprecation is respected. Saying thank you too quickly is boastful. As an individual character, alone or in combination with others, can mean much more than meets the eye, so too can actions. Context and cultural awareness are key. If you trip, the Chinese will laugh. They are not laughing at you, but rather with you to offset the hurt. Well, the Chinese surrounding me may be trying to make me feel better or welcome even, a part of the fabric of their lives, but I continue to feel embarrassed and uncomfortable. I do not like being the center of their attention. I buy a green Mao cap at another booth and quickly leave the market.

—〰—

Today is cave day. Toshiro was right. The Yungang Grottoes do not disappoint. Tens of thousands of Buddhas and attendants grace the rock walls. Some are small. Others—like the forty-four-foot-tall (thirteen-and-a-half meter) Buddha set in the outer cliff face and his even larger fifty-six-foot-tall (seventeen meter) companion in a nearby cave—are giants. Their serene countenances and awe-inspiring height dwarf little me as I stare up with wide eyes. The high skill and devotion of the ancient Northern Wei artisans is well-evident, though in places not without a dash of imagination. Many of the carvings are in ratty condition, from weather and time, from long ago looting and neglect, and from damage during the Cultural Revolution. Headless, faceless statues are sadly common.

The ruins of a fort extend across the windswept plain directly above the magnificent carved cliff face. Its buildings have long since disappeared, leaving only echoes of primitive foundations. Ascending a steep, hardened path leading up the outside of an old mud wall, Peter, then Billy, then I walk out single file along the thinning top of this ancient structure that ends at a watchtower overlooking the edge of the cliff face. We are above the monumental Buddhas. The path is three feet at its widest with sheer drops of several dozen feet on either side. No guardrails. Nothing between vertigo and a hard fall. Scared silent, heart racing (this time from fear, not nervousness), I concentrate on taking pictures to block out the reality of where I am. From up here, two breaks in the outer wall are visible, as are the time-battered remnants of watchtowers in the far distance. Staring out at the high plain, past the crumbling sentinels, I feel the shadows of Ghengis Khan's mounted Mongolian soldiers sweeping over the Wuzhou Mountains towards our defensive backstop. The sun is bright, and the air is quiet.

—m—

The last stop on our brief visit to ancient China is the Shanhua Monastery. I am drawn to places like this. I get a feeling of familiarity deep in my gut, a sense that I belong on these grounds. Billy's interest is more cerebral. He's an analyzer, looking at the religious aspects, thinking on the history. Secreted down a small alley off a main road, he and I walk right by the monastery the first time and only find it after careful hunting. There are no tourists in this part of town. There are not many locals either. In the scruffy front courtyard sits a smaller dragon screen. The monastery buildings do not look good; they are in the process of being renovated. The statues, however, are a marvel. The detail. The setting. The shiny cobalt blue, which the ancient Chinese used so much and which I am so enamored with, remains vivid. The Buddhas have worn spots, but they are still commanding. Statues of soldiers, guards, kings, queens, attendants, and musicians accompany the Buddhas. After so much time, so much conflict, the chaos of communist rule, it is incredible how much of the past survives.

During the Cultural Revolution, Mao sought to eliminate the *Si Jiu*, the Four Olds—old customs, old habits, old culture, and old thinking. He had great success and untold historical structures, sites, and treasures were destroyed with wanton abandon. This is a tragedy, but fortunately, complete eradication was beyond his destructive prowess, his wrath of the ancient, his attempt to insert himself as the end all of power and veneration. A combination of China being too big and brave souls willing to protect parts of the country's heritage ensured that there is still a great deal to see and experience, a great deal to anchor the China of today. The damaged Shanhua Monastery was fortunate to be overlooked for total destruction by the ravages of China's modern history. As for me, I have discovered a piece of preserved and hidden China. The grandeur requires visualization, but I am happy to do so standing in its tranquil courtyard.

—◊—

Our train tickets to Beijing are hard seat, and there are no open benches. After standing in the crowded aisle bouncing and swaying until we do not want to stand or bump into each other any longer, the three of us head to the dining car for a bite to eat and a seat. The train personnel allow us to stay there for the final seven hours of the trip. A middle-aged man sits at a nearby table counting money. He raises his head and declares us to be friends. A People's Liberation Army soldier plops down next to me and looks us over casually. Many of China's three-million-strong army (recently trimmed from four million) are young men in their early twenties like this guy. He asks if we are Russians.

The train passes the same spot where I first saw the Great Wall on the way out (Datong is located outside the inner section of the Great Wall). We follow the wall for many, many kilometers in bright sunshine. At one stop, the wall is right there! So close and yet so far. I cannot wait to walk on it. It's calling me.

We reach school about 9:30 p.m., and I want to crash. I am beat. While washing up, the thought of bed dancing before my drowsy eyes, I say hello to a guy who lives a couple of doors down from me. He invites me to his friend's room to talk.

Ali welcomes me into a mirror image of my room, only cleaner. It is also homier with Middle Eastern-themed posters decorating the walls and tchotchkes on the desk and windowsill. He and Mohammed are reserved, but seem excited to have company. Since they know only a few words of English, our common tongue, such that it is, is Chinese. While Ali explains that they are studying international politics, Mohammed brews aromatic Syrian tea with sugar and passes around three cups. The hot tea is sweet and soothing. If I wasn't in conversation, I could easily close my eyes and drift off.

"We are from Balestan," says Ali. His straightforward declaration stumps me. *Where is Balestan?*

Since I do not want to look ignorant, I nod in faux understanding and wrack my weary brain trying to figure out which country he means. I mentally scroll through the names of various countries. Definitely Middle Eastern, Muslim, maybe Arab. It bothers me that I do not come up with a ready answer.

The topics meander from living in China, to China's place in the world, to international relations generally, and then to the Middle East. When Mohammed comes out with, "The Balestan question is a complicated one," the light bulb finally goes off. He is not saying where they're from. He is saying how they identify themselves.

Balestan is Palestine.

Mohammed and Ali are Palestinian.

Talk about a late-night shock to a tired system. I can only imagine the look that passes across my face. Yes, I was raised Jewish by Jewish parents, but I am not religious. I went through the bare minimum of the motions because my parents forced me to. I have an affinity for certain cultural practices based on upbringing and I do love Jewish deli, but being Jewish is not an integral part of my identity. This being said, I feel my Jewishness talking with these two Palestinians guys who are about my age and also studying in China.

In response to Mohammed's statement, all I do is nod my spinning head. But is it, or need the question be so complicated? To three young college guys sitting in a dorm room in Beijing shooting the breeze in Chinese, maybe not so much.

CHAPTER 6

ACUPUNCTURE

M Y MAILBOX IS empty. Still.

Not one letter. Not one package. Not anything.

I check every single day.

Nothing from my family. Nothing from my friends. Nothing from Jill.

That this list includes my family surprises me. I cannot believe that I yearn for this connection to my old life. With my family, it is not just that I am not a hugger. I am private and not that open. I do not often express my thoughts and discuss my life with them. I particularly shy away from conversations with my mother because they can be draining. I speak in short sentences; she narrates in discursive paragraphs. She wants to know everything; I hit the highlights and move on. With mom, once you begin, you are quickly down the rabbit hole. Anyway, I wouldn't normally write and thus would not necessarily expect them to. This place must really be throwing me for a loop. Or, am I melancholy because I ache? I really, really ache.

As has happened several times in the past, I woke up out of the blue with a wrenched shoulder, neck, and back. The trip downstairs to the mailroom is a journey. The slightest twinge sends radiating pain throughout my tender body.

I want somebody to take care of me.

I do want very much to hear from Jill. I look at her smiling face every day when I get up. Her pictures sit on my desk, framed by the window and the morning sun. We haven't told our folks yet, but we are pre-engaged. It's our step before our formal engagement. A private statement of commitment.

The silence from her concerns me. I miss her. I worry about her. We come from different worlds, but our love will conquer the challenges. I believe this, but why hasn't she written? Does she have doubts? Has she reconsidered that our differences might be too big to bridge? I know little about her family, but enough to recognize that her upbringing was not the conventional, sheltered existence I was afforded. She is streetwise. I will never forget the day she unfolded a little packet of paper to show me the white powder that I presume was cocaine. After a moment she silently closed it back up. It was probably a test to see if I could accept who she is. I said nothing. A year apart is bad enough; not hearing from her is torture. I hope she is OK.

Oh, my neck aches.

—⚏—

I've got to do something about this pain. I turn to Susan. Susan is a new friend, a wavy-haired, Southern California healer in Beijing to hone her craft. She is studying the use of traditional Chinese medicine and Eastern philosophy to treat the body and improve health. Older than me, she radiates a holistic vibe that breeds trust. I am comfortable with her and reach out. I do not think I would have done so to Linda, the other western acupuncturist I met here. I enjoyed our day touring Beijing on bicycle, but Linda's vibe was quite different than Susan's.

Susan gives me a massage. I do not like massages because I am ticklish, but this time I lie there without cringing or, worse, squirming with the giggles. The pressure of Susan's hands is strong as she squeezes and molds my upper body. For someone with a medium physique, there is power in her. The overall sensation is one of pain, but somehow controlled and positive.

When she stops, I release the breath I had not realized I was holding and turn my neck. It is better. I relax.

But the relief does not last and a few days later I am complaining once again.

Susan has the solution and she puts on the full-court press. She wants me to try acupuncture. She explains the history of acupuncture, and the wide range of treatments for which it is used.

"Andrew, the Chinese even use it as an anesthetic during surgery. I swear it will not be painful." She looks me directly in the eyes trying to convey what to her is a given.

She is supremely confident. I am not. I am having a big problem getting over the fact that she is talking about sticking needles in my body. I do not like needles.

"The treatment can cure this so that it will not return. You will not have to suffer any longer." Her passion gets my attention, her voice soothes some of my worries, and I promise her that I will think about it.

Another day goes by and, needles or not, I realize that I have no alternative. My neck is not getting better, and this is not the time or place to be immobilized.

I screw up the courage and decide to give it a shot. I cannot believe that I am about to take this step. I visit a guy down the hall who has extra acupuncture needles and buy a set from him.

I am ready.

I invite Susan down this afternoon.

"Lie down on your bed on your stomach and face your head left to the wall." The doctor is in. I lie down, hoping against hope that she cannot hear my beating heart. The pounding must be audible in the quiet room. To me it is deafening. "Relax. I am going to gently insert each needle. You will only feel a slight prick." She senses or maybe sees my tension.

I close my eyes. The thought of my body being pierced with little metal pain sticks runs on a loop through my mind. I am about to learn what a pincushion feels like. Will it be like getting a shot? With shots, I have found that the anticipation is worse than the reality, a quick stab of usually minor discomfort and then it is over. Will it start off light and grow in intensity? Will it be a horror of pain that does not end?

I am glad Susan cannot see my face. I am pretty sure I have not relaxed as instructed.

"OK, Andrew. I'm done. You can open your eyes." The statement catches me by surprise.

"Really? You just started. How many needles did you use?"

"Eight," she says evenly. "Two in the back of your neck. Five in your shoulder and back. And the last one is in the back of your left hand."

"That sounds like a lot of needles." I try to say this without my voice cracking. "How long will you leave them in?"

"Fifteen minutes." Her answer is quick and quiet.

"I can't feel them much."

"That's the point. I told you it wouldn't be painful." She gives a friendly chuckle. I imagine she hears this frequently from skeptical new patients. "You can open your eyes."

I open my eyes and immediately wish I had not.

I am staring at the last needle. Inches from my face, this thin, evil barb is anchored in the back of my hand, quivering in the air. It taunts me with unfettered imagination.

This is no shot, no quick prick and then it is over. I don't care what Susan says, this is fifteen minutes of quiet agony, knowing that I am pinned to my bed. I should not have opened my eyes. It doesn't matter if the needles physically hurt or not. This is my body we're talking about! To me, the sensation of discomfort in my mind is real. I know they are there. I am trapped within myself.

God, I hope I do not hyperventilate.

Susan senses my ongoing mental anguish. "Andrew, please close your eyes again and relax. Think of a quiet place that makes you feel calm." I try. "Visualize your place of tranquility. Drift away into sleep." She says this as gently as possible, trying to will me to breathe easy.

I fail.

My mind races. My anxiety level spikes through the roof.

Seemingly hours later, but most likely the promised fifteen minutes, Susan removes the eight evil instruments from my body. "Wait a few days and see what happens." My doctor has completed her treatment.

Sitting on my bed alone after Susan leaves, I struggle to get my blood pressure to stop redlining.

CHAPTER 7

WAITING FOR CLASSES

M Y VASSAR FRIENDS are in their third week of classes while I twiddle my thumbs on this mid-September day. I have taken my placement tests. I have been issued a schedule. I have even met two of my teachers at orientation and most of my ten classmates. We are an international hodgepodge, though majority American. I am supposed to have classes today according to my schedule. The only problem is that there are no classes today. The rooms are empty.

Another week to acclimate. This is getting to be a routine. At least it begins on a positive note. I receive my first letter! From mom and dad. Sent eight days ago. The rush I feel at holding the envelope and peeling it open is surprisingly strong. And then another positive note. I realize that my neck feels much better and moves freely. It appears to be holding too. My upper back was a little sore from the needles, but that was it. What do you know? My personal acupuncture professional, Susan, was right. I opened myself up to try something new, and it worked.

I experience more of Chinese society, the types of things you do not encounter on Cape Cod. Babies and toddlers wear open, slit-bottom pants. No diapers for this crowd. When little boys or girls, bare tushes sticking out here and there, have to go, they go. Parents and grandparents help them squat and gravity takes over. I see this on sidewalks. I see this in between moving train cars. I smell this in department store stairwells.

This, though, is not as bad as spitting and much less disgusting than nose blowing. I understand the spitting, even if the hucking sound is gross. With all the dust and grime, it helps clean out your mouth. Nose blowing, however? Watch out. Just the thought of it gives me the shivers. The Chinese put a finger on one side of the nose to close it and then blow as hard as possible from the other nostril. This is a no-tissues endeavor, commenced from about four feet above ground. If one is standing within potential range, gauging wind speed and direction are important considerations.

While fruitlessly trying on padded Mao jackets in a local market one afternoon, I look left and notice two Chinese girls taking my picture. They are journalism students at a nearby school. I model one jacket as they snap away. More than half a dozen Chinese gather around to gawk. I put them out of my mind and focus on my fashion. Unfortunately, the jackets are either a little short or a little tight or not the right color. One of my new journalist friends confirms as much when I glance over for validation. I can imagine the headline in the next edition of their school newspaper: "Foreign Student Models Chinese Jackets at Haidian Marketplace."

My additional week to acclimate coincides with an important Chinese festival, Zhongqiujie, the Mid-Autumn (Moon) Festival. This harvest festival of thanksgiving takes places during the full moon on the fifteenth day of the eighth lunar month. The *yuebing*, mooncake, I ate on the train back from Inner Mongolia symbolizes the festival. A group of us originally plan to visit the ruins at Yuanmingyuan, the Old Summer Palace, to celebrate under the harvest moon. We do go out, but never leave campus.

We instead first watch a Soviet film dubbed into Chinese. Most of the dialogue escapes me, but the plot is by no means subtle. A dramatic disaster movie with a side of unintended comedic relief, it conjures up rather unsettling parallels to living in China. "Picture a movie," Billy sardonically suggests, "with no budget so they have to incorporate all of the disasters into one scene."

There is a plane. The plane lands on a skinny runway high in a mountain at a burned-out airport that is blackened, broken, and aflame. Upon landing, an earthquake strikes. One plane rolls into the terminal. Another blows up on take-off. A torrent of floodwater pours down from higher in the mountain. Nearby oil fields explode. Trains from unseen tracks above tumble down the side of the mountain along with flailing, hapless people. All is on fire. Ferocious winds sweep down and carry more people over the edge of the cliff. The heroes manage to take off in the sole airplane that hasn't been destroyed as blazing gas that looks suspiciously like lava engulfs the runway.

Stumbling spent out of the screening room, we manage only to walk over to Weiminghu, "No Name Lake," the largest of several lakes at Beida. I strolled over here shortly after arriving on campus to sit on a bench and read. I wound up people watching. I wondered then what the Chinese students thought of me, a foreigner, sitting in their midst.

Tonight, most of the activity is winding down by the time we arrive, but small groups of students still cluster around the lake in pockets. Some sing accompanied by a guitar player, while others play *xiangqi*, Chinese chess, as well as poker and games I do not recognize. Two television sets with video games perch on a nearby hill. Smaller kids play table tennis on one set, and students play a fighter plane game on the other. Another group is playing a game that looks a little like pool, except that four players stand around a square table trying to shoot a puck into the opponents' holes. There is a noticeable absence of girls in this makeshift lakeside gaming center. Every now and then a couple will peer in, but only briefly before melting into the night.

—〰—

The next day Billy and I bike the short distance to Yiheyuan, Empress Cixi's Summer Palace. The Dowager Empress diverted much of the failing Qing Dynasty's treasury in the late nineteenth century to rebuild and expand this imperial garden as her private resort after the British torched the nearby Yuanmingyuan. The preserved beauty of Yiheyuan lies in its architecture and the endless paths, forests, and waterways. Stone bridges appear and disappear. We climb the forested Longevity Hill rising up next to the expansive Kunming Lake. There is a sparkling, pollution-free view today of Beida and the more urban outskirts of Beijing. The juxtaposition of old and new is jarring. The classical pavilions, halls, and covered terraces of the Summer Palace are painted in reds, greens, and blues that pop. Russian-style, concrete block buildings dot the distance.

Resting on a railing in the famous Long Walk stretching along the lakeside, I feel that sensation again. The ancient structure makes me tingle. The weighty history buried beneath my feet and in the air and the trees and the water stirs my soul. This awareness, this feeling of "being here," suffers only from the problem that plagues many tourist sites—its growing popularity results in crowds and an explosion in tourist trappings serving the masses. Food stalls sell snacks; souvenir shacks sell trinkets; and people mill around offering to take your picture for a price.

Billy and I return to campus, pick up Peter, and the three of us head to the weekly Saturday night campus dance with our new Chinese friend, Chen. Chen likes hanging around with foreigners and has become part of our circle. He is a young painter from Southern China with wild, wavy black hair and a mission to live life on his own terms, the picture of a true Chinese Bohemian. The dance is well attended, and we attract our customary collection of English-speaking Chinese looking to practice. One of them is Honghua, a plain-looking Beida senior who comes right over to latch on with the foreigners.

Chen begs us to dance. He is bouncy with energy. None of us are dancers, but we eventually relent and each hit the floor with Honghua. It does not go well. Peter, to his credit, tries twice. Billy and I each try once and quit. When I go right, she goes left. When I go left, she goes right. We cannot get into a rhythm. I am not good, but Honghua is worse. This does not seem to faze her, though, and she keeps going. It is not pretty.

I am impressed with the music selection and the fact that some of the songs were not censored. Interspersed among the waltzes, tangos, and more formal dances are Tears for Fears ("Shout"), David Bowie ("Modern Love" and "China Girl"), and Madonna ("Like a Virgin"). Chen, however, is not happy. "The music is too slow. It is much better at the Xiyuan." He proudly informs us that he periodically splurges and goes to this expensive, joint-venture hotel to party.

Tonight's dance reminds me of a high school dance with its collections of people clinging to the walls watching the action, such that it is. Dim lighting. A DJ. I think he is playing reel-to-reel tapes. There are many same-gender tandems out on the dance floor. This is one of many customs that are so different here. Even on the streets, in public, it is not unusual to see either guys or girls walking arm in arm or hand in hand. It's a communal feeling, with no apparent social awkwardness. Several of the Chinese dancers are good. Others stumble around like us. A few of the students are smiling, laughing, and talking while dancing, but most wear serious expressions and are either watching their feet or staring straight ahead.

A Chinese guy dressed in imitation leather pants and a "cool" jacket leaps into the middle of the dance floor during one particularly fast song and takes off on a solo. In a dance style that can best be described as a mix of *tai chi* and *kung fu*, he jumps, bends, twists, and kicks in a flurry of movement. Face scrunched in a warrior grimace, teeth gritted, lips flared, he reminds me of a picture I have seen of one of Emperor Qin Shihuang's Terracotta Soldiers in Xian. This student must be doing something right because when he finishes, a few clap for him. The Chinese never clap. Once a performance is done, it's over. No applause, no whistling, no straggling. You stand up. Silently. You walk out. Silently.

——

If I am going to live like a local, I need money. Changing U.S. money for local currency would be a simple matter in most places. China is not most places. When the communists began opening up the country to more foreign contact in the late 1970s, they wanted to keep control of the contacts. They are obsessed with control. As far as money is concerned, they went so far as to create a second currency for foreigners as a way to limit where the foreigners could go and how we interact with the local populace.

The Chinese people use *renminbi*, the People's Currency. In 1980, the government introduced *waihui duihuanquan*, Foreign Exchange Certificates ("FEC"), colloquially shortened to *waihui*. Foreigners are required to use FEC instead of *renminbi*. FEC can only be used in certain places, like joint venture hotels and state-owned friendship stores (expensive stores carrying a broader line of quality products that limit access to foreigners and the elite). This might be all good and well for tourists passing through, but what about those of us who have to buy fruit and vegetables at the market, get our bicycles repaired at a small shop, and buy paper and pens? Ordinary businesses do not accept FEC.

The answer is that we foreigners get our hands on *renminbi*. Once we have it, no one cares. In the new China of expanded economic opportunities and small businesses, a shadow economy has arisen to assist the experiment in capitalism. I head downtown to the Alley. Sandwiched between buildings in the area bordered by the Beijing Hotel and the Beijing Friendship Store, the Alley is a little private marketplace of individual stalls. Vendors sell clothes, knickknacks, and a host of other items. Several also offer an illicit money changing service to convert US dollars and FEC into *renminbi*. The recent exchange rate is approximately 125 *renminbi* for one hundred FEC. Changing out in the open can be risky since the public security bureau patrols and periodically cracks down. The Alley gives us cover. I let the vendor know how much I want to change and then count the bills in the back of the stall away from prying eyes. Not only do I get more cash, but it is cash I can use.

Today, I also purchase my second snuff bottle. An allegedly Qing Dynasty, blue and white porcelain bottle catches my eye. I violate Rule No. 1 of negotiating as I am sure my face displays my eagerness. The lady wants more than seventeen US dollars. I tell her that I only have half that amount. She offers a trade. However, after searching my knapsack and person, we find nothing of value. I offer her the same half, but now in FEC. I'll let her have the float. She asks me if I have a pen. I pull out a pen I bought in Datong for twenty cents. Thus, with FEC and the pen, I have my bottle.

If I am going to live in China, I want to exercise and practice a Chinese martial art. Thus, at 5:50 a.m. today with my two snuff bottles sitting on my bookshelf and way before the sun rises, I find myself preparing for an *wushu, kung fu,* class. I get up quietly and leave without disturbing Toshiro. Li, our teacher, is a Chinese-American exchange student about my age from Florida. He is skilled in the complex *zui quan wushu,* drunken fist *kung fu.* He offered to teach a class on the basics of *kung fu,* and a small group of us shows up to an empty first-floor classroom in the pre-dawn darkness for the first session.

Li begins with a brief history lesson. *Kung fu* has a proud tradition in Chinese society and embodies mental as well as physical conditioning. It is not something that is mastered quickly or easily, but rather is a lifelong pursuit concentrating on defense and preparation. Li tells us that we will be stretching, twisting, kicking, and punching. We will be learning how to stand, how to think, how to react. "If you are serious about this practice, you will need to learn to *chiku,* eat bitterness." In its simplest sense, this is a Chinese metaphor for working hard. In practical terms, it is a statement of required mental toughness.

To begin our first class, we stretch and stretch and stretch, preparing our muscles and bodies for the movements to come. I feel like a slab of taffy being pulled every which way. Li continues this conditioning workout for a nonstop ninety minutes. He is not mean, but he sure is relentless. When the session is over, I look around the room at several exhausted faces. Sweat mats my hair and drips through my T-shirt. I turn away and hobble back to my room. A searing pain throbs up the back of both legs with each tender step. My thighs burn. My back and shoulders and arms feel like a squashed pretzel. I didn't think my body could contort in such grotesque positions. Every muscle screams at me, scolding my temerity for putting them through this punishing treatment. Forget mental toughness. I drop with a cry of anguish onto my bed defeated. My first *wushu* class is my last *wushu* class. Eating this bitterness is beyond me.

But, I still want to try something. There has got to be a Chinese exercise for the lazy, timid, and weak minded. When I can stand and move with a modicum of dignity, I seek out Li and ask him if there is anything else I can try, something that hopefully won't break me. He considers my request, applauds my continued interest in trying, and suggests *qigong*. I have no idea what this is. Li tells me that *qigong* is translated as energy work. The *gong* is the same *gong* as in *gongfu*, *kung fu*, but the emphasis is on working with the body's internal energy, its *qi*. *Qi* is the essence of the universe, of our beings, and is the backbone that runs through Daoist philosophy on nature and man.

According to Li, *qigong* is a martial art that aims to cultivate the *shen*, spirit, the *jing*, essence, and the *qi*, energy, that are in each of us. Identifying and channeling the *qi* lead to strengthening the *jing*, which leads ultimately to nurturing the *shen*. *Qigong* is all about seeking balance within ourselves and with nature. When we are in balance, our bodies, our minds, and our lives improve. We become formidable. This herculean task is accomplished (if at all) by clearing and emptying the mind of the clutter of the world and focusing on slow, deep breathing. The *qi* is there if we can find it.

The good part is that the practice consists of languid, meditative upper-torso movements with none of the torture of *wushu*. While *qigong* is not physically strenuous, Li cautions that I should not think it easy. Like *wushu*, *qigong* takes decades to master. It too requires the ability to *chiku*, and maybe even more so because of the internal nature of the practice. As much as *wushu* strained my physical being, *qigong* will strain my mental being.

CHAPTER 8

CLASSES BEGIN

IGHTY-FIVE PERCENT OF Beida's students have now trickled onto campus. This is significant because meeting this threshold signals the beginning of classes.

Han Yu, Chinese Language, Level 3 is my first class. This two-hour reading, vocabulary, and listening and speaking comprehension class is taught by Guo Laoshi, Teacher Guo, a 1985 Beida graduate. Stylish in a modern-China way, she is more our contemporary and is excited to be teaching foreign students. The vocab is familiar, and the reading passages are simple, but I need to know many more characters. Characters, characters, characters. I cannot believe how many I used to know that I now stumble over. Not to mention the thousands I do not know. Learning Chinese requires constant repetition and effort. Because nothing is familiar, as opposed to the Spanish and German I have studied in the past, there is no possibility of guessing what a character means. My speaking isn't too bad at this point. My listening comprehension is improving a little. Characters, however, are another story. This will be work.

The university arranges an outing every Tuesday night during the semester for the foreign students. Tonight, we attend an abbreviated Peking Opera show. The opening act is an hour of jug balancing, long-bow maneuvers, magic, "Chinese Hacky Sack" (two people dancing around and bouncing a small pink object between different parts of their bodies), and other balancing acts. One of the girls must be boneless. She bends and twirls like a rubber band, all the while flawlessly balancing bowls of water on her head, her palms, and the soles of her feet.

The opera itself, a merciful twenty minutes, is a cacophonous medley of drums, bells, and gongs led by hidden musicians playing wood blocks and stringed instruments. Four armed, colorfully-dressed warriors protect a flower in a small glade on a mountain. Dancing around, brandishing their swords as they guard this rare and prized possession, the warriors soon depart. A girl wearing a headdress and a white costume with sparkles emerges into the glade. Two sheathed swords hang by her side. She introduces us to the story with a long sequence of dancing and singing. It does not matter that I cannot understand what she is saying because I cannot even hear what she is saying over the music. Ultimately, she is confronted by one of the warriors. They battle and his friends come to help. Our heroine fights them all. Swords having been replaced by poles, the contestants throw, kick, and bounce across the stage in coordinated and ferocious harmony. The maiden proves triumphant and snatches the prize as the vanquished soldiers look on forlornly.

I share a seat on the return bus ride with a North Korean student. Lu is tall and slim, sitting ramrod straight. He speaks a little Spanish, Hindi, English, and Chinese. We speak in clipped Chinese. The basic questions come first and we learn that we are each twenty years old, the oldest of three children, and have a younger brother and sister.

Lu is wearing a pin of his country's leader, Kim Jong Il. I've seen a couple of North Koreans wearing them. They are by far the most unusual ones I have seen. This makes it all the more enticing for my pin collection.

"Do you have an extra to trade?"

"An extra what?"

"Your pin."

His eyes narrowing in confused suspicion, he shoots back, "Why?"

"I collect pins."

Silence. Pin-drop silence. Our conversation crashes to a halt.

What did I say? Is he upset? Bewildered? Something else entirely? I cannot read his face.

Sitting in my own thoughts for the remainder of the ride and for the walk up to my room, I think I finally have it figured out. My request did not just take him by surprise; rather, it was more foundational. I asked a question that should not ever have been a question. I collect pins as a hobby. It is fun, a pastime. For Lu, his pin is not a mere decoration. His pin is a piece of his identity. It is his connection to his social group. It might even be a political requirement. Trading his pin, giving it up for any reason, particularly to an American, is not an option. It is not even conceivable.

A Chinese man stands outside my temporary single when I return (Toshiro is away for a month of work-study). He is about to leave a note. I realize that it is Wang Ping, my New York City roommates' brother. I have not seen him since our first meeting outside of Beida's front gate when I gave him the toy bear for his nephew. He invites me to his home next Wednesday (October 1) for China's National Day, one of the three official Chinese holidays. On October 1, 1949, Mao Zedong proclaimed the formation of the People's Republic of China. Ping speaks slowly for my benefit, but the slurring rhythm of his Beijing accent is heavy and understanding his tones and his words is a challenge. I agree to attend, but am instantly nervous because if I have a hard time understanding him, what will it be like with the entire family? As Ping turns to leave, he asks me to sign his pass to be in the building. He had to leave his ID card at the front desk. As a foreigner, I can go just about wherever I please. As a Chinese, Ping cannot.

Late tonight, I practice *qigong*. I have only had one lesson, but this is the exercise for me. No squatting, crunching or twisting. No strenuous physical exertion. No *wushu*-inspired regret at being alive when it is over. The movements we learned this morning are designed to circulate our *qi*, our inner energy. Li tells us to breathe slowly and deeply and to concentrate on the breaths and our flowing arms. Once we are successful in emptying our thoughts and on concentrating, we will begin to meditate and feel our *qi*. Once we can feel it, we can direct it to different parts of our body to control our inner energy. There is an issue, however (of course there is). My mind is constantly aflutter. Trying to empty it is indeed at least as hard mentally as *wushu* is physically. The goings-on of the outside world and my internal review of this, that, and everything in my life relentlessly intrude into my consciousness. My mind empty would be a vacuum, and nature abhors a vacuum. But, what if I stick with *qigong*? Might I be able to use it to harness my temper and not be so quick to blow up? Being able to process a situation without first exploding would be a welcome change.

—⁂—

Following up our visit to the underground city, Peter and I bike to the National Art Gallery after class to see a photo exhibit documenting four decades of Chinese communist history. Taken by a husband-and-wife team, the photographs show war, historical events, landscapes, everyday happenings, and people, people, people. The exhibit reflects the official story of modern China, of the political heroes who saved the country. Deng Xiaoping and his son watch Zhu De and Peng Dehuai play chess. The original of the famous picture of Deng and Mao conferring at Jinan in 1959 is here. In all pictures showing Mao, the face of each person in his presence is fixed wide with a smile of rapture. This sense of being with their "emperor," their "god," leaps out from the photographic paper. Such unconditional joy and awe in the presence of a politician, possibly anyone, is unfathomable to me.

The National Art Gallery, like many grand Beijing buildings, has a split personality. The first impression of the distinguished exterior is "wow." Detailed craftsmanship is a testament to the dedication and affection devoted to the design and construction of these magnificent edifices. And then one crosses over the transom to find uniformly drab, dreary, and dull interiors. It was the same in Datong with a twist. Our nine-story hotel offered well-appointed rooms, but the bathroom looked like it hadn't been cleaned since the place opened a few years before. There was a billiards room on the top floor with a table, balls, and no cues. The veneer in the larger cities screams modernization, and the Chinese are indeed good in places at applying the wrapping paper, but they often forget to fill the box. They try hard to emulate the first world, but China is a developing country in the throes of epic changes and it just isn't there yet.

As I turn to leave the gallery, a petite Chinese girl approaches me. "Hello. English speaking?" She stands there shyly, a nervous yet expectant hope on her face.

"Yes, I speak English." I enunciate the words the way I need the Chinese to with me.

"I learn speak English." Still timid, she relaxes at my familiar words.

She wants to talk, and screwed up the courage to do so, but the words do not come out smoothly. She is frustrated. I know how that feels. When I tell her that I am an American exchange student and speak Chinese, her relief is palpable. She begins speaking Mandarin, but so softly that it comes out a whisper. Her name is Meilin, and I gather that she is a student nearby. We exchange addresses and go our separate ways. This is a common practice with foreigners. I recently received a letter from another "exchanged addresses friend," a guy Peter, Billy, and I met in Datong from

Taiyuan University. I am proud of the fact that I understood the entire gist of his letter without a dictionary.

After a pleasant morning, the day nosedives. Peter and I return to a restaurant that we liked the first time with decent food, OK service, and inexpensive prices—a college student's nirvana. Today, it is crowded, so we follow custom and hover over a particular table until the people are done and leave. I hate doing it and even more so hate it being done to me. Once seated, we wait close to an hour to be served. We should have taken the hint. Since we still do not read menus well, we do the same as before and order a pork dish, a chicken dish, a vegetable dish, and soup. Instead of three dishes, though, five are brought to our table. We make the mistake of keeping them even though we do not eat much and do not know what they are. One appears to be a plate of pig fat.

Then the bill comes. It is more than four times what we paid last time!!! The operators sensed our naïveté and concocted exorbitantly expensive dishes for the foreigners. I expect to be taken a little. It has happened before, and it will happen again, but this is outrageous. The Chinese would have fought back. They would not take such an affront. They do not stand for being cheated. Alas, Peter and I are not Chinese. We impotently pay and leave chagrined and steaming, not being confident enough in our Chinese to argue

It gets worse. On the ride back to campus, I hit two people with my bike and just miss two taxis. Brakes would have helped. They loosened last week, and I have yet to fix them. I figured they were still about eighty percent effective. I was wrong. At one point, I collide with Peter's back wheel. Off balance, I cannot move my bike away from his and we roll along together until he rides me to a stop (like a cowboy trying to stop a runaway wagon in a western movie). Later, we are riding smoothly when the guy in front of me abruptly turns aside. Facing me, not three feet away, is a lady standing in the bike lane holding a shoebox in one hand. I am hemmed in on both sides. An accident is about to happen. She stares at me, feet rooted to the pavement. At the last second, I shift left, and she leans right. As my handlebars smack into her shoe box, spinning her around, I maintain my forward momentum and then I am past. I glance back wobbly to see if she is OK, and receive a glare in return. Yep, she is OK. My heart races, wondering what the next shoe to drop will be this afternoon. I was going to change money at the Alley, but decide that the way the day is going, I would likely get arrested. I skip the Alley.

—⁂—

Exploring more of the Beida campus, Peter, Billy, and I visit Honghua, the Chinese girl from the dance, in her dorm. We live well in Shao Yuan. Three bunk beds and two double-sided desks fill most of the Chinese dorm room that is not much larger than the room Toshiro and I share. A part of each bed shares duty as a shelf. Drying clothes hang from every available space. Honghua's room faces west so it is bright and cheery in the afternoon. I imagine that the rooms away from the sun must be sad and gloomy. The hallways certainly are. Dungeon dim with only the occasional straining bulb, the high ceilings are cloaked far above where the pale light penetrates. Clothes sway from bars every five or six feet. The halls are dank and heavy.

Honghua is not a shy young woman. She complains bitterly about how unfair it is that the Chinese are not afforded equal opportunities in their own country. Foreigners are given special attention, access, and, comparatively speaking, first-rate conditions. She is spot on. The socialist state preaches the classless free and equal, but Communist China does not walk the talk. Never did. The leaders have always been the elite haves, a perpetuation of the status of the imperial line and Confucian gentry; the masses, the have nots. Now, we foreigners are among the haves, and the masses are still the have nots. I have the luxury of being in this higher class, and it bothers me that I have these privileges. Yet, how would I survive in this society at its stage of development if I was truly among the masses? My western middle-class upbringing is being tested as it is. As for the broader society, classes may be a human reality, but if the differentiation and inequality are not properly managed, then there is oppression. Oppression breeds resentment. The end result is usually combustible.

Another Chinese young person who is not shy is Chen, the wild-eyed artist who likes to party and dance. He has inserted himself into our lives. Tonight, he showers in Shao Yuan. His clothes lie on my bed. While he is in the shower, a friend comes over to look at dictionaries. When Chen returns, we talk. A third knock. Zhao Gaoshan, a Chinese guy I met playing American football on the field in front of the library, under the gaze of the towering Mao statue, enters. It is well that we were playing touch football because the slender Gaoshan would have been destroyed if tackling were allowed. He is a graduate student sent by his *danwei*, work unit, to study computers at Beida. Gaoshan is teaching himself English and we exchanged addresses. Reserved but also not shy about his desires, we discussed trading language lessons. I did not expect him so soon and unannounced. The others clear out, and I help Gaoshan with his English. His grasp of the basics is solid. He leaves when I head out in search of my new best friends, Billy and Peter, to attend the foreign students dance with Chen.

I find them in Billy's room with a Chinese student who speaks excellent English. Philosophy is the topic when I enter. The conversation switches from god and creation myths to China's Autonomous Regions and reverse discrimination. As usual, it is a wide-ranging, high-level bull session among the western students. The English is flying thick this night. These are not light topics. I look over at the Chinese student who is doing his best to keep up with the exchange. I only too easily sympathize with his plight. Excellent English or not, this has got to be hard on him. I would have been mystified if the conversation had been in Chinese.

As I sit, my mind wanders. It can do so because I understand the words, the background, the speech patterns of those doing the talking. They are speaking my language, figuratively and literally. I do not have to strain to comprehend tones, character sounds, idioms, context. I am glad my closest friends here speak English. Now and then, more often now than then in reality, it is relaxing to fall back into a comfort zone. Not knowing the right words and how to express myself, especially when shopping and eating out, is so frustrating. I feel like an imbecile. Speaking English helps me keep my sanity and release tension. Yet, this savior of mine is also a crutch. If I want to achieve fluency in Chinese, whether it be at a restaurant, at someone's home, or in a college seminar, then I need to make much more of an effort. Language proficiency is earned, not gifted. I am in China. If I do not apply myself now, then when?

More than one hour later, I am exhausted by this English debate session and return to my room. As I crash into bed, I remember that I stood up Chen for the dance.

CHAPTER 9

A BEIJING FAMILY

O CTOBER I, 1986. *Guo Qing Jie*, National Day. We have two days off to celebrate the communists' 1949 victory of the proletariat over the decadent, oppressive culture of imperial China. I do the Chinese holiday thing and go visiting. This is the day Wang Ping invited me over to his Beijing home when he showed up at my room last week. Early afternoon, I leave Shao Yuan and peddle out the Beida gate to the bus stop. I park my bike and catch a bus downtown. The crowds are wall-to-wall stupendous. On foot, bicycle, bus, trolley, cab. I am lost in the midst of a loud, pulsating, body-mashing scene.

I am nervous. I am heading to a Chinese home, to visit a Chinese family. Will my Chinese be good enough? Will I understand them? Will I make some horrible linguistic mistake and offend them? This is no-safety-net time. I arrive thirty-five minutes early for my 4:30 p.m. rendezvous with Ping at a bus stop not far from his home.

Strolling nearby streets to pass the time, I discover a large Catholic church screened behind one of the ubiquitous walls lining many Chinese streets. The church is an old cement structure with a small balcony. On the outside of the building is half a confession booth, built for three. On either side of the enclosed portion of the booth, a confessor sits out in

71

the open. The separation between priest and penitent is a piece of clear mosquito netting. Privacy is apparently not an important part of Chinese confession. Come to think of it, Communist China is officially atheist. There should not be any confession, inside or outside. Inside the church, the design on one of the kneeling pads catches my attention. It is a Nazi swastika. I stare at it slack-jawed and cannot for the life of me understand why a church would use this as a decorative motif.

Still puzzled, I make my way back to the bus stop. Wang Ping is waiting. He and his family live in a *siheyuan*, a traditional Beijing quadrangle home located inside a *hutong*, one of the long, interconnected maze of alleyways that are a hallmark of old Beijing. Entering the narrow alley, we thread our way deeper and deeper into the interior. Turning and turning, my normally good sense of direction deserts me. I am a child being led into the dusky unknown. Numerous families sharing numerous *siheyuan* are hidden behind the tall, windowless walls punctuated with closed wooden doors. We pass a duck feeding from a basin. Is he Sunday night's dinner?

In times long gone by, each such home was designed for one extended family, a wealthy family, maybe a family with imperial connections. A front, south-facing gate leads to a spirit screen and then a moon gate. The home is designed so that it will have good *feng shui*, a balance of wind and water—harmony among the elements. The spirit screen requires residents and guests to travel around it to enter the courtyard and provides more than privacy. Since spirits can only travel in straight lines, the screens block them from entering the home and bringing mischief. Through the moon gate and into the central courtyard would open up onto connected buildings on the east and west for the younger and older generations and the main building at the north end for the principal family member. In Communist China, however, many families share one courtyard home, crammed inside wherever they can be squeezed in a place that used to reflect serenity and position.

My hosts live in a cozy, two-room flat. This is their entire home. It is spotlessly clean in a city ever caked in dust. Ping's parents live next door, in what is another part of the old *siheyuan*. Ping and his wife have a five-year-old son in addition to caring for their nephew. I cannot get a straight answer as to how old their nephew, between two and four years old, is. You would think I would know this after sharing an apartment with his parents in New York City. The outer room of the flat is their living area; the inner room, the bedroom. The living room is furnished with a hard couch, a few chairs, a Sharp television, and two pieces of furniture that are a combination of hope chest, bookshelves, and display shelves. Glancing inside the bedroom, I see a double bed, desk, and a Sharp stereo. It is tight for four.

Wang Ping, Zhang, an old friend, and I spend an hour chatting, eating apples and small, tangy oranges, and drinking soda pop. They are dressed in dark trousers and light shirts, untucked. Zhang, though unmarried and living with his parents, hints that he and his girlfriend might eventually marry. They politely offer me cigarettes every fifteen minutes during the entire four hours I spend with them. Smoke swirls around us in the small living room. It is hard to ignore. I try not to choke. Although Zhang speaks some English, the bulk of the conversation is in Chinese. Ping only began studying English two months ago. Zhang's expression is that of a happy man proud to be translating for us even though we all understand the Chinese conversation, even me. My confidence grows.

Ping's father and another family friend carrying his infant son join us. Dad is difficult to understand. I struggle to attach meaning to the numerous sounds he is speaking. The smoky room is not the only thing that is hazy as I try hard to concentrate. The elder Mr. Wang is a manager at the Beijing Railway Yard. Zhang recently transferred to a job working with foreign tourists. Ping is studying English so that he can hopefully transfer from his factory job to a job in a joint-venture hotel. The chance for contact with foreigners, much better pay, and the possibility of future opportunities is the shiny prize. Transferring jobs is a new phenomenon in

Chinese society, one that has been instituted only over the last ten years. Before, your government-assigned job was your career. It might be boring or counter to what you studied or desire, but that was irrelevant. With the "economic reform and opening-up" program (*gaige kaifang*), what the Chinese government calls Socialism with Chinese Characteristics, transfers are now an option for those fortunate enough to succeed.

As dinnertime approaches, I briefly meet the rest of the family. Ping's wife, son, and mother enter quietly and say hello, but not much else. I do not even learn his wife's name. Little nephew is still sleeping. The women shortly slip back out to the kitchen. The viewing, them of me and me of them, is over. At 5:30 p.m., the living room converts to a dining room as a table and three chairs are set up. Ping, Zhang, and I sit around the table. My cultural bias quickly lands me in trouble.

"There are only three place settings. Can I help bring a seat over for your wife?" I ask Ping innocently.

Both men look at me silently for a moment as if trying to come up with an appropriate answer. Ping breaks the silence.

"Andrew, tradition in our culture is that men and women eat separately. The women and children will eat later in the kitchen." He says this with simple, definitive clarity letting me know that I am an outsider and do not know better.

Silence again ensues as I have no immediate response. I can only imagine the confusion etched in my face as I try to formulate my next words. Before my mouth can further betray me, the first of the dishes, eggplant with pork sautéed in oyster sauce, arrives, and the awkward moment passes.

Ninety minutes later, I am ready to burst. A stack of empty plates teeters on the little table, the remnants of an eleven-course meal! The offerings kept coming, and I kept eating. Ping's wife was a conveyor belt entering and leaving the room with more and more food. She produced this feast from a communal kitchen in the *siheyuan*. Hot dishes. Cold dishes. Soup. Rice. We dine on beef and greens, carp, cold turkey meat, tomatoes, beef meatballs, and cucumbers with shredded chicken. My favorite is a mouth-watering veal in a red sauce that reminds me of an Italian dish. I love veal and am not shy. It is delicate and delectable, and I am later astonished to learn that I devoured much of a plate of pork and tomatoes.

Dinner even includes Shandong chicken. Unlike in America, chicken is the priciest meat in China. The time, effort, and expense to produce this feast are not inconsequential. My hosts go all out preparing this banquet for the honored foreign guest. How much of their monthly income did it consume? I am one part sated and one part mortified that they have gone to all of this expense and effort for me. I understand that my visit is rare, even now. Not too many years ago, such a visit would have been unthinkable, a criminal and political offense. I am finally able to compliment the chef when she and her mother make another brief appearance at the end of the meal.

There is much face being given tonight, on both sides. How to describe *mianzi*, face? It is a distinctly Chinese concept. It is a way of living, of acting, of showing respect to others and upholding the respect of oneself and one's family or group. It can be big or little, significant or insignificant. It can be individual, familial, societal, national. My hosts honor me and themselves with their efforts. I, in turn, provide them the status of having a foreign acquaintance (admittedly a situation that could become a liability if the political winds shift). If I do not mess up too badly, then I maintain my own face as well.

Alcohol becomes a conversation topic. I, the non-drinker, have a glass of beer and a glass of red wine with dinner. I enjoy the wine. My hosts bring out a bottle of Chinese hard liquor. The bottle, which they say is the second best behind Maotai, is itself expensive at fifteen yuan (about US$4), but still less than half the thirty-five yuan (more than US$9) cost of a bottle of Maotai. Zhang notes that a bottle of Maotai equals half a month's salary for a factory worker. So this bottle would set a worker back one quarter of his month's salary. I stare at the bottle, fearing that they will open it. If they do, face will require me to drink. I do not think I can handle doing shots. I silently will them not to move to the hard liquor. My efforts are not in vain.

As we continue to talk, Ping states that he likes Americans. "You are outgoing and cheerful." Zhang chimes in, "You are friendly too."

"I think all people are the same," I say. "It's just that the Chinese cannot now be as outgoing with strangers due to 'real-life' conditions." My poorly phrased contribution does not sit well with Ping, but not because of my linguistic weakness.

"Well, I do not like the Japanese," Ping says. Belying the simple words (possibly for my benefit), his face mottles with hatred as he spits out the words with sudden bitter vehemence.

Given the history of the two peoples over the last century, most especially the Japanese brutality on Chinese soil during World War II, his raw emotions are not surprising. I ask him to elaborate, but the wave of passion passes. He would have lost face if he did not control himself in front of a foreigner, a guest in their country, a guest in his home. I admire his ability to restrain himself. It is not a character trait we share.

News of their relatives in New York is eagerly received. When Ping's brother first went to the States, his wife became very sick. I am the first person the family has met who has seen them recently. Thus, as soon as Ping's wife and mother come back into the room, the questions explode, and the Mandarin flies fast.

"Is she OK?"

"How does she look?"

"Is she eating?"

"What kind of food do they eat in America?"

Mom though has the most Chinese of questions: "Is she fat?" An American does not ask such a question. It would be considered the height of rudeness, the type of thing your mother scolds you for uttering. In China, to the contrary, it is a positive inquiry. If you are fat, you are eating. You are healthy. You are successful. I understand where she is coming from and tell her that they are eating well. That is as far as I can go. I want to oblige, but I cannot bring myself to call my fit former roommate fat.

They ask about their lives in America.

"New York City is big and bustling with cars, buses, taxis, a huge subway system, and lots and lots of people. They live in an apartment in a building owned by the university. I rented one of the bedrooms in their apartment. We are all out during the day. I worked, and they attended school. The others come home to cook, eat dinner, and rest and study at night. Your brother and sister are happy and healthy. They miss their son and family very much."

I then meet my roommates' son. I am now his uncle too, Shushu Ande (my Chinese name is Xin Ande). I pick him up and sit him on my lap. He immediately jumps off and runs back to grandma. After that, he will not come to me. I learn that he carried the bear I delivered from his mom constantly and did not stop playing with it until it shredded. He calls his aunt and uncle "mama" and "baba." They are raising him. Will he recognize his real parents when they return? Will he want to be with them? He is too young to realize that he is the carrot guaranteeing his parents' loyalty.

The television, which someone turns on after dinner, is so much background noise as we spend the evening chatting away. Tonight has been the most prolonged, and successful, experience I have had in Chinese. I have been privileged to share a private visit with real China. I am full, comfortable, and satisfied. But, the evening has slipped away, and it is time I return to campus.

"If you are still in Beijing at Lunar New Year, you must come over again."

CHAPTER 10

EMOTIONAL TURMOIL

OCTOBER 7, 1986. Life is confusing.

October 9, 1986. I should explain that.

I've got girls, cockroaches, and classes on my mind. Not even the fact that I have now visited the Great Wall of China alleviates this stress. And such an event has been my dream, a prime reason for traveling half way around the world! I hiked for two hours on the restored Badaling section northwest of Beijing. And yet, what I remember of this visit are platitudes—the Great Wall is gorgeous, beautiful, exhilarating, steep, and slippery. I should be able to paint a mental picture of the mountain-tops and the stone structure snaking across the ridge. I should be able to explain the hardness of history under my feet as I climb one of the grandest ancient fortifications ever built. I should be able to describe the view as I hike farther and farther up into the wild terrain of North China. But I cannot. The details are lost in a fog of emotion. I've got girls, cock-roaches, and classes on my mind.

Jill remains silent. Close to two months without even a note. The longer this goes, the more my mind questions. Concern is mixing with annoyance. If she has a problem with us, with me, then tell me. If not, then tell me. It's eating at me, and I have been moaning about it to my friends with increasing vigor. They ask me straight up, "What kind of a girlfriend does not write?" I have been defending her, telling them how wonderful she is and how there must be a good reason she has not written. Now, though, I am not so sure.

I join an international group of students (a mix of Americans, Canadians, Thai, and Chinese) chatting in a dorm room after dinner. I gravitate towards the other American in the room, a Chinese-American woman with long black hair. Her name is Beth, and she is one of the hosts. While everyone else talks about Canada, Beth and I break off for our own quiet conversation. She is an intelligent woman who looks right at me as we talk. Sitting on the edge of one of the beds in the room, we discuss religion, sex, and abortion. I have no idea why or how we focus on such weighty matters—this is our first conversation after all—but Beth and I strike an easy rapport and keep on gabbing.

Eventually, the conversation turns to us. Beth is from the Mid-Atlantic and has family here in Beijing. Her parents escaped during the Chinese Revolution, and this is her first time in China. Beth shares that she at times struggles with her unique position as both Chinese and American. She looks American, acts American, is American. It is clear from how she dresses, how she talks, and how she handles herself. Yet to the Chinese, she is Chinese and is supposed to act Chinese. They expect her to speak perfect Chinese, to understand, to conform, to be like them. She feels constrained by Chinese customs even when they are not hers: "If I laugh out loud and show emotion, the Chinese roll their eyes. When I express my opinion too strongly, I feel their disapproval." And it goes deeper. She knows that she is in part also a reflection on her Beijing relatives. Her actions are not hers to own alone. Such knowledge is heavy. The concept of face stalks Beth in China.

I tell her about me. When talking about Vassar, I mention Jill. I hit the basics: She is one year behind me, we've been dating for a year, are in love, etc. And then, before I know what I am saying, I launch into, "How can she not write? We're supposed to mean everything to each other. We're supposed to get married someday. The last time I saw her was over the summer in Montana. It's like she doesn't care all of a sudden. What am I going to do?" My voice rises to a controlled crescendo. I feel my face burning when I finally come up for a pathetic breath. Beth listens attentively with a polite, interested expression. I admire her poker face. She's probably thinking that this is the last time she invites strangers to her room, particularly whiny white guys. I am flustered by my outburst and jolted by the extent of my bottled up feelings. Thanking Beth for hosting us and chatting with me, I excuse myself and slink out.

Heading back to my room does not help. I enter, turn on the light, and flip when I find four cockroaches partying on my stuff. A shudder rolls through me. Why is a tiny, insignificant insect pissing me off so? I am more freaked out, scared, than angry. I swat them to the floor and squish them dead. Another shudder roils me.

The next day is D-Day. I have to get a handle on this situation. I declare war. I sweep my side of the room and lay new floor mats to keep down the dust and show crumbs better. I dust. I clean. All of my food, well-sealed though it may be, gets tossed. The sole survivor is a factory-sealed bag of cookies. Having cleaned, I discharge an entire can of roach spray in our room, mostly on my side.

Toshiro's side is too crammed for much spraying, but I do what I can. I can feel that his food, pots, and pans are harboring a mess of roaches. I do not think that this problem is all a result of his former Indian roommate's issues. There must be a nest under Toshiro's bed, but I do not want to spray there for fear of wrecking his stuff. I gag when I find several of the pesky buggers at each end of my mattress. The bile rises in my throat, and I try to breathe deeply and calm my mind, as Li keeps instructing during our *qigong* classes. I cannot seem to kill them all. I use roach spray faster than I can re-supply.

I make a decision. I will be content with a demilitarized zone. If

I cannot see the roaches, I will be at a calculated peace. With all the hubris of a liberal arts upbringing, I am an overly simplified embodiment of Philip Slater's "Toilet Assumption." Slater, who we studied in sociology class, writes in *The Pursuit of Loneliness* about the "...notion that unwanted matter, unwanted difficulties, unwanted complexities and obstacles will disappear if they're removed from our immediate field of vision." Slater is talking about our collective societal response to social problems, to how we treat and respond to racism, poverty, the family, our environment, and our very lives and lifestyles. I'm obsessing about cockroaches. Slater points out that, "When these discarded problems rise to the surface again...we react as if a sewer had backed up. We are shocked, disgusted, and angered, and immediately call for the emergency plumber...to ensure that the problem is once again removed from consciousness." These are bloody roaches.

My trifecta of gloom is complete. One of my teachers is a disinterested ignoramus who spouts the dry monotone of bureaucratic propaganda class after class after class. A friend of mine walked out in between quizzes last session, and I forced myself not to follow her. I stuck it out for the last fifteen minutes of class, but only in body. I closed my book and lay my head on my desk. These were firsts for me! I am a good student. The actions went unnoticed.

I do have one class that I love. Guo Laoshi, Teacher Guo, the 1985 Beida graduate, is lively, interested, and caring. A bright spot in a long day. We're writing and role playing. As Zhang Laoshi, Teacher Zhang, reminds us, we need to think in Chinese to speak in Chinese. She channels Professor Chin at Vassar: "We must understand different cultural tendencies that are reflected in language and actions. This is how we will be able to ultimately speak the language and understand like a native."

Modern Chinese is vernacular, an oral language that is generally credited to the populist 1919 *Wusi*, May Fourth Movement. Before this time, classical Chinese ruled the day, and what was said and what was written were not the same. Knowledge and the written word were the provinces of the Confucian elite, the scholars. Commoners didn't merit such attainment. With vernacular, *wo shou xie wo kou*, my hand writes what my mouth speaks. It is the unity of written and oral communication. It is a way to bring knowledge to the masses.

But Chinese is still a language of metaphors and allusions, of historical context and philosophical depth. You have to know the backstory to get the front story. Understanding characters and sentence structure are not enough on their own. The Chinese pepper their speech with four character idioms and longer proverbs. You need to know the importance of the referenced mountain, the pine tree, the peach, the so-and-so king during the so-and-so period of the so-and-so dynasty. These nuances and cultural inputs form the basis of the millennia-long back story. The Chinese learn this from birth. It is infused in every teaching of their parents, in every interaction with society. The foreign student does not, and this is a challenge we face. Two-dimensional words must be understood in connection with their three-dimensional reality. That is what it means to think and communicate in Chinese.

In discussing the beauty of autumn, I write, *shumu you henduo hongye*: "Trees have many red autumn leaves." A true, but plain statement. I'm thinking in English while composing in Chinese. This is not a recipe for fluency or sophistication.

Teacher Guo reads my attempt and constructively offers a more melodious Chinese way of saying the same thing, one that incorporates backstory. Her suggestion includes a four-character Chinese idiom at the end and reads, *shushang dou fahongye, qiuse wucai binfen*: "Red autumn leaves on all of the trees, the autumn scenery blazes with color."

Now why can't I write or think or express myself like this? *Wucai binfen*. Four simple characters that mean much more than the sum of their parts. Shorthand for a fuller expression and description of life, of brightness, of vibrancy. Five (*wu*) colors (*cai*) means "many" and can refer to the splash of blue, yellow, red, green, and violet in a rainbow. Coupled with an ancient term for numerous (*bin*) and another character meaning a jumbled many (*fen*), they combine to mean a riotous profusion. Together, they paint a picture of broad color, a vibrant autumn scene with the trees changing, the season alive. It paints a picture that the English translation does not do justice.

I am inspired to try my hand at Chinese poetry:

AN UNCOMPLICATED DECLARATION

Winter will soon arrive,
The weather's cold, the wind blows hard.
Everyone hides their faces away,
Even the bicyclists do not ride.

    The leaves on the trees have all fallen,
    The boats on Beihai cannot be seen.
    The flavor of the food has no taste,
    But friends I certainly have.

        A person said...I do not like
        The winter season...
        Everything dies,
        Everything is meaningless.

            I do not agree.
            We can consider
            Whatever makes us happy,
            What can be done to have a good life.

Gaoshan and I meet on Wednesday evenings, and today is Wednesday. When I speak like an American in Chinese, which is most of the time, he corrects my misplaced subjects, my poor choice of verbs, my stilted construction. He is quiet and conservative, straight and narrow to the core, and a sweet guy with seemingly no mean bone in his body. Thus, if asked to predict the top one hundred topics of potential conversation tonight when we would stray from studying, I would not have come close to the two we discuss: drugs and prostitution.

It starts innocently enough. There is a reference to Marilyn Monroe in his English text. I explain that she was a famous American movie star with blond hair and a curvy figure. I have difficulty explaining well-endowed in Chinese, so I resort to hand gestures. I'm apparently not that good, and it takes a moment before his puzzled look fades into recognition.

I tell him, "She accidentally killed herself with an overdose of drugs." "Are drugs a problem in America?" Gaoshan asks me earnestly. I have his interest.

"Yes. They are a huge problem impacting all of our society, including young children. The government is waging a losing battle against the drug dealers and the widespread use of drugs." This conversation taxes my Chinese. I wish I could express myself more artfully. I have to use the occasional English word and try to help him understand.

He absorbs this and then, as matter-of-factly as if I said I brushed my teeth this morning, says, "I've heard of marijuana and heroin, but China does not have a drug problem. We used to before the Communist Party came along. Now we do not."

My impulsiveness takes over, and I blurt out with bite, "Yeah, right, Gaoshan. Marijuana is everywhere. It is here, and I would wager there are other drugs as well. You can find controlled substances in Shao Yuan if you want them."

He stares at me a bit shell-shocked for a moment. I gather that he does not believe me, but then the conversation segues to "street girls," as he phrases it. I do have his interest. He is curious about America and wants to know more. He remains sitting back straight on my bed, but now he leans towards me as we talk.

I tell him that prostitution is rampant not only in the US, but also in every large city around the world. There are no hookers parading around Tiananmen Square, but they must be around.

Gaoshan does not challenge this, but, almost rising from the bed, he tells me that, "Drug use is totally bad. People have money and the ability to feed themselves, but choose to spend it on drugs instead. That's not right. One is responsible to look after oneself. Wasting money on drugs is useless and disrespectful towards one's duty. Prostitution might also be illegal, but it is often stimulated by dire need. Young girls don't have money and need to eat. They have no choice."

It is my turn to be a bit shell-shocked. I was not expecting this heart-felt rush of sentiment. While not yelling—that is not his style—this is the most animated I have ever seen Gaoshan. There is conviction behind his words. It is also the most I have heard him speak in one go. I pause, in part to make sure I am correctly processing this amount of Mandarin and in part to formulate an intelligent response.

"Gaoshan, it is not that clear cut. You can get addicted to drugs because of need, poverty, and force, the same as prostitution. How about girls and women who are runaways who are forced into both? How about someone who accidentally gets hooked on drugs, say because of medication, and cannot stop?"

Gaoshan is adamant. He sympathizes with prostitutes and has not one iota of compassion for drug users. To him, the issue is black and white. The latter have a choice and are negligent in squandering the means they have to live without drugs. Prostitutes on the other hand are driven by a necessity to live and get a pass.

I am exhausted when Gaoshan leaves. My brain hurts. I am proud that I held my own in this conversation, but I need to decompress. A couple of western friends stop by and we chill listening to George Carlin's "Indecent Exposure." I quickly return to my comfort zone. The leash remains, though maybe it loosened tonight.

—〜〜—

A few weeks ago, I received a letter from Meilin, the girl I met at the National Art Gallery who was so happy to learn I speak Chinese. I haven't written back. It takes me time to find someone to help decipher her cursive Chinese, and well, I am lazy. I do plan to write her, but before I do, another letter arrives. I quickly find a translator.

"Andrew, the girl who wrote this letter expects an answer from you, man. This is serious. You can see it in the words she uses and how she phrases them."

Deep breath. I can deal with this. Is this an obsessed, nineteen-year-old Chinese girl or someone simply excited to correspond with an exotic foreigner? *Boy, am I full of myself*. I write her a simple letter and mail it the next day.

Later that same afternoon, as I walk downstairs I pass a Chinese girl walking up. I glance at her and keep going. She squeaks softly, but loud enough that it catches my attention. I turn back because I think she wants to ask directions.

"Have you received my two letters yet?" There is intensity in her quiet voice.

Oh crap. A cold awareness clears the fog. "Meilin, how are you?"

She attends school on the other side of the city. The bike ride must have taken her a minimum of an hour. What is she doing here? As required of the Chinese, she left her student ID at the front desk. It is in the written record that she came to see me. I hesitate and then, because there is no other practical option, I invite her to my room.

I sit at my desk. Meilin sits on a corner of my bed. *What does she want?* She has something to say, and when she begins, she becomes a Duracell bunny in a plain sweater with mussed bike hair. Her words and thoughts come tumbling out a mile a minute. I ask her, almost pleading, to slow down. I understand maybe a quarter of what she says. Her soft voice and high pitch make it even more challenging. She has pictures to show me.

We share albums, another common Chinese custom, like exchanging addresses. I begin to feel like there is some sort of ritual at play.

When Meilin sees Jill's photographs on my desk and in my album, the energetic speed-talker falls silent. She closes her mouth and sits immobile. I am at a loss. Her eyes lock onto the pictures. Mine search the wall. The beating of my heart—not the pounding that I heard so acutely during my acupuncture treatment, but rather a normal, everyday beat—is the loudest sound in the room. I think I have the answer to my question of Meilin's interest. Of the photo of Jill and me smiling and holding each other at Yellowstone, the only thing she eventually manages to chirp out is that the scenery is beautiful. We exchange a few more banalities, and she leaves to pick up her ID and her bicycle for the return ride to her campus.

I glance at Jill's pictures once alone. Her pictures may still be everywhere, but that does not mean all is well. Since the dam opened with Beth recently, I have been thinking about my relationship with Jill. I want to know if she wants to be with me, if she cares about me. Is she willing to keep the commitment we talked so much about? I wrote her a letter trying to sum up my feelings, to ask these questions. It rests on my desk unsent.

—⟶⟵—

Pulling open the drapes this morning, I stand mesmerized as the east sun fills my hanging crystal and floods my room with a brilliant rainbow.

I mail the letter to Jill. I am glad I do. A few hours later, though, I feel strange, body tingling, heart racing, blood thumping. I go to Billy's room to calm down. This doesn't work. I make myself scarce and practice *qigong*, seeking to recover my balance. Standing silently, I go through the motions as Li has taught us. Empty the mind. Breathe deep. Concentrate on the feeling of the breath. Breathe deep again. Slow down. Concentrate on how the breath moves throughout my body. Feel the *qi*. Move the *qi*. Before I can take a third deep breath, however, thoughts of our relationship, the good and the bad, crash back in. The flood gates re-open, and there is much running around and around in my head. I have again failed to quiet my mind.

Why am I feeling this way? At first I think that mailing the letter to Jill must be the cause. I told her how I feel and asked questions that require answers. Will she reply? Will she not reply? I dread confrontation and have now sown the seeds for potentially just that. What if she replies and the answers are not positive? At the fringes of my mind another concern thrums quietly. What if my answers to the same questions are not positive? At even further fringes of my mind, lurking in the deep shadows, hides a potential zinger. What if my burgeoning friendship with Beth is scrambling my senses? My meltdown during our first conversation in her room did not repel her, though I hardly suggest it as a reliable first impression maker. The early rapport has held, and Beth and I have been hanging out. Shao Yuan is a small place. Whether it is in the cafeteria or the front courtyard or someone's room, we see each other a lot.

I like spending time with Beth. From unburdening when Chinese society gets to us to exchanging light banter to gentle, friendly flirting, we are comfortable with each other. But there is a physical draw. Her piercing eyes, which sometimes have a haunted gleam to them, are captivating. When she comes down to talk, she usually lies on my bed (there isn't anywhere else to sit). A couple of times she has come down to borrow something wearing only a robe. I can't help but notice. She is tall and shapely and fit and fills out the robe nicely. Listen to me. I have a girlfriend. Beth has a new boyfriend, an American exchange student she met here. This is just loneliness, an infatuation, a distraction from the truth. These confusing situations drive me nuts. I prefer to stick to myself. I want to go about my business without bothering anybody or being bothered. I wish to hell I had a girlfriend who would write! I love her!! She is making me crazy!!!

CHAPTER 11

PRIVILEGES

THE JOINT-VENTURE GREAT Wall Sheraton Hotel is the plushest hotel in Beijing. Sam and I ride through the outer screening wall, which is part cheesy replica of its namesake, into the inner courtyard, and past a faux section of wall with turrets and a mini-golf course. The compound is big. There are restaurants, a beauty/barber shop, a massage/acupuncture place, and a car rental outlet. In a city with few private cars or people who can afford to own or ride in them, the latter stands out. I glance at the phone operators behind the reservation desks as we enter the lobby. I have heard that they are secretly multi-lingual public security officials who monitor all calls.

After trips to the Friendship Store and Ritan Park, with an intervening stop to change money at the Alley, we need the hotel's bathrooms. And what bathrooms they are. Shiny, white, US-made Sloan Value Company toilets and Illinois-made hand dryers. Clean and modern, a place where one can relax. Sam and I take a breath and smile. Another Massachusetts native, he and I have bonded over the Red Sox, who are in the baseball playoffs and making a deep run. The last time they made the World Series was when I was nine-and-a-half in 1975. Now, they are in the post season, and I am far away.

We explore this palace of luxury. The lobby gleams. I can imagine that the rooms have soft sofas, large mattresses, private bathrooms, and space to be alone and pampered. The billiards room, however, is disappointing with cheap tables and a hucked two ball that doesn't roll. For twenty FEC an hour, I expect more. Patting the large wad of ten *yuan renminbi* notes in my pocket (I changed money for a friend too and am carrying way more than I am comfortable with), I fortunately still have FEC left.

This whole FEC thing is already getting old. The government recently announced that FEC would soon be abolished. No more Alley trips required. Three days later, they indefinitely postponed the abolishment. At the same time, they hiked telephone, telex, and telegraph rates by an initial fifty percent to be followed by an ultimate rise of eighty percent. Are they trying to rationally consolidate the economy or soak the foreigners and the native Chinese? I doubt they know.

The hotel swimming pool is small and shallow, and the bottom vibrates with what can most politely be termed a queasy green moss. A "No Topless Bathing" sign perches on the near-empty pool deck. I shake off the sight of the hairy water and join a group of Hong Kong Chinese in the outside elevator for a sightseeing ride up to the top floor, the twenty-first. Notwithstanding its issues, the Great Wall Sheraton is the pinnacle of Beijing hospitality. For now.

China being China, the government is building the Kunlun Hotel diagonally across from the Great Wall Sheraton with no foreign partners. The current construction zone is designed to be bigger and grander and even more of a statement than its joint-venture neighbor. And it will be one hundred percent Chinese. To the Chinese, bigger is not just better, it is a sine qua non. It is another part of the Chinese backstory. Sam, a student of society, attributes this to an ingrained Chinese arrogance. To be shown up by *waiguoren*, foreigners, in their own country is the ultimate loss of face. Ergo, they must outspend and out lavish any venture with foreigners. It is a twist on the phenomenon I witnessed at the National

Gallery of Art when I met the in-hindsight overly intense Meilin. The box to be wrapped must be the biggest one around.

Sam decides to hang around the sheltered confines at the Great Wall Sheraton. I want to shop and head over to the Lido-Holiday Inn, another joint-venture property. This is a day of Western decadence. It is open to me as a foreigner in China and is one I can ill afford. But this does not stop me. The Lido is a fifteen-to-twenty-minute bike ride from the Great Wall Sheraton. It's more expansive, but not as plush, with a recently opened supermarket, delicatessen, and drug store to complement a twenty-lane bowling alley and restaurants.

I am on the hunt for M&M's. The supermarket is like any in the US, but the prices are two to three times US prices. The three 250-gram bags of M&M's, can of Del Monte Fruit Cocktail, and Kit-Kat bar in my basket total more than fifteen dollars.

I ask the young cashier if I can use RMB to pay for my things. "*Keyi yong renmibi mai dongxi ma?*"

"*Bu Keyi.*" "No, you cannot" is her terse reply. And she is not done. "When you change money, do you get FEC?"

"Yes, I do, but I prefer paying in RMB because it saves me money." Then, brain fart in process, I naively explain to her that when foreigners change money on the street, they receive more than one hundred yuan in RMB for one hundred yuan in FEC. *What the hell am I saying?*

She stares at me incredulously. "How do you know that?"

I quickly tell her that I am smart and hustle out of the store. I return to the Great Wall Sheraton, and Sam and I indulge in bowls of expensive homemade ice cream before leaving for campus. If I thought enough ahead to have a budget, I blew it this afternoon.

I am exhausted. We rode all day and still, as soon as I return to campus, I am convinced to re-mount and bike down to the Yuyuan Xueyuan, the Beijing Language Institute, for a Saturday night dance. A foreigners' rock and reggae band, The Beijing Underground, is playing. We sneak Honghua in sandwiched between Sam and I disguised in a Vassar sweatshirt and Dartmouth hat because the dance is not for the Chinese. Subterfuge is not necessary for the several "cadre kids" at the dance. They have good *guanxi*, and entered as themselves. They sit at tables watching and listening with detached self-possession. They are cool, and they know it.

—◆—

The next night, eleven pairs of Chinese eyes swivel my way. I sit at one end of a sofa in a three-room flat at Renmin Daxue, People's University, facing a good chunk of my language buddy Gaoshan's family. A relative of Gaohsan's works at the college, and this is his place. Gaoshan's family is staying with him during a visit to Beijing. It is like an awkward first date with your girl's entire family. Mom and dad, his older brother, his sister and her husband, the relative and his wife, three playful nephews, and Gaoshan. Gaoshan is happy to be the fulcrum of this get together. The relative is Gaoshan's father's younger brother's wife's third something. Sounds like a cousin. The Chinese have this complex naming hierarchy, which makes for a simple matter of identification to those who master it. I have not.

We drink tea and munch sunflower seeds. The flat has more heat than I have at Shao Yuan (which until sometime in November is none). A seventeen-inch color television broadcasts a game show off to the side. Dad is prim and well-dressed in a grey Mao Tunic. Gaoshan tells me that his father is a real renaissance man who practices *wushu*, *qigong*, and *taijiquan* and is an accomplished calligrapher. Mom's effusive with an appealing gentle quality to her. I have trouble understanding the fast-flowing conversation. I am better at pretending I understand what is being said to me, but most of it blows by me in a blur. This can and does lead to its own problems, for example like now when someone asks me a question and I stare back nodding mutely not realizing it was a question. Gaoshan helps me out where he can.

I know I speak like a little kid. My vocabulary is weak. My sentence construction is sad. And yet, as usual, everyone complements me on my Chinese. "*Nide guoyu shuode hen hao.*" "You speak Chinese very well."

I try to be polite in response. "*Mei you, mei you. Wo guoyu feichang cha.*" "No, no. My Chinese is very poor." I hope this is the correct formulation and not American Chinese construction.

Another man sits in the corner, unobtrusive and silent. I finally ask Gaoshan who he is. Turns out he is Gaoshan's friend as well as the family driver. Wait a minute. His family has a personal driver? Gaoshan grew up in a small city in southern Hebei Province, several hours from Beijing. He attended college there and works for a utility office. So does his father. Their *danwei*, work unit, provided the car for the long drive to Beijing. And this must happen enough that they have an assigned driver. I think on this for a moment. Gaoshan's family has some pull. At the end of the evening, they extend an invitation: "We have plenty of room at home. Please. Please. You must come visit. You will be our guest." A car and a lot of space at home? They definitely have some pull. Closer to heart this night, we eschew more mass travel for the short hop back to campus, and the driver and the five-year-old nephew give us a ride in a new, loaded, five-speed Nissan. The first thought I have is that if I visit them, maybe I can take it for a spin.

I am such a hypocrite. I condemn the privileges of the elite, what with their access to cars, foreign goods, education, and leisure time, and then here I am enjoying those same fruits. I criticize the Western influence, but I keep jumping right in to my benefit. It might be access to the Friendship Store and fancy hotels. Tonight, it is a private car swaddled in luxury and privacy. I have the freedom and opportunity to choose and receive.

The Chinese do not and are, not without good cause, paranoid of the government's power. So many are trapped in the fear of their own minds. Decades of draconian political and social movements and oppression and privation and death can do that. The Chinese guy I met in a friend's room the other night wouldn't hear of going to the Western dance; Honghua jumped at the idea even though she would need a disguise. Gaoshan and

Honghua never *dengji*, register, when they enter Shao Yuan; others do as required. Small steps? Maybe.

It is not that most people know when to stop, it is that they don't know how far they can go. The government doesn't worry about Gaoshan and painter Chen (he now regularly showers at Shao Yuan because his nearby room in a courtyard home has no hot water or heat) because these are little things and it knows that the vast majority are not going to push for more significant rights. They've been held down so long, they aren't equipped to fight for their own well-being. Or have they accepted these limits in a Faustian bargain for a stable life with subsidized food, shelter, healthcare, and lifetime jobs (the iron rice bowl)?

Whichever it is, to me it is like living on a treadmill. You move and move and make and make, yet you never get ahead, never get anywhere other than where you began. China will never be able to break the glass ceiling of true development and achievement because so many people are being excluded from the process. Such a country will be able to grow to a certain level, but eventually it will stagnate. The system is self-defeating. They say you cannot miss what you never had, but shouldn't everyone have the opportunity to decide whether or not they want to shoot for the moon?

We watched a special showing of Lu Xun's *Ah Q* at the Renmin Juchang, People's Theater. The play is a critique of traditional Chinese society. Drinking, joking, fooling around, and knowing his boundaries make up the entire existence of the protagonist, Ah Q. And what does it get him? Nowhere, except shot at the end by the revolutionaries who overthrow the ruling imperial system. It is a dehumanizing, depressing commentary on the potential of life. And has anything really changed?

—w—

I am privileged. I am apart and above the masses, the *laobaixing*—literally the "old one hundred names," referring to the hundred most common Chinese surnames to which the vast majority of the Chinese population traces its roots. Besides the freedom to come and go as we please, we also have access to aspects of Chinese society reserved for the elite and special. We foreigners are often viewed with awe, but I can't help but feel that the Chinese people must feel an undercurrent of disgust at the disparity of our treatments.

I heard a story about two Beida Chinese History students who wanted to form a study group to discuss the more deleterious aspects of communism. They went too far even in this new environment of Socialism with Chinese Characteristics. The students were subsequently expelled, arrested, and jailed for their actions. Sam knows of a group of students who tried to organize a gathering last spring to discuss a reinterpretation of Marxism to show how China has strayed from the path. They, too, were expelled, arrested, and, so Sam surmises, sent away to "reform through labor" (*laogai*) in the gulags of remote Qinghai Province. Banging rocks in the desert for the crime of questioning Marxism.

With the opening to the West and the influx of new people living, studying, and working in the country, the communist government is fighting to control what and with whom we come into contact. There are open and closed cities and areas. Gaoshan's city is closed. Not only am I not supposed to visit there, but I am also not supposed to stay with a local family. We are told to use separate money in separate stores. The Party wants, yet is afraid of outside contact.

This segregation upsets the ever-earnest Sam, and he laments the effects: "At my old school, Beishi Daxue, Beijing Normal University, the old direct contact between the Chinese and foreign students is being split. It had been one of the best places for living with the Chinese. They are now building a new foreigners' dorm, their very own Shao Yuan. No more direct living and sharing and experiencing between the two groups of students. Separate food, separate mail, separate classes. It is sad."

All of which brings me back to painter Chen. After making the agonizing decision to trade him my red Vassar College Class of '88 pin for a

Mao pin tonight, Chen pulls out slides of his paintings. His landscapes are good, but his portraits are out of this world. He gives me several snapshots of his sketches, landscapes, and portrait oils. He asks if I would send them to the Vassar Art Department. I agree. As I prepare to send him packing for the night because he is falling asleep on my bed, he proposes another trade.

"If I get accepted by an American university, I might have trouble converting my RMB to foreign currency because I am a Chinese citizen." He says this casually as he pulls himself up. I am not yet sure where this is heading. "You owe money to Beida for your studies and living here. What if I help pay your fees in China and your parents help pay my fees in the United States?" His bombshell drops.

This is a significant request. It is the kind of thing that calls for a definitive answer. My throat constricts and my heart starts pounding. Nervous energy and decisional panic grow as I begin sweating. I have known Chen for less than two months, which is to say I do not know him well. What is it with some Chinese? Meilin was looking for a personal relationship. Chen is looking for an economic relationship. Gaoshan and Honghua do not seem to want more than cultural exchange with foreigners. Wow. Look at me. I am a hypocrite. Chen is fighting for his own well-being. He is shooting for the moon. And my response? Unease, distrust, and opposition.

"Thanks Chen, but I already have what I need. And my parents are a little strapped with three kids and all." I hope the last part is a white lie.

"That's OK. I understand," he says quietly. "I might be able to find someone else to help." He doesn't push the matter.

The wave of agitation passes as Chen leaves my room. He covered well, but his shoulders slouched, and I know my refusal hurts.

CHAPTER 12

CHINESE CRUTCHES

THE CANDLELIGHT FLICKERS. This is the fourth power outage in twenty-four hours. My, oh, my, how life can change in a matter of days. Today is my father's forty-eighth birthday, and I sit here in my room immobilized. My plans for the day, which is also Sam's birthday, included dancing at the Lido disco and a celebratory meal. They did not include being trapped on my bed in the dark with no food. They did not include my right ankle ballooning to the size of a bloated tennis ball. I'm trying to maintain a stiff upper lip, but dammit this is torture. As the lights come back on, I lean my head back against the wall, close my eyes, and whimper.

———

I played basketball this afternoon on the courts in front of our dorm. About an hour ago, after a lengthy, full-court, fast-paced four on four, I had the ball near our basket with Sam in between. Although I was playing better than usual (which admittedly isn't saying much), I lost the ball. Spinning to chase after it and Sam, my right ankle rolled with three staccato cracks that echoed across the clay surface. The stark sound got everyone's attention. I hobbled for a minute before it hit me. My hearing became muffled. I was overcome by light-headedness, blurry vision, and severe nausea. I folded to the ground and remember thinking that the world looked askew.

Sam and another friend, Sato, ran over and half carried me on their shoulders across the courtyard to my room at Shao Yuan 2-323.

"How you feeling?" Sam asked through the haze as we hobbled up the stairs.

"Terrible," I croaked.

"You don't look so hot."

That's good. I'd hate to feel like this and look good. This is what I wanted to say, but I was not up to it.

My head cleared once I sat down. The power was on. Perched on the side of my bed, I immersed my swollen foot in a bucket of frigid water. A shock of glacial cold ran through my body as I leaned back against the wall.

—⁂—

I open my eyes. My ankle is the size of a softball. The throbbing increases.

I cannot swallow pills. I have tried. I know what to do, but I drink the water, it passes right over the pill glued to back of my tongue, and I get this bitter, soggy mess in my mouth. Twenty years old, and I need to drink two Bufferin diluted in hot water. Aided by Lifesavers, I manage to finish the entire nasty, granular, bitter cup. Sato comes back and gives me pads that are supposed to be better than Tiger Balm to wrap around my ankle while I sleep. Susan, my doctor, heard about the accident and swings by with an offer to stick needles in my left leg to ease the swelling in the right.

Billy and Peter bed sit with me. Peter brings me dinner. They are good friends. They "commend" me on my athletic prowess. The power fails again. In the dark, I shovel food into my mouth with my chopsticks, hoping that the dead fly Peter found in his dinner earlier didn't have any friends.

It's late. Susan gives me an acupuncture treatment and applies her medicinal *qigong*. She notes my pallid face with concern. She asks me to relax, to listen to her soothing words, and clear my thoughts. I want to be a good patient. My left leg twitches as she inserts the needles. Her hand is steady. My heart is not. The individual beats cause my shirt to rise and fall in my mind. The pounding *thump-thump*, the image of those three-inch-long needles quivering like toothpicks in Jell-O squares, these aural and visual sensations are more than I can handle. Susan feels the swelling anxiety, the *qi* energy surging in and around me. She does her best to keep her untethered patient under control. "Close your eyes, picture a tranquil place." In a tiny, empty space in my head, somewhere along the fringes, I recognize that her efforts are having an effect. The swelling moderates and the pain subsides. My mind, however, remains untethered.

The acupuncture worked for a while, but I still cannot apply pressure to my foot. I wheel over to the Beida Hospital with help. Our timing is inconvenient. The staff is on *xiuxi*, rest break, and we are turned away. Closed means closed. We return to Shao Yuan to cool my jets for an hour. Then, we return. Another trip using my bicycle as an awkward, makeshift wheelchair.

Tom, an American friend who speaks the level of Chinese I wish I did, is my savior, my translator and runner. I pay one Chinese yuan, twenty-seven cents, to register and am sent to the Outpatient Office. The guy gives my ankle a couple of agonizing squeezes and sends me off to be X-rayed. The machine is ancient. They do not offer me one of those heavy, protective aprons the dentist gives you when he scans your teeth. It looks like I am going to be irradiated.

My time in the hospital is itself an odyssey of pain. I hop back and forth between both ends of the floor from office to office. No crutches. No wheelchair. No assistance. Because I am a self-paying student, the school doesn't cover my medical costs. The X-ray and the repulsive-looking medicine each cost fifteen times the registration fee. This being said, relatively speaking, the hospital is remarkably clean for China.

A well-meaning technician eventually comes out and speaks to me in measured English. "You are good. You have no factory."

No factory? What the hell is he talking about? Where's Tom? Where's my dictionary? I apparently cannot communicate in either Chinese or English. I stare at him blankly.

He repeats that I have no factory and looks at me expectantly.

I wrack my brain, confusion wrinkled on my forehead. *What is a factory? What don't I have?* His demeanor and tone imply that it is a good thing. At last, I figure it out. The lightbulb brightens, and I break into a relieved grin. I have "no fracture." Nothing broken, just a bad sprain.

The prescription is to *xiuxi*. Good old bed rest.

The nurse spreads warm black paste on my ankle and wraps it tight. Tom gets crutches from a nearby building. They are a good size for me and a bargain, a fraction of a cent a day with an eight-dollar, don't-steal-me refundable deposit.

I hobble back to the dorm ever so grateful for the assistance of friends. I cannot imagine facing all this alone. Pain, panic, and incomprehension render me useless. The visit to the hospital is tiring, and my wrapped, still-swollen ankle once again throbs. I lean the crutches against my desk and sink gratefully onto my bed. The everyday mattress feels as glorious as I imagined the mattresses to be at the Great Wall Sheraton.

I do need to rest.

But I do not listen to the doctor. I do not listen to myself.

Instead, there is a knock at my door, and I go out to see a play, *A Farmer's Nirvana*, with a group of classmates. I sit next to a girl named Yoko, a Japanese classmate with a bubbly smile who does not speak

English. We chat briefly during intermission and then more in depth on the bus ride back. I feel confident in my end of the Chinese conversation with her. I also felt like I understood more of the play. Am I concentrating more because of the pain? Maybe there is something to being injured.

On the bus ride she tells me, "Because I am studying abroad for a year, when I return to Japan others will no longer consider me true Japanese. I'll be a half-breed—part Japanese, part foreigner." This floors me. Yoko loses her native Japanese-ness by studying abroad? She becomes other in the eyes of her country! In a homogeneous society like Japan, not being the same is bad. This bothers me. America does not stand for this. The other is not other. We are all one. Yet, Yoko came to China anyway. This demure young woman has spunk. She defied the probable contempt of her countrymen to chart her own course.

Yoko helps me to my room. As we enter, I see the photos of Jill displayed on my desk. Not so unusual. She is my girlfriend. But then, out of nowhere, standing there with this person who has graciously accompanied me and my sprained ankle upstairs, I blow up about my relationship with Jill. In Chinese. I've never spoken Mandarin so fast or probably so incoherently. My tones are tentative when I am calm. I can imagine how nonexistent they are when I am unhinged. Poor Yoko. She stands there shocked. Her face that likes to smile is frozen in mute incomprehension. Here she is trying to help a new acquaintance back to his room, and the crazy American starts ranting like a lunatic. I am not even sure if she knows what I am ranting about. Why am I so upset? I am embarrassed that I still have the pictures on display. I am angry that she sees them. I hate that I have not taken control of my emotional life.

Yoko retreats as quickly as she can. I take three large gulps of air. What just happened? I crutch down to see Beth. To talk with a friend. She is with her boyfriend, Joe. We hang out. The topic of Jill and Yoko does not come up. Chilling helps me calm down, to come off the anger high. When I have interrupted their time together long enough, I tell

Beth privately about what happened as she accompanies me to the door. "Andrew, why are those photos even still up?"

They are not anymore.

—⁓—

Days later, I am in pain as one of my nannies, Billy this time, and I walk-hobble over to the campus post office. My "well-sized" crutches suck. They are short. The sides of my body are chafed raw. The grip is too narrow. My palms have blistered. Each step is a grueling exercise in awkwardness.

Mom sends me a care package: my blue sweats and an AC adaptor. I asked for my grey sweats because the blue ones are tight. The AC adaptor is a more expensive brand. I appreciate her offering to help, but why can't she listen and only do what is requested? This is a pattern for as long as I can remember. She does her own thing. I respect attentiveness to the request. I do not expect anything more, and I do not like anything less. I have no patience for tangents. It is a back-and-forth that plagues the two of us. She annoys me, and my emotions get to me. This time is no exception. Angry and not thinking, I plug the new 120-volt adapter in without the converter, again. Soon, I hear the sizzle and watch it fry as had the first.

Still smoldering (me, not the converter), I host an impromptu party. Peter and Billy come over, and we are soon drinking rum and cokes and eating a pineapple and bananas. Yes, I am drinking. I must be steamed. Chen joins us to play cards after showering. Honghua and another girl stop by. I am sure none of them registered. We play bottle caps, a variation of spoons. I'm buzzed. Chen is smashed—at least I hope he is because otherwise he would not have stuck two yellow bananas in the top of his pants.

Four hours later, I hobble up to my friend Beth's room to leave her a note. She is awake and hears me at the door. My party high—or was it the rum?—wore off, and I am down and want to talk. Beth is my go-to listener. I trust her instincts, feel comforted by her empathy. I'm still fixated on Jill. How dare she not contact me since the summer? I consider her my now ex-girlfriend. I tell Beth that if I haven't received a reply to my letter by next weekend, I will call Jill collect and demand a response. Beth verbally smacks me upside the head.

"What! Andrew. Listen to yourself." She is animated now as well. "Why on earth would you call her? To tell her you're breaking up as you already did in your letter? That makes no sense." The disdain in her words wallops me.

Did I break up with Jill in my letter? It was implied, but I am not so sure.

CHAPTER 13

RELATIONSHIPS

I DO NOT HAVE to wait for next weekend. After more than two months in China, I receive my first letter from Jill.

"Do you still want to share the rest of your life with me? I wouldn't blame you in the slightest if you didn't..."

What do I want? I love Jill, but something in our relationship has always felt a little off, and it gnaws at me. Is it the drugs? Economics? Life experiences? A number of times I became angry for no apparent reason, and not just because something did not go my way. These realizations shame me and, in no small part, scare me. I know Jill loves me deeply and that she'd do anything to make me happy. Is this enough? What is the intersection of love and lust and compatibility? We have the first, most definitely the second, but what about the last? How do you know that someone is the right person, the one? Do I want Jill in my life, as my wife, or do I just want to be with someone, anyone? Beth asked me recently if I am in love with the idea of being in love. Billy thinks I'm in love. Whether love or life, I fear being uncommitted, the lack of a settled path. I put two of Jill's pictures back up and almost immediately take them back down. I'm such a wimp, an emotional Weeble.

—⁄⁄⁄—

For the first time in two weeks, I wear two sneakers. I walk gingerly with the cane Toshiro keeps in a corner of our room. It is a fine piece of craftsmanship with an elegant inscription:

May Your Good Fortune Be as the Ever-Flowing Waters of the Eastern Sea/
May Your Life Be as Long as the Ageless Peaks of the Southern Mountains.

It is Daoism, the marriage of the natural and sacred, encapsulated. The Eastern Sea represents bounty, promise, the land of the Daoist Immortals. Mountains are the stepping stones to heaven, spiritual and physical connections to the higher plane. The Southern Mountain is one of the five great mountains of China. Who would not want plentiful good fortune and perpetual life in a home of the gods? It is what emperors of China have sought for millennia. I feel the power of the couplet as I make my literal way once again in China.

I feel liberated, no longer trapped in a cage. At day's end, I unwrap the long piece of rapidly crumbling gauze that was the hospital's ace bandage and remove the flexible cardboard lathered in medicine paste. The concoction burned all the hair off my leg, leaving a black-rimmed, irregular circle of baby-smooth skin on my ankle! I soak my foot in warm water. As the blood begins circulating in my newly freed foot, my leg feels funny. I hobble downstairs to call Dr. Susan. By the time she arrives for another house call, my ankle has swollen up with ugly black and blue bruises covering my smelly foot. The odor is overwhelming.

Susan inserts a needle at a major *qi* point near the top of my left foot. It connects three main energy corridors in the body. This should relieve the blockage that causes my right ankle to balloon. Renewed circulation will lessen the symptoms and the pain. As the needle pierces the skin of my good foot, however, my world erupts. My leg bounces. I am definitely twitching. All I can see is bright, blinding light. I turn a ghostly pale and feel myself lifting out of my body. It is the most surreal experience, both awesome and terrifying. I am actually rising above myself. This is happening. My mouth opens, but I cannot speak. Susan senses the situation. She quickly removes the needle, and I spiritually and physically settle back into my shell, the journey aborted. My vision clears, and a hint of color returns to my face.

Giving that energy intersection a wide berth, Susan places another needle on the top of my left foot, near the middle. As the needle again sinks below the surface, all five of my toes feel like they have been blown apart. It is excruciating. The throttled breath escaping my clenched lips is unnatural. I blindly grab at the mattress, seeking stability. My back stiffens against the wall as I subconsciously retreat from the source of the terror. Susan removes the needle, concern and the faintest passing confusion flickering in her eyes. Acupuncture may be more than my untrained and unrestrained mind can handle. I want to leave my aching ankle unwrapped for the night, but Susan suggests otherwise. I let her rewrap it.

"Susan, I appreciate you helping me out. I must be the worst patient you've ever had," I offer sheepishly.

"You just rest, and everything will be fine. Everyone responds to acupuncture in their own way." She is kind to the end.

Susan leaves me alone, and I realize that my shirt is soaked with sweat.

After two more days of cane walking, I remove my new ankle brace and hobble to the shower. The brace is so much more convenient than the gauze bandage. I was lucky to find it downtown. As I walk to the shower, red-hot flames of pain shoot up my body with each step. My throbbing ankle is still swollen. The short walk to the shower room leaves me in another cold, damp sweat. The water helps, but it is not until I have the brace back on that it calms down.

—⁓—

The Red Sox march on in the baseball playoffs, and Sam and I listen to as much of the games as possible on my 9-band shortwave radio and devour all of the UPI teletapes a friend's wife picks up at her job with ABC. Sam is the only other New Englander I have met since George and I went to the zoo in August. Sam and I have similar reference points, whether it be baseball or geography or experiences. In a limited way, it is our slice of shared American backstory. In this case, it is the excitement of the Sox back in the World Series after eleven years. It is also the innate fear of a Red Sox fan that they will blow it, like they did in 1947, 1967, and 1975.

Listening to the playoffs here is an adventure. I am in an episode of my favorite TV show, M.A.S.H., huddling with a group of diehards around the radio in our remote outpost straining to hear a broadcast that keeps fading in and out. During Game 3 of the ALCS, the Sox were leading the California Angels 1-0 in the top of the fifth inning. Two outs. Bases loaded. Billy Buckner at the plate with an 0-2 count. The announcer begins, "Here's the windup, *BZZLPP.*" Sam and I strain to get our ears even closer to the shortwave. What happened!! The AFR signal comes back, long enough to discover that he grounded out, and then disappears for good.

After being down three games to one in the Championship Series, the Sox win three straight to get to the World Series. I think of Pudge, Yaz, Dewey, Jim Ed, Fred, Rico, Rooster, Denny, El Tiante, Spaceman, and the rest of the 1975 team that raised and then crushed my nine-year-old spirits. They remain many of my favorites throughout the years. The 1986 World Series pits the Red Sox against the New York Mets.

For Game 1, I am again down on my knees, ear pressed up against the speaker trying in vain to hear something, anything. We move the shortwave around, we attach various wires as homemade antennae, we use ourselves as human antennae. When we finally lose the signal with one out in the bottom of the ninth during a great pitchers' duel, I go out and call the American Embassy looking for the final score. It is closed on Sunday and the two Marines on duty either do not know or won't respond to the crazy American looking for sports scores.

I have a sick feeling in the pit of my stomach after they blow a two-game lead and are tied two games apiece. I see it in Sam's eyes as well—the weight of history rearing its demoralizing head. Neither of us says anything. We do not have to. One look shares our collective foreboding. This sounds melodramatic, but it is a Red Sox fan thing. The Sox win Game 5. They lead the Series three games to two and can clinch in Game 6.

In Game 6, the Sox are up five to three in the bottom of the tenth. The Series is theirs. Two quick outs. I can taste victory. Two quick strikes on Carter. Two strikes, two outs, no one on with a two-run lead. Sam and I bounce on the floor of my room. This is really going to happen. And then? Then the world spirals out of control. Three straight singles. Bang. Bang. Bang. Like knives to the heart. Steamer throws a wild pitch, and the score is tied. Buckner bobbles a ball and Game 6 is over. It figures that we did not lose the AFR signal for this game. Sam and I sit shell-shocked.

The torture continues with a rain out of the last game. When Game 7 is played, the Sox lead three to nothing heading into the bottom of the sixth. Is it possible? Do I dare believe? Of course not. With one out in the inning, the bottom again falls out. It had to. The Red Sox lose the game eight to five, and the Series four games to three. Sam and I look at each other in agony. Another chapter of our backstory is written, and we listened to it from the other side of the world.

—⚶—

Yoko celebrates her birthday a few days later. I have not had meaningful contact with her since my meltdown after the play. I would like to show her that I am not completely off kilter. I give her a birthday card handwritten in semi-legible Japanese. I have an idea how to say what I write, and Beth helps me make it sound intelligible, if not completely readable. I show the card to Toshiro and get an "Interesting." I leave the card under Yoko's door because she is out when I go up.

She comes up to me at lunch today and in English politely says, "Birthday card, thank you." Not much contact, but I feel good.

Beth tells me that she is going to Taiwan next semester. She's not happy here. Having cadre relatives is too much of a drag. They have no qualms about reminding her (expressly and otherwise) that her American thoughts, mannerisms, and actions are a reflection on them. She wants to be herself, but also feels the connection. The news hits me. I'm going to miss her. More than just a confidant, we are also flirting friends—a shoulder touch here, a suggestive look there. She likes to laugh and brings me along for the ride. She is more grounded than I am. I can go to her whenever I want. Her presence is increasingly a focus of my being in China. This is not to slight Billy, Peter or Sam. I have developed a strong bond with each of them. We are close companions sharing this most out-there of journeys, but let's face it, Beth is way cuter. Not having her here will be a big void.

I am *suibian*, casual, now. Society still bothers me and the *mafan* is a challenge, but increasingly it takes a lot to rile me and even more to shock me. Why am I not as on edge? Could it have anything to do with the fact that I am drinking alcohol more regularly? I successfully navigated around it at Vassar. Peer pressure was not an issue. Now, I hang out with friends drinking the North Asian nights away with vodka and Kool-Aid, screwdrivers, rum and cokes. Nothing straight up (I still do not like the taste), and not to too much excess, and still without any pressure. My drinking is an organic reaction to processing the inputs of life here, and it appears to have a salubrious effect on my outlook.

I do not worry as much about appearances, physical and social. I still keep mental checklists of what I need to do, want to do, should do, but if an item remains undone, I do not obsess about it. The pressure on me has lessened. Back in the States, the pace is always running from this to the next. How are my grades? What will I do when I graduate? Did I come across as an ass the other night? Why am I so emotionally weak? Here, my existence is limited to here. It is coping and handling the present. So maybe it is not that I am *suibian*, but that the bubble I am in allows me to ignore all the other. Whether this is good or bad is more than I can process for the now. As if I need immediate proof of this, that it is an illusion that I am more casual in attitude, when my Chinese pen conks out every other line or so in my journal, I lose it, snapping the pen in two. Andrew is never too far from the surface.

—⁓—

Yoko stuffed me but good tonight. It was my own fault. I disturbed the rules of the societal game. I am not doing anything, so I go up to her room to say hello. The birthday card went over well, so maybe there is a chance for friendship. She is studying and seems very surprised to see me. She doesn't invite me in and, after a minute or two of small talk at the door, she kills the encounter. "I have to study. Goodbye." Slam.

I stand there for a moment with the door in my face.

I leave in a snit. I mean, I only want to be friends with the girl, but she won't let me. Is she afraid I am trying to hit on her? Am I? The disparate customs among countries can be so inflexible. It's often hard to remember them, keep them all in order, to understand. For our part, I've noticed that Americans are always the loudest, least restrained, and most likely to have fun even if we embarrass ourselves in public. Even shy Americans are not very restrained, relatively speaking. Restraint is an Eastern concept, not a Western one. And maybe what Yoko told me the night of the play is involved. She must struggle mightily with how her society judges her because she chose to leave the motherland to come here to study. I was intruding. In any event, that is that.

—⁓—

The weather today in Beijing, the end of another autumn week in China, is gorgeous. My open window catches the warm air. The trees on the other side of the tennis courts sway in a gusty wind. The flared roofs of the Chinese dorms in the distance shine in the sun. I recall the landscape scroll paintings at the Beijing Art Gallery—rocky mountains and cascading waterfalls; misty clouds shading pine trees perched precariously on craggy outcroppings; little, tiny people walking on little, tiny paths, entering caves.

I spend the day with Beth. She and Joe broke up. That did not last long. She needs someone stronger. The split is to my benefit because a woman dating is not going to hang out with another guy that much. She takes me to the regular campus *shitang*, cafeteria, for lunch. Unlike at Shao Yuan, the Chinese students have to supply their own bowls, plates, spoons, and chopsticks. We walk around to the back of the cafeteria building and present our bowls to a guy who scoops rice from a large bathtub. A huge pile of raw cabbage waiting for another day's meal sits in the dust on the ground nearby. We pick up the rest of our food inside. It is a nice day so we eat outside. My bowl of melons, eggs, mushrooms, and carrots is tolerable (better than the food at our foreigners' cafeteria). Leaning against a cement wall, I dig in my chopsticks and put a healthy bite in my mouth. On the second chew, I hear a loud *crunspshstc* and spit out a large pebble.

The next day I take Beth to the Beida hospital after she sprains her ankle jogging. I have never liked running, but then I am not as fit as Beth is either. I loan her my crutches, and we walk around campus. Toshiro yells at me for taking "a cripple for a walk." He would not be pleased if he knew we then rode the bus downtown to the Great Wall and Lido Hotels for a Western break. Dealing with being American Chinese, dealing with her breakup, and dealing with her accident. A Western break is definitely on tap. We have talked about traveling to Hong Kong together for winter vacation. That would be a fun trip. I enjoy being with Beth. She enjoys being with me. Why not spend vacation together?

Fate then intervenes to push our relationship to the next level. Days later, at the end of a bad day where she re-re-injures her ankle, I help her back to her room. Beth is close to tears.

"Stay with me," she asks with a vulnerability that melts me.

We lie on her twin bed holding hands. Quiet. I hear her heartbeat inches from my own. I feel some of the tension float away from her. When her roommate kicks us out, we head down to my room. We resume lying on my twin bed, talking and resting. Toshiro stops in and then leaves again. It is late. Arm in arm, the warmth of our bodies connecting and comforting, Beth and I eventually drift off to sleep.

I am awake enough when Toshiro comes back to hear him gasp. When Beth wakes deep in the night, I bring her to her room and drift back downstairs as in a dream.

We fell asleep as friends, but woke the next day, in separate rooms, as something else. I confess the obvious attraction. The smile I receive in return stirs me. Our slide towards a relationship quickens. We continue to confide in one another. We share our fears and our likes. I cannot remember a deeper connection than I feel with Beth by my side. Spending time with Beth brings a tingle to my being.

—⚬—

I feel good. Things are flowing smoothly. I am finally accomplishing, seeing, living, experiencing. My Chinese is stronger. I'm listening to myself more, paying attention to my tones and pronunciation. Conversations are more comfortable, not as trying and draining. Toshiro edits my weekly writing assignment for Guo Laoshi, the teacher and class I care most about, and confirms that while still simplistic, this week's work is better than last week's. This sense of accomplishment is exciting and makes everything seem real.

Yet soon thereafter, in the immature world that is my emotional life, I ask Beth, my now new girlfriend, to look at an official Dear Jane letter I write to Jill, my ex-girlfriend. I failed Jill's white powder test, which was but a symptom of a more fundamental issue, yet did not actually break up with her. Well, I kind of did. But did I? What is more lame, beginning to date a woman before expressly breaking up with another woman or asking the new woman to look at the break-up letter? If Beth is looking for a strong boyfriend, she missed the mark.

I tell Beth things I have never shared with another soul. Things I maybe didn't realize myself, about my hopes, my insecurities, my paranoia. I have always been private, closed-off. And yet these sentiments now pour out of me as through a valve with no stopper. Years of silence wash away into the receptive ears of this stunning woman who does not seem to mind my ramblings. She allowed a friendship to be born notwithstanding my less-than-stellar first impression. She stuck it out as she learned more about me. And we have grown together for it.

During one such session, Toshiro comes in, picks something up, and leaves with a firm slam of the door. I feel bad, though not so bad that we stop doing that which drives him nuts. I want to talk with him, but he will not or cannot. He is Japanese. He is Buddhist. He is the embodiment of reserved. The door slam is the first communication of his displeasure in any way.

When Toshiro comes back, I am alone.

"Toshiro, I know that seeing me and Beth together in here bothers you. I sense your anxiety. I am sorry." He may not want to talk in such blunt terms, but I see no other way.

"Ande, meshi." "Andrew, it's nothing." He responds calmly, but directly. If I said this, it would be trite. Coming from Toshiro's lips, it sounds like the perfect Buddhist non-answer answer.

"If there are times when you prefer that we are not here, let me know," I offer.

"If I have work to do, I will tell you."

This is good. I think we have made progress.

CHAPTER 14

ROMANCE IN CHENGDE

A STRONG GALE BLOWS. Only yesterday a pleasant November breeze caressed my face as I strolled the quiet, tree-covered paths and empty roads of campus. Alone with my thoughts, I discovered myself standing on the shore of the Lake With No Name. I looked down into the reflection of my face and my body in the mirror at my feet. Now, as I head downtown to buy train tickets for a weekend getaway with Beth, late-autumn leaves fall like snow. A Gobi tempest stands me up every few meters. The streets are a swirl of disruption. I hope this change is not a portent of things to come.

The bus ride back to campus does nothing to allay this unease. I do not shy away from the crowds or fret the bus stop frenzy this time. Instead, with free hands and traveling by myself, I give myself up to the jam-packed bus. The gloves are off. I worm my way into the middle of the masses on the sidewalk and launch. I shove. I hit. I push. It is me or them, and I do not intend it to be them. I scrabble my way onto that bus. With authority. I will not apologize. I have no regrets. My adrenalin surges, and I smile.

Still holding money in my hand as the 103 Bus arrives at the zoo, I shuffle off with the crowd and do not pay. I planned to cab the last leg to

Beida, but still happy with the first part of the trip, I jump onto another bus without thinking. In hindsight, I should have stuck with my first idea. The last leg of the bus trip descends to madness. Arriving at Zhongguancun Village, two girls behind me begin fighting. They scream. Arms fly. The taller girl has the advantage. When the doors open, the shorter girl falls backwards out of the bus. No one catches her. No one notices. The taller girl thrashes long after the shorter girl is gone.

A weekend away sounds like a good idea.

—⁓—

Five a.m. Beijing is dead, dark, and frigid. We catch an early bus at the west gate in less than ten minutes and pick up a trolley at the zoo. Beth shivers in the trolley's frozen interior. I wrap my arm around her to little effect. We do not talk. Traffic is light. The train station is calm.

Our soft-seat train car, which is empty save for a group of about ten Cantonese tourists, is heated. Beth's teeth slowly stop chattering. She and I hold hands and each other much to the interest of the attendants. *Check out the foreigner and the Chinese girl being quite affectionate and close.* They offer us hot water no less than eight times. We are heading northeast to Chengde, the summer retreat of the governing Manchu Dynasty during the eighteenth and nineteenth centuries. The train climbs into the mountains, crosses the Great Wall, and heads farther and farther into the wilderness of North China. We cat nap. We relax. The dense urban landscape falls far behind. Our first trip together has begun.

By early afternoon, we are there. The front desk staff at the hotel gives us a discount with our student ID cards and assigns us one room as requested after looking at us for a moment. Management, though, has second thoughts about an unmarried Caucasian male and Chinese (American or not) female sharing the same room and repeatedly sends the hotel staff up to check on us. They unlock our door, jiggle the handle, and pretend like they are about to enter our room. Then, they go away, until the next visit. It is unnerving.

When we checked in, they told us we could pay later, but they call a little while later, question Beth in English, and tell us that we have to pay now. Beth is having none of it and lets them know it: "We are not coming down now. We'll pay you when we go out for dinner." She hangs up before they can continue.

Notwithstanding these official interruptions, which do stop after Beth tells them off, we are together, and we are alone. It is just us, in a private room with a private bath. Such simple luxury. I have found my Chinese hideaway to share with my hideaway companion.

Today is ours. We have been moving towards this moment for weeks now. We both know what is about to happen. We both want it to happen. The late afternoon sun shines through the thin curtains, filling the room with a suffused light. Within these four walls, all is quiet except the beating of our hearts. We reach for each other and fall into bed together for the first time as lovers. I breathe in the sweet smell of Beth's hair lying across my shoulder. Her chest rises rhythmically up and down against my own. Our legs lie interlocked across the sheet. We soak in the closeness and are one.

Eventually, the pangs of a different kind of hunger tug at us, and we get up to go out. First, we pay for our room as promised. Our dinner is Mongolian hotpot at a nearby restaurant. We select what we want from the main table and wait while they bring us the raw meats, seafood, and vegetables. A hotpot with boiling water sits on the center of the table. Using our chopsticks, we drop pieces of beef, pork, and shrimp as well as fish balls, *doufu* (tofu), bok choy, and cabbage into the bubbling pot. We add sauces and spices to taste and cook our own dinner. *Qishui*, soda, is a foreign concept in Chengde. The beer is weak and therefore not too bad. We eat and drink our fill.

At the end of a fabulous day that began far away in a dark, cold

Beijing, we turn in at 8:00 p.m. We talk. We make love. I drift off to sleep, arms wrapped around the most wonderful woman in the world.

—⚬—

Waking up refreshed twelve hours later, we shower in our private bathroom and head out to explore. The attitude of the people in Chengde is the polar opposite of Beijing. Their lives are less rushed, freer, more relaxed. The vibe in the community is tangible. One can breathe. It is infectious. Beth tells me that she more readily accepts her Chinese side here in Chengde. Yes, she is still other, but the pressure of Beijing recedes, as too do the expectations and obligations. It is a joyous thing.

The city, so lively during the summer tourist season, is empty. We have not encountered any other Caucasians. We browse two large out-door markets. The *baicai*, cabbage, is green and robust. The meat looks fresh and tender. The apples are crisp and juicy. We sample sweet pastries. We watch *jiaozi*, dumplings, being handmade in a *xiaochibu*, a hole-in-the-wall café—a dollop of chopped meat mixed with chives and ginger, folded one by one into individual little rice flour wrappers, closed with a pinch and dropped into boiling water.

The raison d'etre of Chengde is the lush mountain resort of the emperors north of the city. This walled compound encloses an expansive imperial palace and gardens that were designed by the same hands that created Yuanmingyuan, the Old Summer Palace, in the Beijing suburbs near Beida. The imperial family came here when even Yuanmingyuan sweltered in the summer heat and humidity. To welcome their subjects, showcase their Buddhist bona fides, and make this far-off retreat a show-case of their rule, the Qing emperors recreated eight famous palaces and temples from around their empire spread among the surrounding hills beyond the mountain resort. Chengde is a veritable museum of ancient Chinese architecture, and I cannot get enough of it.

We rent bicycles for a palace hunt. The bikes are big and ungainly, but once we figure out their quirks and personalities, they take us where we want to go. We ride east-northeast out of downtown, cross the railroad tracks, and arrive first at Pulesi, Pule Temple. This temple resembles one of my favorites, Beijing's Temple of Heaven. The cobalt blues, reds, and golden flared roofs on large worship halls and smaller study chambers sparkle. Crenelated block walls open into inner and outer courtyards. The view out from the upper platform, the round main hall to our backs, spreads from the plains to the distant mountains, today shrouded in haze. More than two hundred years of history saturates the wispy blue sky and fresh air hovering over the temple.

Across the expanse looking north and northwest sit several of the remaining outer temples, including our destination in the far distance, rising layered up a mountain side: Putuo Zongsheng Temple, the Chengde model of Tibet's Potala Palace.

We have a problem. The Chengde Potala is located on the other side of a river and the bridge is not close. Beth and I ask the man at the Temple of Heaven if there is another way across. He points us to a shortcut, and we soon find ourselves riding our bicycles on a dirt path following close behind a tractor pulling a trailer filled with huge, squealing pigs. I sense their anxiety. They know their destiny. The plaintive squeals are heart wrenching. I want to glance at Beth to see if she feels the same, but cannot because I need to concentrate on the rustic path in front of us.

We come upon the "bridge." It is all of three feet wide, about twenty feet long, and constructed of mud, hay, a few large wood planks, and a whole lot of wishful thinking. The porcine tractor pull veers off and begins crawling down the riverbank and into the water. Holding our collective breathes, we timidly venture out onto the bridge. So far so good. It does not give way. Becoming braver, and without any alternative, we then quickly scoot across. We pass the tractor climbing up through the mud and are soon peddling across peasant farmland. Beth and I are by ourselves in a part of China that time has passed by. It is hard to imagine being farther from Cape Cod than I do at this moment.

By the time we find the main road, it is time to eat. Beth and I stumble into a small alley with numerous little carts and stalls selling soups, snacks, and *baozi*, buns. We pick one and enter. The courteous owners wipe off one of their little tables. They go out of their way to find us clean utensils and bowls. We watch them making the steamed *baozi*. Beth retrieves two bowls of soup—wonton for me, *doufu* for her. She loves *doufu* and says this is the freshest and best she's ever had. She inhales the fragrance of the broth. I see delight in her face as she takes in each spoonful. To me eating *doufu* is like eating gelatinous, boiled paper. I'd rather go hungry. The handmade *baozi*, on the other hand, are the best I have ever had. The soft white exterior hides a succulent shredded meat buried deep within. These are medium sized and delicate. You take a bite and cannot help but beam as you savor the flavor. I ask the owners if I can take their picture. They won't let me. I think they keep saying "we are unworthy." We leave with full bellies, a fond memory, and no picture.

When we arrive at the Chengde Potala Palace, we enter through the Han Chinese Main Gate and pass through the Tibetan Mountain Gate, but do not get much farther. The buildings, including the main temple at the top, are padlocked tight. We have to be content with looking around the lower grounds, up the mountain at what might have been, and south towards the rear of the mountain resort. Peddling back to the hotel, we go the wrong way. Getting lost leads us on a forty-five-minute detour to die for. Amidst the rising peaks of mountain landscapes, Beth and I pedal through farms and fertile fields, dodge pigs roaming the streets, and are again deep within old China. The miles flow by effortlessly as we explore. We are energized, not exhausted. The temperature drops, and the gradual incline of our morning ride transitions to a friendly downhill ride on the way back into town.

Later that evening we go for a walk and come across a promising-looking restaurant. I put myself in Beth's hands; she has a great nose for good Chinese food. We have quickly developed a pattern. I secure the table; Beth selects the food. This time we eat stew in crocks. Beth savors her chicken. I eat a meat that may be *yangrou*, lamb, and mouth-watering *guotie*, what *jiaozi* dumplings become when pan fried instead of boiled. Great *guotie* bring delight to my face. The cold, weak beer again hits the spot. A man at the next table stares at us. He is dressed simply and nurses a small bowl of soup. Beth ignores him, but his preoccupation with us bothers me. Is he curious about this foreigner paired with a Chinese woman, as so many have been on this trip? Maybe, but not tonight. When we get up to leave, the man pounces. Emptying whatever we have not eaten into our beer bowls, he picks up my used chopsticks and digs in. Looks can be deceiving. He was watching our scraps, not us.

We wake in the morning and return the bikes to the bike rental shop, which doubles as a cloth store. The clerk is an affable, fifty-something lady, a local with a cigarette dangling from her mouth. Another pleasant experience in China. I am still surprised each time it happens. Chengde revelations keep on coming.

It is a fall morning, more polluted than yesterday, and Beth is cold even in her white turtleneck and winter coat. We take one last long walk around Chengde. Our public displays of affection, today walking hand in hand or with my arm around Beth trying to help her stay warm, are causing a stir among the local populace. Who is this couple? Where is that woman from? Is she overseas Chinese? Local? Why is she with the white guy? I notice the stares, but am surprisingly not bothered. I am either mellowing or proud to be seen with a gorgeous woman on my arm. Let them judge. I've got the girl.

We discover more amazing food markets and buy sour balls, apples, mandarin oranges (more than a pound for less than thirty cents), and pastries. Beth recognizes something at a handcart vendor and pulls me over excitedly. I look down skeptically at a large rectangular slab of whitish something, half covered with a cloth, sitting on a table along a dusty street. Beth tells me that it is glutinous rice laced with hawthorns, nuts, and sugar. Her eyes open wider, and the corners of her mouth turn up. It must be good. The vendor slices a thick hunk, places it on a paper plate, and sprinkles powdered sugar on top. We pull our chopsticks out of our bags and break into the sweet and sticky confection. Beth is right. This is delicious.

Eating is the major pastime in China. Pleasant food memories from Chengde are going to have to sustain me when standing in line in the cafeteria back at Shao Yuan. We order the handmade *jiaozi* at another little *xiaochibu* café for an early lunch. We cannot eat the entire six *liang* (twenty-four dumplings), but come close. Beth says we do right, we give face, by ordering more than we can eat. She explains this to me in another hopefully-not-too-rare instance of her Chineseness comfortably coming to the fore. Later, after walking some more, Beth buys a bowl of fresh *doufu* soup. While the hot soup spreads throughout her chilly body, I click away, taking pictures of local street scenes. A panoply of bamboo cricket cages spills along the sidewalk from one vendor. Piles of sweaters and long underwear overflow the tables of several clothing vendors. Bicycles line the street, and a group of young school children march by in a pack. We walk down one *hutong* alley and buy a *jin* of fresh carrots (about three). The real China resides in these back streets, alleys, and markets.

We check out of the hotel and walk to the train station because the day has become warm and pleasant. Passing a school, we stop to watch the little children play. We enter a nearby farmer's market hand in hand. We arrive at the train station a few minutes before departure. We have hard-seat tickets, but want soft seat. We trail behind two other Caucasians (who knew there were any others in town?) and follow them onto the soft-seat car.

We are stopped.

"Where are your tickets?" The official is stern, but not angry.

I hand them over.

"These aren't for this car." A matter-of-fact pronouncement.

I lie. Affecting surprise, I come out with, "Really, we asked for soft seat. They must have given us hard seat by mistake. Can we please stay?" I am still in a relaxed mood and my voice must show it.

The conductor barely pauses before saying, "No problem. Pay another two dollars per ticket and you can move into soft seat." Another unexpected, pleasant experience in China. Maybe I should see if there are any universities here that accept foreign exchange students.

As the train chugs down the mountains, passes through the Great Wall, and reenters China proper, I hold Beth in my arms, her head resting on my shoulder. At some point I doze off and wake to find that she has written in my journal:

11.17.86. The mountains of Chengde were quite beautiful. I'm so glad we decided to take this trip. I had a great time. I never would have thought I could be so happy with someone before. It's a different feeling. There are many things I want to write now but I can't seem to pen the words. For years I've wanted to come to China but once I reached Beijing I felt disappointed. Now I feel a little different. Beijing is not China. Perhaps I'll stay for the year. Having you around is a great incentive. Don't feel bad, I don't want to [lose] you now that I've found someone who makes me feel whole again. I'm shy with words sometimes but when I'm with you I feel very comfortable. The train ride back to Beijing is lovely. I feel tired, happy, and rested. Chengde was a great little town bustling with local flavor. I'll buy you lots of soda when we get back to Beijing. I want to travel all over China with you and discover the many sights and pleasures China has to offer. I'm looking at you now and thinking how much I love you.

CHAPTER 15

VISITING CONFUCIUS

I CANNOT CONCENTRATE IN class and want to be anywhere other than sitting through four rote hours of intellectual boredom. I want to be with Beth. Yet I cannot be with Beth the same as in Chengde. We cannot hold hands. We cannot publicly show affection here in this staid once and current imperial capital that is our home. Beijing is formal. Beijing is rules. Beijing is where she has relatives. Trying to act like friends when all I want to do is reach out and kiss her bottles me up.

We escape in the afternoon and bike northwest away from Beida to Xiangshan, the Fragrant Hills. Every time I think of the Chinese name Xiangshan, the Chinese name for Hong Kong, Xianggang, comes to mind. The *xiang* is the same. It means fragrant. *Shan* is mountain. *Gang* is harbor. Hong Kong is the Fragrant Harbour. But that *gang* is third tone; it falls and then rises in pitch. There is another *gang*. This *gang* is first tone; it stays level. This other *gang* means anus. My fear is that when I head south for winter break I will accidentally tell people I am off to the Fragrant Asshole. It is very easy to embarrass oneself in Mandarin.

A few weeks back, Meilin wrote again and invited me to come to Xiangshan with her to see the fall foliage. I had not heard from her since she showed up unexpectedly at Shao Yuan. I had no interest, but wanting to be friendly I wrote back accepting the invitation if a friend who also wants to go comes with us. Billy had volunteered. She did not respond and hopefully never will. Today, with Beth, a strong headwind makes for a slow ride out of campus and into the hills. Beth's bike is not in great shape. Leaving it outside to the elements at the Zhongguancun Market for the last week wasn't the smartest idea. Her back tire springs a leak, and she is forced to pedal twice as hard to keep moving. The short ride takes us one-and-a-half hours. We walk our bicycles up the steepest part near the end. Beth is beat.

Xiangshan pales against the majesty of the Chengde mountain vistas. A sad few *hongyue*, red autumn leaves, stubbornly and forlornly cling to the trees. The chairlift to the summit reveals the unappetizing Beijing smog off to the southeast and a belching Four-Mile-Island-like chemical plant to the southwest. It is not a fair comparison, but I cannot help it. The positive is that Beth sits next to me and close. The diffused sun warms us after the chilly mid-November ride up. The exposed chairlift ride down is raw. We stop in a store at the bottom to warm up and then fly most of the way to campus, leaky tire and all, with a strong wind now at our backs.

I have a package waiting from mom. I tear into it with anticipation to find an UNO game, candy, three ACE bandages, ink, a Red Sox yearbook, my other grey sweats, and an adapter.

The sweatpants and the adapter set me off. My frustration switch must be on autopilot. "This is unbelievable. Is that woman incapable of listening to the simplest of requests?"

Beth looks over at me questioningly. She can sense another outburst coming.

"I specifically asked her not to send the gray sweats and the adaptor. Is it really that hard to pay attention?" I am shaking at this point, angry and loud.

"Darling, it is not that big a deal. Don't wear the pants or use the adaptor. Why are you so upset? She is trying to be helpful."

"I know, but. Aaagghh. She drives me out of my mind. I...I...."
I pick up the adaptor and hurl at down on the mattress. *Why can't my mother listen?*

I stomp around a bit more and then sit down deflated. It is always like this. My emotional state is like living without context. It is not just with my mother, but it certainly is best encapsulated by our interactions. She does what she thinks best even when it is not what we discussed or what I want or what I expect to happen. I explode at this and then feel drained and depressed. If only I could remember that this would be the result before it began each time.

Beth remains quiet while I come back into my mind, and now looks at me from far away as she says, "I wish my mother cared or knew how to." *Ouch, I really do not have anything to complain about, do I?*

—⟶⟨⟨⟨—

I need to find some perspective on my own life. I jump at an opportunity a few days later to seek out China's past while hopefully finding my present. Sam and I leave Friday afternoon for Qufu, the ancestral home of the Kong family in Shandong Province. The Kong family's most famous relative is Kong Fuzi, Master Kong, or, as we know him in the West, Confucius.

The trip starts inauspiciously. I have the top berth of our hard-sleeper car for the overnight trip, and Sam has the bottom berth. I look up as the middle berthee comes in and am flabbergasted to see my ever-so-amiable roommate-san, Toshiro. My jaw falls open. How can China be such a small country? Toshiro chokes when he sees me and says nothing. Sam glances at him, tries to stifle a smirk, and whispers in English, "Andrew, it is damn lucky you are traveling with me and not Beth. Otherwise, he'd probably commit sepulku." If I had been feeling better, I would have smirked too. As it is, my sinuses have been aching all day and the bouncing and rocking, the back and forth, the incessant up and down of the train ride exacerbate the pounding in my head. I sit in quiet misery. Neither of us speaks, and Toshiro spends time away smoking. As night falls, I use the built-in restraining straps to keep from flying off the edge of the upper berth bed and thrash around like an institutional hostage until a few hours of restless semi-unconsciousness take hold. When we arrive in the morning, my roommate has already left.

An early morning bus from the train station in the oppressively foul Yanzhou deposits Sam and I in Qufu, a small, out-of-the way city that has been restored to a great degree from the ravages of the Cultural Revolution.

Leaving the bus station, we ignore the persistent cycle rickshaw drivers and hike into town. It is unexpectedly warm for November 22, and the pleasant walk helps to finally clear my head. At 7:00 a.m. on a still-gray Saturday morning, we stroll north on Gulou Dajie, Drum Tower Road, pass through a memorial archway spanning the road, and approach Qufu's Kong Family Forest. Two ladies wearing facemasks sweep the dusty paved road using broad, fan-like straw brooms. The vendors have not yet arrived; their sidewalk kiosks are boarded up. We are some of only a few about. It is quiet in China.

Sam and I talk about the women in our lives. I excitedly share the news of my new relationship with Beth and our travels to Chengde. Sam is equally excited in talking about his fiancée. She is from Taiwan and is living in the States. Theirs is a true love story. Her parents want her to marry for money and power in Taiwan in an arranged union. She wants Sam. He won the girl.

We fall silent looking up at the watchtower gate at the southern entrance to the forest before climbing the gate to stare into what is in reality a gigantic cemetery for Confucius and legions of his descendants. Looking back from the way we came, there are half a dozen bicycles, two horses, and a smattering of people milling about on the straight-as-an-arrow Drum Town Road. There are no cars or buses or trucks. Turning back toward the forest, there are hundreds of acres and tens of thousands of living trees nestled in wooded solitude. What better place to find perspective? We climb down and enter the past.

Two-and-a-half millennia of people from one extended family are buried in the earth here. That is a lot of people. Their remains are the dirt upon which I trod. Their memories are in the early-morning breeze rustling through the trees. They are descended from arguably the most influential Chinese person of all time. What has come to be known as the Confucian Code, his Analects, was developed during a time of great chaos and lay down a philosophical and ethical tone for government and family life in traditional Chinese society. Rigid and patriarchal, the ultimate commandment is beneficial social control as the means and end of high moral attainment. Relationships of respect and ritual—child and parent, wife and husband, ruler and ruled—govern societal interactions and result in social order. The Confucian way is collective. The Confucian way is proper conduct. The Confucian way is virtue.

Stone grave markers dot the forest. A recent grave of a Kong ancestor is covered with brightly colored paper burial bouquets. A granite ram and a *bixi*, stone tortoise, sit among the trees, autumn leaves scattered all around. A proud warrior, right hand leaning for all time on his sword, stands sentinel off a path. Deep within the forest, I find myself standing in front of memory steles honoring Confucius and then his tomb. A soaring granite monument with cursive yellow script running vertically up to a carved, round-edged tablet brings home to me the presence of his mortal remains. This was his backyard some five hundred years before Jesus. And Jesus has been gone a long time.

The day is young and the forest is ours. I move over to a low wall and sit down to think. It is hard not to in such a consequential place. The Cape Codder in Qufu. The boy and the sage. The Confucian way is not the individualism of America, it is not my history, and I am not a good Confucian. My relationship with my mother knocks me out from the get-go. My emotional eruptions impair my relationship with Beth in the eyes of proper conduct. I most certainly rebel at what the government tries to dictate. Ritual. Respect. To what extent do these flow through me? Is there a common good that may also be my good? I shrink at the realization that I am but a superficial thinker, a mite within this place and this space.

Yet, being here, right now, looking out onto this history, enveloped by its remains, excites me and wraps me in its embrace. It is one of those rare moments when I am monumentally content, at peace. The quiet of nature outside is mirrored by a quiet inside. I need to hold onto this clarity when my internal workings are not so serene. I have never been religious, and wonder if this feeling is what it means to be spiritual.

Twenty-five centuries of Chinese history flash through my mind—the locally grown Confucianism and Daoism continuously switching places in a battle for the soul of a people. One is based on strict control and order of the fabric of life; the other flows on its own path through the way of nature. Chairman Mao tried to eradicate each as a taboo old custom. Just as he tore down the old walls and the immense gates that protected and defined Beijing through the centuries, so too Mao made it his mission to erase the philosophy and the religion of China. Social order was Mao's end goal as it was for Confucius, but Mao was to be the pinnacle of all facets of that order, to be unquestioningly respected, revered, and worshipped, to be followed blindly to the ends of the earth with nary a peep of dissent. This was his key to social order.

And yet, notwithstanding Mao's fervent and destructive efforts, much of the old survives. The principles of this long dead man buried before me are a significant part of this legacy. Confucianism remains the unofficial Philosophy of State even in late twentieth century Communist China. Not by name maybe, but by effect. It flavors, often not consciously, the entire Chinese ethos and is rooted here. Seeking social order has proven to be a timeless state of collective being.

As the sun continues its march higher into the morning sky, filtered light falls among the forest floor and shadows move in time with a daily tempo. More and more people are now out and about. A mother and her young son pose for a photograph in front of Confucius' tomb. It is time to go. I rise, and we leave the Kong Family Forest.

CHAPTER 16

THANKSGIVING NEWS

THANKSGIVING EVE, CHINA time. Three days since returning from the whirlwind thirty-eight-hour trip to Qufu, I receive another letter from Jill. Two in fact. The first was mailed ten days before, in the morning, saying how wonderful everything is and how much she loves me. The second was mailed ten days before, in the afternoon, after receiving my "friends" letter. Talk about timing. The second letter asks that I never contact her again: "We cannot be friends because I have too many feelings for you."

I look at the letters lying on the corner of my desk and sit in an anxious chill. I feel horrible. Not about breaking up. But I caused stress, angst, in another. I made a decision with consequences, those consequences happened, and now I have to accept the result. I made the right decision. And yet, the desire to avoid controversy itself led to controversy. Once again, I demonstrate my emotional indecisiveness, my inability to rise to the occasion, to own me.

A knock at the door.

Billy comes in. I think back to the early trip we took to Datong and the Yungang Grottoes. I think of the many conversations we have had about life and the universe. He is just the analytical person to help me come to grips with Jill's letters. He at one point told me he thought she and I were in love and that it would last.

"I am glad you are here." I show him the two letters.

He sits on my bed and reads them, but seems distracted. "Andrew, I want to tell you something." Being a bit preoccupied, I do not sense the weight in his words. "I'm leaving China." In the face of my silent, wide-eyed response, he continues, "At the end of the semester."

I think my eyes must be bulging out of their sockets.

"I know this is a surprise. I have been thinking about it for a few weeks now. I wanted to study abroad and Peter and I were studying Chinese so this seemed like the place to be."

I try to say something, but the words remain lodged in my throat.

"I enjoyed our trip to the Grottoes and like hanging around with you and everyone, but I can't do this for the full year. Asian history is not my passion, and this place is out there."

I can see the depth of reasoning in his eyes, the set of his shoulders. This was not an easy decision. A new set of emotions floods through me, and my heart tightens. I want to tell Billy not to go. I want to tell him that his presence here is a comforting reassurance in such an alien atmosphere. I want to tell him that I cannot imagine an end to our frequent evening bull sessions and comradery. But I am floored by the news and for once am rendered speechless.

Thoughts of Jill vanish.

⸻

The sun sets. My crystal on the window pane hangs still. I close the drapes and stew. Jill's letters are away. Billy has gone to tell others. This run-up to Thanksgiving, my first away from home, keeps getting heavier.

Beth arrives and finds me in a funk. Not one to let this go on for too long, she leaves and then returns with a dinner of egg salad on white bread with real mayo, potato chips, and orange soda. I do like white bread, and the soda hits the spot. Where did she find the makings of this soothing meal? I cannot stay depressed when my girlfriend spoils me with food and attention.

Toshiro is away, and Beth stays over. After making love deep in the night, Beth looks over at me and says with affection that could melt steel, *"Women feichang heshi, tebie heshi,"* "We are extremely compatible, especially suitable for one another." It sounds better in American-inflected Chinese. We are perfectly matched.

—⁓—

Thanksgiving Day, China time. Beijing University is the site of the self-proclaimed "First Annual Beijing Turkey Bowl."

On a patch of dusty earth about an eighth of the size of an American football field, a large group of foreigners and six Chinese students, close to ten players per team, take part. We are a motley crew playing two-hand touch. I wrap my ankle in one of the real ACE bandages my mother sent. I am sore, but manage a couple of good plays. Rules are lax, and the score is not important. Being outside and playing is fun, and it is only the appetizer to the day.

Thanksgiving dinner is the entrée. This is no Cape Cod family gathering of my youth around the antique dining room table that we open for special occasions in my parents' living room. My father is not standing at the head of the table carving a twenty-pound turkey. There is no turkey.

The ever-resourceful Sam secures us a classroom. He only has to ask half a dozen people before permission is granted. There are fifteen of us feasting, an international group of classmates and friends hanging out and swapping stories. The menu is eclectic and includes chicken, mashed potatoes, mashed sweet potatoes, real bread stuffing with onions and spices, garlic bread, cauliflower, spinach, a huge fruit salad, wine, beer, chocolate pudding, sautéed carrots, and apple pie. We are not going hungry.

The improvised evening comes off spectacularly. The food is delicious.

I am particularly fond of the creamy mashed potatoes and homemade stuffing and devour more than my fair share. The company is great. The after-dinner conversation spirals downward into a riveting, two-hour dirty joke-athon. I laugh so hard that tears fall from my eyes. This is *not* a Norman Rockwell Thanksgiving celebration.

I make out, too, because I am excused from washing dishes. I help straighten up the room and return several of the borrowed items that have been cobbled together for the night to their rightful owners. And then I am relieved of duty.

Beth is unfortunately not among us this evening. She is visiting her brother at her uncle's place and is then catching an 11:00 p.m. train to Guilin. She'll be gone sightseeing in far-away Southwest China for ten days on her own. I return to my room dreading being alone. Opening the door, I am surprised to find Toshiro sitting at his desk. It is a good thing that I had already cleaned up and removed most of my stuff from his side of the room. We speak civilly. He tells me that he'll be in Qingdao when I return (I am leaving tomorrow). He is away more than he is here, which works out well for both of us.

When I awake early the next day, it is Thanksgiving Day, American time. The twelve-hour time difference still takes getting used to. Rolling out of bed at 6:00 a.m., I walk briskly in the freezing cold to Beida's 24-hour Long Distance Telephone Office to call home. The office is locked up tight. I trudge back to my dorm and wait until Shao Yuan's own office opens at 7:30 a.m.

I am at the head of a long line, and fortunately, my call is the first to connect. I speak with the whole family, but the longest with my mother. My kid sister chuckles the whole time. My uncle pops on the line for a hello. The phone booth is paper thin, and every now and then I hear people remarking about my conversation. I call collect and am on for about twenty-five minutes. They finished eating an hour or so before and had been hanging around hoping I would call. I promise mom that I will call again on my birthday in a couple of months.

CHAPTER 17

TERRACOTTA HASSLES

THE TERRACOTTA WARRIORS. The Big Wild Goose Pagoda. An intact Imperial city wall. Xi'an, the cosmopolitan Tang Dynasty Capital of Chang'an (Forever Peace), has it all. The acknowledged first emperor of China, Qin Shihuangdi, he of the founding Qin Dynasty some eight hundred years before the Tang, established his capital of Xianyang and built his palace nearby. He mobilized his buried army east of the current city. Xi'an is a place of antiquity. It is a place I am excited to visit.

The train chugs nineteen hours southwest of Beijing. Two of our hard sleeper mates sit with us. Neither speaks English. One is a quiet, friendly People's Liberation Army (PLA) soldier. The other guy's a trip, a real gas. Mid-to-late fifties, receding hairline, graying hair, glasses, and a bit of a belly. He's gregarious and talkative with a quick mind, everyone's effusive grandfather. His four children are grown and have left home, no extended family sharing one apartment. He works as a conductor for the railway and is heading south for a meeting. Our new friend is well traveled for a Chinese citizen. Because their mandatory residence cards and assigned work units restrict where they can live and work, the Chinese are generally local creatures. It is unheard of to travel the way we foreign students do. We have a freedom they can only dream of, if they want to.

I am traveling with Alex, a Chinese-Canadian classmate. Alex may not know it, but I am forever indebted to him for he was the one I tagged along with that evening I met Beth. He is a good travel companion as we venture deep into the Chinese heartland because, unlike me, he does not get flustered. I have witnessed him accept Chinese society with an evenness to which I can only aspire. The long train ride passes with animated conversation about Alex's native Canada, drinking, jobs, music, and food. A lot about food. The Chinese love to ask how much our Western goods and food cost in *renminbi*. Like the young guys I met in Inner Mongolia, the Chinese here are astonished by such fantastical amounts. They seem to get psychic satisfaction that they have what they need for so little.

As a conductor, grandpa lives comfortably with his wife on a bit more than fifty-four dollars a month. He tells us that the PLA soldier makes US$135 a month. Our new friend loves to laugh. Crumbs splatter as he eats. Classic Chinese, he pushes food on everybody with great relish. He is intrigued by Alex's Sony Walkman. Alex loans it to him, and we watch as he puts on the small headphones and listens quietly to *Bridge Over Troubled Water* and *Parsley, Sage, Rosemary and Thyme*. A little boy in the next berth looks in, and our conductor pal plays with him too, even letting him listen to Alex's music. Alex smiles as his cassette player makes the rounds of our corner of the train.

Our new friend (if he tells us his name, it escapes me) shares a traditional Chinese language word play with us: "You know about Chinese moonshine, *baijiu*, White Spirit, right?" He looks at us expectantly and then continues on without missing more than half a beat. "OK, so we also call it *Ba Jia Yi* ("Eight Plus One"). Do you know why?"

The only polite, and in this case honest, answer is no.

"Because *ba* (eight) *jia* (plus) *yi* (one) equals *jiu* (nine). Get it?" His eyes light up and his belly bounces as he gives us the punchline. The character for "nine" has the same sound as the character for "spirit alcohol."

It is not only the heavy use of poetic metaphor and idioms that make learning Chinese so difficult. It is also these types of puns and word plays. And these vary by region to add another level of ridiculousness to learning the language. To be fluent in Chinese is to think in Chinese. The ability to do the latter informs the speaking and writing of the former. It is more than just understanding inside cultural knowledge, which is critical; it is also being up on the slang of societal context.

In English, we learn twenty-six letters and know that sentences for the most part are noun, verb, object. We conjugate our verbs. We pluralize our nouns with the addition of a simple letter or two at the end. We can read and speak any arrangement of the letters even if we do not know the word's meaning. This is not the case in Chinese. I struggle to break free from the noun-verb-object mindset, to be able to think more like the Chinese, to be better able to communicate. Another of our hard sleeper mates returns and after a spell of conversation looks at Alex and me and states with no malice, "You speak and write like third graders." This may be true, but we are practicing our Chinese on this train more than if we stayed on campus and attended classes.

At 7:00 a.m. today after leaving the Xi'an train station, Alex and I face central Chinese *mafan*. Crammed on a packed No. 5 bus, wearing a full pack, squished up against a heaving mass of Chinese locals, I cannot move my arms. I vaguely feel something, a sense of a tug at my side that raises the hairs on the back of my neck. Sliding off the bus at our stop, I reach down to my side pocket in my khakis and reassuringly pat my envelope of money. It would have been reassuring had the envelope still been there. I have been robbed, pickpocketed on the No. 5 bus. All of my *renminbi*, 290 *yuan* (US$78), is gone!! I have my wallet with FEC, but this is cold comfort. As I am discovering my loss, one of Alex's lenses pops out of his glasses as he steps down to the ground. His glasses are not as blocky as Billy's, but they have the largest lenses I have ever seen. Alex

141

swoops down and luckily retrieves the fallen lens intact, no small feat in a surging crowd.

The *mafan* continues. Arriving at the Shengli Hotel, the Victory Hotel, we are told that there is only one dorm bed left. We do not believe the clerk and stand there arguing with her. OK, I am arguing while Alex attempts to persuade. A subtle difference to be sure. She sticks to her story, but eventually acknowledges that there might be another bed opening up later on.

This is a game to her.

"We'll wait."

A guy in the lobby (a fellow traveler) comes over and quietly tells us that there are two beds available in the dorm room right now. While I hover at the counter distracting the clerk, Alex sneaks upstairs to check it out. She doesn't like me in her face and tells me to leave. I ignore her.

When Alex returns, he not only confirms the empty beds, but also that others up there will soon be leaving. We begin dancing with the clerk once again. A Chinese he-said she-said. She insists that there is only one bed available. This is communist bureaucracy at its finest. Why are we fighting? Why do we need to? They have beds and are in the business of providing them to people who are willing to pay. We want two beds and are willing to give them money in exchange for the accommodations. Makes sense to me, right?

"Please, go upstairs and check for yourself," we practically implore her.

One of the other ladies at the counter relents and goes to check for herself. She comes back down, looks at her colleague comrade, and silently a new card is made up so we can have two beds.

Alex and I drop our bags and head out for a walk. We walk, and walk, and walk. We are encouraged in this by inconvenient bus schedules, extreme crowding, and my paranoia about pickpockets. Alex and I travel well together. He possesses bountiful energy and is curious to see the country. What we see, however, leaves something to be desired. Xi'an, the city, is drab, ugly, and grungy; a stereotypical concrete Soviet jungle with all the charm of smog. A few people accost us asking to change money.

Roaming outside the imposing city wall in front of a government office building, we meet an overly-friendly woman. Alex and I are chuckling over a used condom lying on the ground nearby and its ramifications for pure communist society when she approaches. She starts talking, and we, unfortunately, listen.

"Do you wanta changeh money?" She pronounces this with the sing-songy quality that such phrase is said in English by non-English speakers.

"No thanks." This should be the end of it.

"Do you want girls? I can help you find girls in Xi'an."

"No thanks." Now she is becoming a bother.

"Can I have two FEC?"

"What? We don't think so."

"Why not? Two *kuai* is worth nothing to you."

She is right, of course; however, on top of everything that has already happened today, this woman is causing us to lose our patience. Even mild-mannered Alex is getting slightly perturbed. More *mafan*. We turn and walk away before saying something we might regret.

—⁓—

The second day begins better with a sumptuous breakfast buffet at the joint-venture Jinhua, Golden Flower, Hotel. We indulge in repeated trips to feast on fluffy scrambled eggs, fried eggs, bacon, sausage, hash browns, and fresh fruit, all washed down with close to a gallon of fresh-squeezed orange juice. After deliciously overeating, we make use of the hotel's seriously phenomenal bathrooms. I will never under appreciate the value of a clean toilet, particularly after gorging at a buffet and not wanting to use the scary hotel toilets.

Alex and I stroll along the paths and around the lakes of Revolution

Park, past a Ferris wheel, dilapidated go-carts, and a dragon train. The weather is gray, and it briefly flurries. After watching a loud and smoky fireworks display celebrating the grand opening of a food market, we spend a few minutes with a group of Chinese taking part in an impromptu sidewalk class. A woman has hung a large abacus on a tree and is teaching how to use it to count. We pass an open-air meat market with large hunks of speared raw meat hanging from a metal pipe on the sidewalk, another piece swinging on a hook from a forlorn tree.

We climb the 1,200-year-old Big Wild Goose Pagoda south of the old walled city. A long time ago the pious Chinese monk, Xuanzang, walked to India to collect Buddhist teachings for his Tang Emperor. He returned on foot two decades later as a Buddhist scholar with many hundreds of sutra scrolls and writings, statues, and sacred objects. In recognition of the journey, knowledge, and glory brought by Xuanzang to the Middle Kingdom, a successor Tang Emperor constructed the Big Wild Goose Pagoda to house this Buddhist legacy. The complex has survived wars, earthquakes, and Mao.

Standing in the thick of this antiquity, I should feel the same weight of history, the same awe, the same contentment that I felt standing peacefully in front of Confucius' tomb in Qufu. But I do not, on all three counts. This is because notwithstanding interludes of normalcy, *mafan* continues to be our ever-present Xi'an companion. I've never encountered more hassle or been angrier than in this god-forsaken hole. At times, I am barely able to contain myself. We have no equilibrium here.

Enthusiastic explorers or not, Alex and I tire from so much walking. Someone again tries to rip me off on the crowded No. 5 bus. I hear the zipper, but the pocket is empty. We constantly check and hug our bags. We continue to be harassed by "changeh money" guys. The pedicab people nag us. The sales lady at the Shaanxi Provincial Museum will not give us Chinese prices even after we show her our student ID cards. The people of Xi'an are dirty looking and unfriendly.

I keep trying to remind myself to let the journey come to us. I am not a very good listener. We experience Communist China first-hand—the *mafan*, the aggravation, the frustration. Alex and I take turns losing it. Yes, even Alex. First, I melt down and spiral out on a Chinglish cursing tirade at everything and everybody. Once I vent and have deflated, Alex begins shaking, then yelling, and comes seconds away from slugging two guys who will not leave us alone. This is the first time I have seen Alex descend to my level, and I am unsure if I should be saddened or comforted by the company.

We decide to leave Xi'an and head to the train station. We wander aimlessly around the huge building trying in vain to find a door. It would be like the communists to build a grand edifice and forget to include access. After a fruitless search around the perimeter, we learn that tickets are sold outside in Xi'an. We stand in line for ages with the locals, watching beggars sleep and people shove and cut in line, and buy the next available tickets, standing room only the next night, for a seventeen-hour ride further southwest to Chengdu, the capital of Sichuan Province. Anywhere will be better than here.

—⁓—

We have one day left to get through before we can escape, and we have not seen the famous Terracotta Warriors. It is December 1, 1986, and we are the only two Westerners on a twenty-five-person bus tour. Most of the several stops are unmemorable, but not all. At the six-thousand-year-old Neolithic village of Banpo, the field of small clay urns, some with intact covers, gives me a chill with the realization that each once contained the body of an ancient young person who never grew up.

At the still unexcavated tomb of Qin Shihuangdi, the first emperor, we pay our fee and climb a set of stairs to a platform at the top of a barren hill. If he is under us, then the Chinese masses are marching all over him in high tourist delight. Today Emperor Qin is Mr. China, the unifier of a land that had been beset for centuries by feuding fiefdoms. He cobbled together and expanded the Great Wall. He instituted a system of laws and centralized the government. He lent his name to the country and its psyche. At the same time, he was a brutal, ruthless tyrant who burned books, held no quarter with those who disagreed with him, and conscripted an entire life-size terracotta army, complete with live concubines, to guard and serve him in death.

The commercial leeches are out. This is obviously "Pick on Alex and Andrew" week. People hawk chintzy items and pester us to change money. The tomb site is bad. I tell the beady-eyed men, women, and children to "drop dead" in English. I give them the finger. Patience is not a word in my vocabulary today. At one point, I storm down the steps of the bus at a little kid who won't quit. He gets the message and flees. The bus driver glares at me. What is most frustrating is that I can't tell the hucksters to piss off in their own language. My knowledge of slang is non-existent, and my ability to articulate tones and sound coherent when I am flipping out is a fantasy.

Although my unhinged reaction to the stifling weight of *mafan* clouds my ability to appreciate my surroundings in depth, I do come back long enough to recognize that the emerging buried army of clay of the First Emperor of China is spectacular. From the visitor catwalk high above the pit being excavated in Vault 1, I watch the archaeologists toil to bring to light the untold ranks of soldiers. Some stand at attention; others kneel in defensive or offensive formation. The myriad faces of the soldiers and horses gaze at the world with lifelike detail, even now millennia after the original paint has faded and only dusted terracotta remains. The statues were built in stages, separate torsos, hands, and heads all slotted together to form each whole. There are numerous missing hands and heads. Wooden weapons have long since rotted away. The chest of one soldier lies on the dirt with a hand resting where his head should have been. A group of broken heads lies nearby. A soldier in the back remains half buried in sand.

—⁓—

When the tour bus returns to the Victory Hotel, there are cabs out front. Alex checks us out. I run upstairs and hastily throw whatever isn't packed into our bags. I have become alter-Andrew and do not give Alex much choice in the matter. I keep pushing and rushing us out. The cabbie rips us off, but this is because I accept his price without bargaining. I am in that much of a hurry to flee. I am beyond thinking rationally.

Arriving more than eight hours before our scheduled 1:00 a.m. train, we put on our most sad-sack looks, approach the attendant, and lie.

"We asked for tickets for the late afternoon train, but they gave us the early morning train by mistake. Can you please help us make the right train? We can't miss it."

The lady looks at us for a moment and without a word or hassle changes our tickets to the earlier train. We must look that pathetic (or crazed).

Running onto the platform for the train to Sichuan, we jump onto Hard Seat Car No. 1. With more luck (we deserve it, don't we?) this train originates here in Xi'an, and we have assigned seats. They are not soft sleeper nor soft seat nor even hard sleeper. They are hard seat, but a board bench is better than the floor for an overnight-plus ride. An off-duty train employee, a Russian-speaking student of Soviet studies, slides in next to us and begins talking and will not stop. It is a challenge to keep concentrating on his endless discourse as we head deeper into China's interior.

Evening turns to night. The temperature in the crowded car rises incrementally with each passing kilometer. It seems like everyone but us is smoking. The early December air outside is cold so no one will let us open the windows. A thick cloud of smoke fogs the increasingly dark, dank space.

Alex and I choke. We gag. My eyes sting when I close them. My throat is frogged. Even the Soviet studies major finally stops talking as everyone retreats into themselves.

We are wedged in tight, my restless feet captive under the hard-seat booth table. There is nowhere to move, to get up, to stretch. I take my right foot out of my boot to shake it a little, but it does little to calm the irresistible urge crawling up my leg.

The weight of pressed humanity and the suffocating sensation of being caged expands onto my chest and throughout my being. My skin is alive with an eerie feeling. I itch under the long sleeves of my sweater.

Exhausted and overwrought, I wrap my eyes with my cashmere scarf and lay my head down on the table trying to get some measure of comfort, of relief, of escape. The noxious taste of cigarettes circles around and through my makeshift mask.

I fight the panic welling up inside of me. There is no comfort. No relief. No escape. I steal a glance at my watch and sag with the realization that only 240 minutes of the seventeen-hour journey have elapsed. Time is not crawling, it is stagnating.

Everything is hazy, and I cannot empty my mind of swirling thoughts.

CHAPTER 18

GREEN AND CLEAN IN SICHUAN

A LEX AND I stagger into the Sichuanese sunshine as a mega-disgusting duo. I dozed little all night and am cranky. My mouth tastes chalky. We have not showered in days. The fur on my arms feels mossy, and my oily hair is matted to my scalp. Alex's clothes are dust-covered and clingy with stale sweat. His magnified eyes droop behind the large lenses of his smeared glasses.

We immediately get into a fight with our cabbie over the equivalent of one U.S. dollar. The jilted driver follows us into the lobby of the Jiaotong, Traffic, Hotel, moaning to everyone in sight. He walks back outside and starts in again with his cabbie friends. Our resolve wavers, but when we offer him an additional two yuan, he stomps off shouting as he goes, "*Buyao nide qian.*" "I do not want your money."

We need to shower before we can rest, but the hot water will not be available for several hours. We head out for a walk hoping that we will not offend too many people.

Even in our bedraggled state, it is obvious that Chengdu has a charm that Xi'an and Beijing could maybe fantasize about in their wildest dreams. Leafy, green trees line the roads. A river courses through the city center with clear, sweet-looking water. Walking paths, sitting areas, and more healthy green grace both banks. The scale of the streets and buildings and neighborhoods is more human. The atmosphere is that of a large Chengde, friendly, warm, and open. There is none of the staid Imperial presence of Beijing or the gray Soviet monolith of Xi'an.

We enter a small restaurant for an early dinner. The owners welcome us with friendly smiles. They speak Mandarin, but with a heavy accent that it is virtually another language. China's leader, Deng Xiaoping, is a Sichuanese who speaks with a well-known hard-to-understand diction. We have trouble communicating, but these people can cook. After days of tension, we instinctively relax as we absorb the intricate flavors of each bite. Noodles lathered with a rich dark sauce. Vegetables infused with local seasonings. At the end of our meal, my mouth stings with the spiciness for which the province is famous.

We continue walking. It is not warm, but pleasant; the air is clean. A little boy joins us. He says hello and bye-bye in English, but other than that we do not have the foggiest idea what he prattles on about. He is clearly happy to accompany the two foreigners down the street. We come across a large group of young Chinese at the side of the river and hear the sounds of English. Alex is more knowledgeable than I and explains that this is a so-called English Corner, a hip new social scene. We speak with a few girls and learn that they gather in this little park twice a week. At one point the breeze shifts, and I cringe. The odor is pungent. The girls are either polite or desperate to practice their language skills. We reek.

—⁂—

Returning to the hotel, we discover that the promised in-room hot water is just that, a promise. We switch to Plan B and head to the communal shower room downstairs. At this point, hot water is hot water. After stripping off pants and jerseys and sweaters that have soaked in days of endless sweat, coal, cigarettes, dust, and anxiety, we pile them on a bench. They lie there with a form that is almost lifelike.

Precious manna falls from the shower nozzles. I generally take a quick shower. Today, I stand for ages under the steady stream of water, letting the encrusted grime and angst wash down my body and out of my mind. I lather and rinse twice. I shampoo my greasy head twice. We all but destroy Alex's bar of soap and surface as new people.

Being clean, comfortable, and presentable, we are once again hungry and want to sample as much of the famed local food as possible. We stop at a café and eat what I believe is pork with broccoli stalks and twenty wontons apiece. It has been a while since I have eaten fresh vegetables. The wontons are bite-sized wonders. All of this food (our second dinner) should have filled us up, but no. After a short walk, the scintillating aromas coming from nearby restaurants draw us back in.

As we approach, the owners of two adjacent restaurants compete for our attention.

"Are you hungry? Come here!" shouts the first owner. "We have the tastiest food. Try our soup. It is mouthwatering." Four friendly people walk over encouraging us to try this restaurant. One of the girls offers us the soup for free.

"No. No. Come here foreign friends," cries the owner of the neighboring restaurant. "Our food is better. It will satisfy you."

Their accents are still a challenge, but the Mandarin comes through. Eventually, the first group sways us and we follow them inside for our third dinner.

Meat is well seasoned in Chengdu. The chicken is juicy and tender. The rabbit tastes like chicken, but is too bony and spicy for our liking. I down half a bottle of beer trying to quash the flames searing the inside of my mouth. My lips cry. I glance over at Alex and am comforted by the pained expression on his face, my comrade in gastronomic misery.

A Tibetan man comes over and sits next to me, the only non-Asian in the room, and starts jabbering. Others have to translate. He is a follower of the Dalai Lama. It is a one-sided monologue that soon becomes annoying as we try to eat. He says something to the extent that Chengdu and Tibet are equally good places to travel in and that next time I go to Tibet I should have fun. He keeps calling me *meigui*, American Ghost, though not apparently pejoratively. He repeatedly utters something about the two of us and gives us the thumbs up sign.

Returning to our hotel, fully sated and ready to collapse, we find that there is no heat. While it may be mild outside, our room is anything but when the sun goes down. Alex and I shiver through the night. Chengdu is damp. Our towels won't dry. They remain heavy with moisture. Our belongings are beginning to smell musty. The clothes we arrived in from Xi'an are threatening to mold, and we throw them away.

The next morning we head out hunting for warmer attire. I find a pair of cotton-knit sweat pants for twenty-two yuan RMB, the people's currency. I offer the sales lady fifteen yuan FEC, our Foreign Exchange Certificates, because my theft-depleted RMB supply has run out. And what happens? Murphy's Law, that's what. Because we have to use FEC, the local populace has no need for it and does not want to accept it. The sales lady protests that she has no place to spend it, but I persist (what choice do I have?). I explain that my RMB was stolen in Xi'an and plead my case. "I'll freeze without heavier pants. I have no other money to pay. Please." Either I get through to her or she wants us to go away, but in either event, her face eventually relents and we settle amicably on sixteen yuan FEC.

The sun rises late in Sichuan because the Communist Party dictates that the entire country operate on one time zone—Beijing time. China is about the same size as the continental United States. This is a large area to share one time zone. The K.I.S.S. ("Keep it simple, stupid") principle allows the news, trains, and planes to be on a coordinated schedule, but it messes with the normal rhythms of sunrise and sunset the further west you venture.

We roam the back streets of the city. People give me the eye, but behind the looks lies something attractive, not hostile. A toddler peaks out from under a white sheet painted with a red cross hanging in the doorway of a clinic. A grown daughter wearing a bright red jacket strolls along a market street with her mother. A man in a blue Mao jacket bicycles by transporting chickens hanging from baskets. Old men smoke their pipes and play mahjong with cards instead of tiles. We pass two kittens tied up on leashes in a doorway. The cry of *Mai Wenba*, newspapers for sale, from a lady riding her bicycle through the neighborhood echoes in our ears. The local dialect is incomprehensible. I buy little baskets from a lady on a street corner and figure out how much she wants with hand signals and guessing.

We climb the forested hill in People's Park and circle the central lake. The park is alive with children at play, their parents, and their parents' parents. This is family time. Alex and I sit on a bench in a crowded playground. There is a train, animal-shaped slides, see-saws, swings, go-carts, and merry-go-round-like rides for the little ones. Two girls stand up on a swing set seat facing each other and propel themselves back and forth, higher and higher, until they are horizontal with the ground in a blurring back-and-forth. People row out on the lake. A young couple is off on a quiet, private boat ride. The park and playground are not pristine, but there is no pressure, no visible bureaucracy. It is a simple afternoon outdoors.

On our way to a nearby shrine, we stop at a pharmacy. Alex has a doozy of a cold. Stuffed nose. Achy sinuses. What with Xi'an, the overnight train, the nighttime chill, and the damp, it is no wonder. The pharmacist asks Alex what is wrong.

"Give me your hands." He takes Alex's pulse in both wrists. "Stick out your tongue." Alex lets him examine it. "Mix these two packets of powder in boiling water three times a day." He offers to boil the first dose and hands it over.

Alex eyes the concoction with suspicion, but chokes down the first cup of thick, bitter brew. The scrunch on his face tells me all I need to know. We walk on.

The shrine and its garden are connected to a park. The garden is lush, lush, lush. And clean. Such a change from the dusty Beijing we are allowed to see. Entering a quiet tea garden, the patrons openly stare with curious, friendly faces. Ah, a different China, away from the communist machine and Marxist rhetoric. Do Chengde and Chengdu represent a surviving culture? Might it possible to be happy and satisfied in this People's Republic?

We stop on the way back for lunch. We want hotpot. I select my raw meats, vegetables, and seasonings from the serving table and bring them back to our table to the steaming metal pot/wok in the middle. Sliding and placing the ingredients into the boiling water, I cook my own lunch. A tall cylindrical chamber releases steam up and away from us. As each piece is finished, I remove it with my chopsticks, dip it into a small bowl of peanut oil, and pop it into my mouth.

The food tantalizes at first with a nice, tasty flavor. But then, seconds later, an expanding ball of fire grips the central part of my mouth and radiates out to my tongue, teeth, gums, and throat. My face flushes. Sweat bubbles on my forehead. My head tightens. I am the swelling mercury-filled thermometer tip of a childhood cartoon setting to explode. This is pain. Somehow, and I still do not know how, I finish my meal.

I need something sweet to try and temper the inferno roasting my mouth. I find Shanghai-made chocolate gelt in a nearby store. The pseudo-chocolate flavor is familiar, and I think of Chanukah.

—⚓—

Our last night down south. We watch a two-hour Western show called *North Beach and Rawhide* starring William Shatner on the clunky television set in our room. It is dubbed into Chinese with no subtitles. We fall asleep after the first hour.

The next morning is our last meal down south. We pull out chopsticks from the ten-pack we carry and enjoy a *baozi* (steamed bun), a pork dish, and soup with pork. Food has become the central focus of our existence. Alex and I are now Chinese. After our breakfast, we leave our chopsticks at the restaurant in tribute to all of the good food we have enjoyed in Chengdu.

CHAPTER 19

MISSING FRIENDS

ETH HAS NOT returned to Beijing. There are three letters from her among the baker's dozen from friends and family I have waiting at Shao Yuan when I return. She wrote last Saturday, last Sunday, and last Tuesday. That's the date of her last letter, Tuesday. Why is this important? It is important in the emotionally insecure reservoir that is a deep part of me.

I heard a news report on my way back from Sichuan that a tiger killed two people and injured three others in Kunming last Wednesday. Beth was due in Kunming last Wednesday. Beth, she who had written me three of the four previous days, apparently stopped writing at the exact same time as the tiger attack. According to the news report, two of the injured have yet to be identified. And I have no word from her since then! The wheels in my neurotic mind are in overdrive.

I am being crazy, right? These two circumstances cannot possibly be related. It is too fantastic. Just a coincidence. Why is it then that this scene of potential dread consumes me? Why does it seem that if something is not bad in my mind, something is not right? Now I am moping and anxious. I cannot study for my big test tomorrow. When I finally call it a night, my rest is anything but peaceful.

To add insult to injury, two members of my support team are leaving. Sam has been distraught since Thanksgiving when he learned that his fiancée succumbed to the relentless parental pressure and returned to Taiwan. He and I had just returned from Qufu, our trip to commune with Confucius. We had enjoyed a pampered, Sunday morning breakfast buffet extravaganza at the Jianguo Hotel. Sam then called home for the holiday and heard the news. His fiancée had not been able to reach him before she left. Sam hasn't eaten or slept much since and for days has walked around Beida in a dazed stupor. He bursts out crying with no warning. His future road ripped from him, Sam is leaving. He is not totally sure when or to where or to do what, but he says he cannot remain here. He might try going to Taiwan to see her. It is a gut punch to all of us. What words of comfort can one give in such a situation? How does a person begin to process and cope with such a volcanic life change?

Billy is leaving too. Unlike with Sam, I knew this day was coming, but that does not make it any easier. He and I have been close this past semester. We discovered a hidden Buddha refuge in Datong. He offered to be my anti-wingman with Meilin. We debated geopolitics back and forth. He is not shy about calling out the inequities of the social experiment we humans undertake throughout the world. We commiserated over the daily inanities present in country. In the end, the "what" of these evening bull sessions didn't matter so much as the fact that he was here. His presence has been a comforting reassurance. I am going to miss him.

I have to face that several of my travel companions, my hang-out buddies, people who are important to me and help make this experience so much more fulfilling and bearable, will be gone. Their looming absence already weighs heavy in my heart.

—⚬⚬⚬—

I am still in an anxious, self-pitying funk the next day when a friend appears at my door. "Andrew, Beth's roommate has a postcard for you upstairs."

"She does? Is it from Beth?" I ask in a semi-manic breath.

I race upstairs, practically tripping in my excitement. And there it is. The words are initially beyond the point. The card is from Beth. In her handwriting. Mailed last Wednesday. She sent it to her room by mistake. A weight lifts from my distraught heart. I silently laugh at my unfound fear, knowing that the next such event is not too far around the corner.

Beth sounds lonely. Traveling alone takes a toll, having to field all of the locals' questions by herself, with no break for days and days, with no easy access to comfortable conversation in her own language. I know. I so hope she's back soon.

In my solitude, it dawns on me that the holiday season is fast approaching. I haven't sent cards to family and friends back home and now have no chance of them being remotely on time. Our lives here, how and when we do what we do (or do not do), are on a separate path. China runs to its own beat with separate schedules, holidays, lifestyles, culture. I'm cut off and segregated from my upbringing, my customs, my comfort zone.

—⁂—

And then, two days later, great news. Beth returns. Her cab rounds the corner and enters the U-shaped entrance drive of the Shao Yuan complex. I skip downstairs, excited to have her back in my daily life. The one person who can make me feel completely balanced has returned. Unfortunately, she's sick. Her stomach's queasy. She is beaten down emotionally from her trip. She caught flak for being a woman traveling alone. She barely managed to get the Civilian Aviation Authority of China (CAAC) flight from Kunming. At least on this flight the CAAC, the lone airline of the PRC, did not live up to its nickname, "China Air Always Crashes."

Beth might be exhausted and ill, but she is happy to be home and has brought gifts (I like gifts): a black cotton fisherman's jacket from the famed southern village of Yangshuo; a shoulder bag embroidered in a rainbow of bright colors by the local Minority Nationality; and a kaleidoscopic Yi

Nationality hat with tassels and earing-like ornaments on either side that the women wear in Kunming.

"You should have seen me, darling. I actually wore the hat part of the way back because I had no other place to put it. People looked at me funny." She frowns at this recollection.

"You must have looked beautiful." I am sincere, but biased since everything makes her look beautiful.

"Yeah, right." She mock sneers with a wide grin on her relaxed face. Beth shows me several stamps she found for her collection and then lets me in on a secret she is keeping. With a twinkle in her eyes, she pulls out a Mao pin and hands it to me. "I know you have been looking for another one."

I hug her and give her a big kiss. This is terrific. This is my second Mao pin, and I share with her that I will soon have a third as well. A Chinese guy I met brought fifty pins from his large collection to Beijing and has agreed to trade me one for my Beatles pin. My collection is growing.

—∞—

Later, when Beth and I are lying on my bed reunited, Toshiro returns from his shower.

"Do you want us to leave while you change?" I ask to be polite.

He smiles, bats his eyes through his black-framed glasses, looks down a little, and nods.

OK. Not with a roar, but rather a silent whimper, he responds! I had to ask, but at long last, he answers. Maybe I have been subconsciously pushing him because I want a response. Beth's roommate takes it all in stride. She's a workaholic, so while she plugs away at her desk, Beth and I talk, rest, or sleep. Her roommate gets into bed when she wants to sleep, and we take the hint.

Beth and I get up and leave the room.

When I come back, Toshiro has returned from drinking with his friends. It makes him talkative, and we have a real conversation. Sitting on our respective beds, facing each other, he is relaxed. His guard is down. For forty-five minutes, an eternity based on our past interactions, we speak of his goals, his life, me and Beth. He shares that he and his girlfriend, a salesperson in a Tokyo department store, are getting married next fall. I catch a smile. I learn that he is a Buddhist philosophy major who doesn't particularly care for Confucius and wants to be a professor. And travel to India. "I cannot be true Buddhist because I like to drink and eat meat. But, some Buddhist sects can marry, so I'll be OK if I ever decide to convert." If Yoko is not pure Japanese because she has studied overseas, what does that make this man?

CHAPTER 20

ANXIOUS MOMENTS

"I'M LATE," BETH announces one morning a few days on as we are getting ready for class.

"Late? Late for what?" I ask distractedly as I get my books together.

"Late, *late*, Andrew." She emphasizes the repeated word. I am still not getting it. I look up questioning. "As in my period." She announces with exasperation. Her eyes meet mine. Her nervous face bores into that of her lover. My frozen, slack-jaw response is probably not what she hoped to see.

There is no way my eyes do not reflect the dread instantly spreading through my body. My chest contracts. My brain sputters. I cannot think. Then this: "But how?" My voice rises an octave. *OK, that was stupid.* I need to take a deep breath.

"Do I really need to explain it to you?" The edge to her voice sets off alarm bells.

I am flailing, but can't seem to shut up. "But we used a condom."

"Yeah, well maybe it didn't work." The retort is sharp. I cringe. She is pissed. And scared.

Still, I can't stop the words from tumbling out. "How could it not work, you saw how thick it was," *OK, that was even stupider.*

Beth stares me down like the babbling idiot I am and spits out with resigned contempt, "Andrew. You're not helping."

No shit. Fortunately, I do not say this out loud. I am finally out of words. *Pregnant? Here? Now? I am not sure I ever want to be a father, but I sure as hell know I do not want to be one now. I am barely holding me together.*

"If I am pregnant, I am going to have the baby." Her statement is firm.

I am not emotionally stable enough, or intellectually strong enough, to attempt a comeback to this statement and it hangs out there.

We leave for class with a mountain of unsaid conversation on top of us. We do not talk of marriage. We do not talk about whether the child will have an involved father. We do not discuss other options. We're both thinking about them, but neither brings them up.

Today becomes tomorrow and tomorrows after that. Beth is adamant about "I'm having the baby." As this most potentially life-altering of life-altering events hangs over, well, everything, we try to cope by going on with life normally. Until we know for sure, what else can we do? If we do not, I'm afraid the worry will eat me away. What is normal anyway? How do I make decisions such as these? Is there even a decision here for me to make? We are two twenty-year-olds staring into a yawning abyss and desperately hoping we do not fall over the edge. We need each other, yet are retreating internally.

—⚡︎—

I need to clear my mind, to escape the thick tension of Shao Yuan. With my friends Peter and Alex, and a Chinese student, Bao, we head back to the Great Wall for an afternoon. Bao is one of only twenty Han people at the Nationalities College, all basketball recruits. He is tall for a Chinese guy, but about average for a Westerner. Ascending once again at the Badaling section, we turn left and hike past the crowds toward the steeper, unrestored portion of the Great Wall. We run up one section undeterred by the nearly perpendicular stairs. This is a mistake. Heart pounding, pulse racing, I stagger in a poor third. Doubled over gulping in precious air, I am not sure if Bao, the only athlete among us, won our impromptu and ill-considered race.

I look up toward the horizon and an image of Beth's tender, worried face crosses before my eyes. I scream out over the North China wilderness. The echo from up here is strong. My companions join me, as do the few others nearby, and for a short while, there is much hollering and reverberating in these mountains. It does wonders as a temporary stress release.

We scramble down an unrestored crumbling section and jump off onto the jagged terrain. In ancient times, we have left civilized China and are hiking in the lands of the barbarian Mongol hordes. We are with Ghenghis and his grandson, Khubilai. The wind is ferocious, our footing precarious. We are one slip away from long, hard falls. I relish the openness, the empty space, the ability to not concentrate on what might be.

We return to the train station early and decide to walk around. We attract the attention of a station worker who begins following and will not leave us alone. It is dry, and he wants to make sure that we do not smoke and cause a fire. Even after being reassured that the smokers in our group will not light up and going so far as to offer him the cigarettes to hold, he remains glued to us. Another worker shows up and tells us that the train to Beijing is at another station.

"OK, where is the other station?" we ask.

He clams up. We leave even though we sense that he is lying just to get rid of us.

The Chinese can be real jerks when they want to be. But apparently not this time? We walk. Exiting a dank, narrow tunnel, we see other tracks up ahead with a train pulling in. We, and the Chinese walking near us, sprint the last kilometer or so up a dirt path to the train. My ankle throbs. We arrive panting to discover that we raced after the wrong train. We mill around totally bushed in the windy cold another forty minutes waiting for the correct train.

—◇◇◇—

The anxiety remains in Beijing. Beth and I continue to ignore the ever-lengthening period of time, her queasy stomach, and her general malaise. Burying scary possibilities, we head downtown to pick up care packages at the post office. Beth introduces me to an American-Japanese bakery with sweet breads and soft buns. We change money. I buy a "Qing Dynasty" snuff bottle from a lady I have done business with before, while Beth purchases an "antique" cookie jar. The vendor's stories of their origins are fanciful, and we bargain. The veneer on our lives remains unbroken.

Gaoshan, my English-language tutee, invites me to his dorm room with a request. I jump at the chance to go out. He taped an English-language news report from Radio Beijing and asks me to translate it. The newscaster is discussing nuclear proliferation and disarmament with an Australian official. This is specialized vocabulary. I think I convey most of the meaning to Gaoshan and his roommates. Very. Simply. My ability to discuss Reagan, Iran, and Nicaragua in Mandarin is limited, and that is being generous.

I attend the inaugural All-Foreign Student Show to honor Beida's week-long tribute to 1986's International Year of Peace. Beth is not up to going, so I offer her ticket to Gaoshan. When he has not appeared by 7:25 p.m., I leave without him. The cadres make a big fuss. The show is filmed and excerpts are to be televised afterwards. It's in the newspapers. What a production! Some of the skits and dances are good, but the hammed-up finale is nauseating. Marxists love to portray everything in society as wonderful and happy. What bullshit! It's so fake, so transparent, and oh-so pompous. Life is not all peaches and cream. The Party cannot believe it to be truth. They cannot be that deluded. No, they understand that if they convince people that nothing is something by saying it enough times, or at least keep them from questioning this nonsense, then they retain control and maintain power over society to their exclusive benefit. Can this Marxist thought order work for Beth and me too?

I meet Peter and his fiancée, Kate, near Qianmen downtown for lunch and then a visit to nearby Liulichang, the traditional cultural arts district lined with Imperial-style buildings selling books, antiques, and knick-knacks. Peter and Billy came to Beijing because of Kate, their Chinese exchange-student language instructor back in New York. Kate is *Beijingren*, a native of Beijing. It's difficult to picture Kate growing up here, though, experiencing the Cultural Revolution and being a *xia xiang* student—sent down to the countryside away from her family as an elementary student to toil for Mao's vision of the world. She looks like a Westernized American-Chinese. She stands straight and proud with a confidence that belies the turmoil of her upbringing.

I can go shopping. I can visit Chinese friends and go out with American friends. I can see shows. I can pile on many diversion excursions. But my nerves are on edge. Beth remains on campus physically and emotionally ill. She is only getting later. And later. We do not take chances. We take precautions. How could they not work? This uncertainty, our (my) dodging discussion, our (my) going on with everyday trips and tasks; is this real? Where is my life heading? Listen to me. This is not so much about me, is it? What is going through Beth's mind? She is in pain overnight. Everything hurts and aches. I walk up to her room about 4:00 a.m. to get her aspirin and tranquilizers. She eventually falls asleep in my bed. I lie down in my new sleeping bag on Toshiro's bed.

We hang out, talk, and do nothing the next day. Beth cuts out a number of snowflakes from colored paper and strings a chain of them in the window. The room looks Christmassy. Later, she goes upstairs to rest. I write a letter:

> *My Dearest Beth,*
> *I love you both as a great friend and a great lover. I hate to see all*

of this happen. What you need is a strong companion to help ease your worries. I am attempting to do that. I realize I'm probably not doing too well which pains me incredibly. My cowardliness and fear are no excuse for letting you down. I only hope I'm worthy of giving you the comfort you now need.

You mentioned in your letter to your sister that you wouldn't marry me. That's probably for the best since neither of us is really prepared. But you are also too young to have children. You are much stronger than I, yet I know how tough having a child would be. I'd love to be around even if we weren't married.

As we were walking tonight, I realized that our not getting married would probably mean the end for us. You would have the child; I wouldn't be around. I'd never be able to come back. The resentment on your part and guilt on mine at you having raised the child by yourself would see to that.

You may never see this letter, yet I believe you already know its contents. You're incredibly scared and depressed. I so wish I could help. I guess my being here does something. Is there anything else I can do?

I'll make any sacrifice if it'll help. I love you and want you to be happy. This letter's been poorly written, but my intentions are good and true. You have a promising life ahead of you regardless of when you have children. I hope I'm around to enjoy it with you.

MY HEART IS YOURS,
ANDREW

CHAPTER 21

RELIEF AND REALITY

THIS POSSIBILITY OF becoming a parent is the most terrifying experience of my young life. The uncertainty. The lack of control. The thought that the future may be transformed beyond all expectation, and before I even have an expectation. The potent fear that I will not measure up to the challenge. All compounded by being halfway around the world, far away from everything I otherwise think I know and understand. Damn communist condoms.

And then, after too many days of internalized terror and substantive silence, when the pressure cooker of the unknown threatens to blow more as each hour passes, when we begin to consider that we might have to accept that "it" is so, then, that which we could not muster the fortitude to discuss suddenly no longer needs to be.

When Beth tells me that her period has at long last arrived, we collapse into each other's arms in relief. Our life can go back to the way it was. But can it? This experience cannot but affect us both. I feel the pregnancy-scare adrenalin surging once again. While Beth rests upstairs, I borrow a Mozart tape from Toshiro and listen to Requiem Something or Other. Possibly not the best selection. The music is tense and stirring.

Looking into the mirror of one's soul is hard. What you see might not be all that appetizing. I am a good person and hopefully well meaning, but I can be petty and self-centered. I can be arrogant and condescending. I want what I want, when I want it, and when I get a head of steam up, you want to step aside.

I am quick to anger and suspiciously paranoid. Little things set me off. My mother sending the wrong items. A cabbie trying to squeeze an extra dollar here and there. A schedule not being kept. These are little things, minor in scope, but I view all through the lens that everyone must have an angle to screw me. I wonder why I have this chip on my shoulder.

To make matters worse, I am also a nudge. In my worry about Beth, about her depressed and quiet thoughts, I incessantly bug her with "How are you?" "Are you OK?" "What's wrong?" The responses to such annoying questioning become increasingly peeved. This is partially a function of the fact that I struggle with making decisions. My indecisiveness when scheduling or shopping bothers me and others no end. "I think I'll buy that." "Do you think I should buy that?" "I want it, but am not sure if I should buy it." "No, I definitely want to buy it." "What do you think, should I buy it?" I seem incapable of controlling myself. I'm obviously looking for approval, but even after I get it, I am not satisfied. I do not trust my judgment and question the judgment I am seeking from others.

All of this from my girlfriend possibly being with child in the Middle Kingdom. But the introspection continues. This mirror to my soul is a deep one.

I thought I'd beaten China and my U.S. anxiety, but it was an illusion. I'm better, but it's still there. I do not want to burden Beth, but she's my closest friend here, and I have to talk. For good or bad, I've lost the ability to internalize my angst. Before I never opened up, kept it all bottled inside. Now, I am uncorked.

China's a bleak place. The Communist Party has seen to that. What I cannot figure out is why I still have interest. I do not see hope for the present China. All I see is stagnation. Foreign businesses will revolt and leave after a couple decades of losses, leaving China high and dry. Society will not advance. You reap what you sow. The Chinese feel so superior and mighty—everyone must bow to them. As in earlier centuries, China is the center, and the world revolves around the emperor, be it Khubilai, Hongwu, Shunzhi, or more recently Mao and now Deng. All must come and pay tribute for the honor of receiving an audience. But the joke will be on them. Foreigners will out-produce and outdo the Chinese. The Chinese superiority complex will ultimately be a self-defeating anchor.

—ɷ—

Beth is off with relatives. We are both still recuperating from our ordeal. I cannot focus on work. I am irritable from irregular sleep, yet all I seem to want to do is sleep. I look in the real mirror and see heavy bags under black and blue eyes. I force myself to get dressed and go out for a walk.

Silent, white snow falls on China's capital. Several inches bring Beijing to its knees. Buses stop early evening. Cabs and street life disappear. A Siberian cold wave sweeps down from the Gobi Desert.

I am padded and warm, wearing Vassar sweats, army pants, socks, boots, T-shirt, my new cashmere sweater, chamois shirt, gloves, hat, scarf, and a heavy winter coat. I think of my family back in the States lighting the Chanukah candles each night, eating fried potato latkes, of my brother, sister, and I receiving small gifts and usually, one larger gift over the eight nights of the Festival of Lights.

It is dim outside; not many people are out and about. The bracing air washes away some of my lethargy. Weiminghu is iced over and covered once again with snow. Bo Ya Pagoda, white on the eaves, rises in the distance. The paths, benches, and trees are quiet and beckoning. This is my refuge. Two students throw snowballs at each other, hiding behind makeshift snow barriers. Another group appears to be trying to practice speed skating. As I walk across the frozen lake, weird reverberations echo below me. I get off the ice.

Unbelievably, I long for the US. This is a mind-numbing realization. What I want more than anything tonight is to hop in the car, drive to McDonalds for a Big Mac, rent a movie at the video rental store, make popcorn, and crash in front the TV. I want convenience. I want ease. I want familiar. I so want a break from the constant *mafan*, the trouble that is China. I want... my American life? Bowling at CapeBowl; playing Cosmic Encounter in marathon sleepovers with friends; body surfing at Nauset Beach. I miss home.

I want life to not be a constant grind. There is so much in Beijing that I have yet to see, but it is such a hassle to get there. My classes are not challenging. My study skills are stagnating. I do not dream of going home early. I will see this through, but I cannot wait to leave China for winter break. The middle of January is circled on my calendar.

CHAPTER 22

THE ACCIDENT

UNFORTUNATELY, LEAVING CHINA does not come fast enough.

Late Sunday, nearing midnight, Beth and I use the kettle to steam heat our cold room as we huddle and cuddle below the blankets. The same unsanctioned hotplate we use to cook meals when we cannot handle going to the cafeteria now serves as a makeshift heater.

Perched on a chair next to the bed, the steam rising from the open kettle is not a lot, but it may be helping to fight back the frost straining to form inside our room. Beth and I are together, sharing our warmth and company. We've been talking for hours. The perfumed scent of her hair tickles my nose. I feel the beating of her heart next to mine. I am safe and content. The world is out there. Tonight, others can have it.

"We should really shut this down and get ready to sleep."

"OK," she murmurs.

"I'll do it."

"*Mmm.* Alright."

As I throw back the blankets and begin to rise, I stumble. Maybe my foot gets caught on the edge of the blanket. Maybe I am rushing because I know it will be cold. Maybe I am just a klutz. Whatever the reason, as I fall, I instinctively reach out for something to hold onto.

Before I realize what is happening, it is a blur of motion that is over in seconds, I grab Beth and she gets pulled toward the edge of the bed with me. Her leg swings out, crashing into the chair, her pant leg catches on the kettle, and boiling water pours out.

Laying on the cold floor looking up at her, there is an unnatural quiet before she rips off her sock and our eyes rest upon her blisteringly red, raw leg. Beth goes into shock as I stare in silent confusion. She begins shaking and then quietly screams. I sense more than hear her anguish. Finally, she cries. In the blink of an eye, our safety and contentment have shattered.

Settling Beth back on the bed, I lurch out of the room and run down the hall calling out for Peter. He has returned from Kate's and comes back to sit with Beth while Alex and I search for the *fuwuyuan*, the attendant on duty downstairs to call the hospital.

My mind is not yet comprehending what I have done. Bundling a coat around Beth's trembling shoulders, we place her on a bicycle and wheel her through a deserted Beida campus to the university hospital in the dead of Chinese winter night.

The hospital sees us this time. They clean the wound. It has not got down to bone, but it is a significant burn. They put something on her leg and wrap it in a bandage. There is nothing else they can do now. There is no pain medication.

"Go. Rest. Come back in a couple of days for us to check on her leg."

The reality of the situation hits me as I am pacing back and forth in the hospital. My clumsiness has traumatized my love. I have hurt her body. I have caused further emotional torture to an already strained mind. What do I say? What do I do? What can I possibly do? This is not how I hoped the New Year would arrive.

They send us back to the dorm, still in the dead of Chinese winter night.

PART II

SECOND SEMESTER

学期二

CHAPTER 23

NEW YEAR'S FIREWORKS

T HE ROMAN CANDLE streaks out from my second-floor window over the Shao Yuan courtyard. Darkness briefly transforms to shadows. Toshiro's bed is littered with Roman candles, firecrackers, bottle rockets big and small, and a gaggle of sparklers. Two empty Great Wall wine bottles and a cold pot of tea sit on my desk. The first part of our New Year's Eve party is a success.

We continue to usher in 1987 out at the lake, Weiminghu. Standing on the snow-covered ice, Alex, the confident Canadian, grabs a Roman candle and begins to light it.

"Alex, make sure you hold that thing tight, OK?"

"I've got this. Don't worry." He says this dismissively.

We should have worried.

He lights the candle. He is holding it gingerly. Too gingerly.

As the first of the missiles blasts out into the night sky with a loud screech and a kick, the candle base shoots out of Alex's hand onto the snow-covered ice behind. The second missile shoots out horizontally, skimming the snow towards the island. The candle turns with the kick, and the third missile heads straight into a nearby group of students. As the Chinese students scatter, the fourth missile dances along the ice like a red flare streaking through the night onto a section where the snow had been cleared.

Chaos. Chinese and foreign students alike jump, flee, and scream. For several minutes, it is unexpectedly loud in our corner of Northwest Beijing.

Beth is with us. We wheeled her over on Alex's mountain bike. Her leg remains a bandaged raw wound, but the medicine they apply every few days when the dressing is changed has made the pain more tolerable. There is no sign of infection. I admire Beth's stoicism in facing this ordeal.

Standing next to her, I light a Roman candle. I hold it tight. The first missile exits and explodes inches outside the cylinder in a blinding flash. *BANG!!*

What happened?

The concussive blast washes over us. My right ear is numb. There is a perplexed glaze on Beth's face. I instinctively toss the cylinder as another missile exits.

"Run!" Not the best thing to do on a burned leg, but we are reacting, not thinking. The candle empties. We are once again running for cover as missiles shoot this way and that. The shock of silence gives way to a hollow echo as our hearing slowly recovers.

After a few more youthful antics that one is wise not to tell your parents about until long afterwards, we head back to shore. Alex, riding his mountain bike on the cleared section of ice, tumbles at the far end of the lake with a booming echo that comes at us from above and below. The North Koreans are still at it when we return to Shao Yuan, the walls shaking as they slam dance across the hall.

—✺—

A couple of nights later, another type of fireworks. Beth's bandage gets soaked during a shower. Peeling it off, we stare down at the inner gauze coated to her leg by dried pus and matted blood.

Should we try and get to a Western hospital or stay on campus?

Of course it is snowing, it is dark, and there are no cabs either here at Beida or down the street at the Friendship Hotel. Why can't these things ever happen during the daylight hours?

Beth is scared that her leg might be infected. I don't disagree and lose the ability to be helpful. The two of us sit their indecisive. The four walls of her room seem to close in.

Indecision leads to confusion. Confusion leads to fear. Fear leads to an argument.

Anxious, I make an inane comment about her leg not looking that bad and that we should calm down and not rush out. And with that, the dam is broken.

"What! How can you be that insensitive? Why would you say something like that?" She is frightened and hurting.

I stammer, my heart beating rapidly.

"You don't care about me, do you?"

Hysterical energy engulfs my entire body. I sit rigid.

"Get out!" The room reverberates with her fury.

Bursting into tears, Beth sinks back onto the bed.

I want to say something, anything that might be helpful, caring, practical. But, shamefaced, I cannot. Such situations already seem beyond my control; having them occur in such alien surroundings only heightens the tension. Confused and flustered, I get up to leave, beginning to move towards the door.

But I do not leave. An awkward silence, a stalemate, descends upon her room. Beth whimpers in pain and fear; I am a mass of quivering nerves. A friend happens in on us a few minutes later and takes charge.

I call the campus hospital. They do not want to see her. "Why didn't you come during daylight?"

Because we didn't know of the problem then you lazy, mother-fucking, turtle egg! This is what I want to say, not what I do say. Not being able to coherently vent in Chinese, even though I know this particular swear, but also recognizing deep down that it would be counterproductive, we go around and around on the telephone. If nothing else, I do not quit.

"Aiya. Alright. Bring her over."

"Thank you. We will be right there."

When we arrive, they are eating and make us wait until they are done. When they decide that they have let us stew long enough, or more likely, when they simply decide to get up for a change of pace, they send us back to an exam room. The doctor we finally see turns out to be a competent and compassionate woman.

I keep up a running chatter to distract Beth as the doctor cleans the wound and gently peels the gauze off. Beth grips my arm and cries. Staring directly up at the ceiling, her wet eyes radiate pain. It sears my heart. I hold my breath awaiting the prognosis. *Let it not be infected. Let it not be infected. Let it not be infected.*

The doctor examines the now-clean wound, looks up at us with a caring expression, and calmly announces that there is no infection. A collective rush of air escapes us both.

"The healing is coming along well. You should be changing this dressing every day." The previous doctor most recently told us every five days. No matter. There is no infection.

Beth, still limping and in a good deal of pain, goes to her uncle's the next day for the weekend. Her uncle and his married son and family share three units that have been combined into one large living space with a Western-style toilet and makeshift shower. They are not *ganbu*, government cadre. The accommodations are compensation for Cultural Revolution losses. A third of the apartment belongs to Beth and her family, but she is generally not comfortable there. Her brother and sister-in-law come to pick her up. They are polite, but distant, and I get the distinct impression that they do not like me much. They do let me hitch a cab ride with them. It is a quiet ride.

Leaving Beth with her relatives, I buy an ice cream and wait twenty-five minutes for the bus outside uncle's building. When it arrives, it is full. Mimicking the Chinese, I force my way up anyway. I am now standing where the back door wants to close, half-sitting on the ticket seller's little booth. Thus squished, bodies stacked like vertical cord wood, we wait another twenty minutes while people at the middle door continue trying to shove on. Since he cannot move until the doors close, the driver leaves the bus for a smoke. He actually gets up and walks away. People begin laughing at the absurdity of our situation. What else can we do? In our rush to get to where we are going, we go nowhere.

Eventually, the driver returns, the doors close, and we begin our crawl downtown. It takes a while, and another cab ride, but I finally arrive at the *Gong An Ju*, Public Security Bureau, to apply for exit and entry visas for our winter trip. The PSB is slick. I walk in. There are no people in line. I hand in the two applications, visas-passports, green cards. The lady hands me a receipt and says, "Come back on Monday." In and out in four minutes. Our tickets to freedom are being processed, and the experience is civilized.

Amazed at my success, I walk over to the Commercial Press on *Wangfujing*. We have been searching without success for a popular, little red Concise English-Chinese/Chinese-English Dictionary. Today, they are in stock. I buy five. I follow this with a trip to the big drugstore to buy condoms, and even this goes without incident. I am in a zone.

—⚋—

Fireworks are happening in the community too. The *International Herald Tribune* and *South China Morning Post* run significant coverage of recent student unrest here in Beijing. The government-owned *China Daily* is silent other than printing editorials against *luan*, chaos. Stability is the mantra of the authorities. A clamp down has been announced.

The other night more than four thousand students marched to the house of Beida's president to demand the release of students who had been detained for speaking out. They then marched all the way to Tiananmen

Square. It's like a nine-hour walk. The march began after an all-day rally ended about 9:30 p.m. Halfway to Tiananmen on the freezing cold night, the marchers were informed that the detained students had been released. I heard that a few hundred persevered and made it to the square at 6:00 a.m. the next day.

The protesters have guts, I'll give them that. They are passionate. I might agree with their demands, and they might have similar minor successes, but they are unrealistic. They want freedom of speech, the right to choose their own careers, and political freedom. Admirable, but not practical demands in this society. This is not a Western democracy. They will not succeed.

—m—

The worst fireworks are often in the family. When Beth comes back from her weekend with relatives, she is down, rambling on about how life sucks, her fears, depression. She wants to return home in March. Now, she's not so sure. Her energy's sapped. She's been sick for a while and sleeping a lot. We're all tired. She is being pulled in opposing directions by her family and is not happy with either choice. A good deal of the stress revolves around a potential loss of face for the family in China if she leaves early. Her actions continue to be not just her own. While venting, she tells me, "My brother thinks you lack common sense because you didn't take me to a big hospital right away."

What? I have no problem when she tells me that she has more common sense than I do. She's my girlfriend. And she's right. I have more book sense than street sense. I know this. I am not blessed with an abundance of self-confidence—I constantly want detailed instructions because I am afraid I'll screw up. Improvising is not my strong suit. Yet for all this, I get along pretty well. *But anyway, who the hell does he think he is?* I want to tell Beth this. To stand up for myself. But, I do not. As I so often do in uncomfortable situations, I mumble a weak, "Yeah, I know," and say nothing further.

His statement stings. Who is he to judge? He doesn't know me. He wasn't around that dark night of the accident. I might have been able to do better. I'm sure of it, but I wasn't a total disaster. Scared witless, we quickly immersed her leg in cold water and got her to the closest hospital as fast as reasonably possible. It was Beida's hospital and not a foreigner's hospital, but the latter was far away in a sleeping city in the middle of freaking China! We followed instructions given us both times at the campus hospital. Beth's now been to a foreigner's hospital, and according to her, the story is the same. Her leg appears to be getting better, and there are no signs of infection.

So all this means I have no common sense? Maybe it does. What do I know? I am a twenty-year-old out learning about the world and myself. It is not always that easy.

CHAPTER 24

TURNING TWENTY-ONE

I CELEBRATE MY TWENTY-FIRST birthday by buying a gin and tonic for Beth. In China it would not matter if I was sixteen, but it is an important principle even if I do not drink it. Beth treats me to lunch downtown at one of the restaurants in the China International Trust Investment Corporation (CITIC) building with Peter and Alex. Billy and Sam are gone, but Peter, Alex, and I remain tight. Together, the four of us dine on the tender meat, crisp vegetables, and fresh noodles of my birthday lunch, all steamed, sautéed, and fried in tantalizing sauces. This is more than enough to hold me for the day, and I gratefully skip the dreaded cafeteria dinner waiting back at Shao Yuan.

In less than two weeks, we will leave China. The anticipation builds daily. There are good days. There are bad days. Looking forward to time away brings a measure of calm. We chose a quick, three-hour flight to Hong Kong. Sure, it is vastly more expensive, but it will shave thirty-three hours off the express train trip. We both call home, and our parents agree that HK is the place to go. They each generously agree to wire us a much-needed US$1,500. Dad tells me that he wore the padded army hat I sent him in New Hampshire. A communist Red Army hat must have been a sight in the White Mountains. My brother gets on the line and quietly asks if I need contraceptives. I should say yes, but I do not.

My last call of the day is to Anne Brennan at the *Cape Cod Times*. My hometown paper is covering the demonstrations in China and got wind that I am here. These events remain front-page news in the Western press, even though they have ended here. We speak for close to thirty minutes. I talk about the demonstrations, my life, my thoughts on the "China experience," my impressions of the people and society. I mention the need to be circumspect so as to avoid getting into trouble.

Once I hang up, however, it hits me that while I can talk the talk, I am less successful in walking the walk. I am here while the pent-up emotions of the students are boiling over. Beida is the epicenter. On the walls near the post office in the center of campus students surreptitiously post daily *Dazi Bao*, Big Character Posters, expressing their desires and concerns. But I do not immerse myself in them, do not comprehend the detail, and have only looked in on the conversation happening only meters away. Do I have a real inkling or knowledge of what is happening? Probably not. What am I doing? What aren't I doing? I do not stray far from my Western cocoon in China. I need to force myself to take regular Chinese college courses with the Chinese students. I need to make more of an effort to improve my fluency and listening comprehension skills. I may be doing and seeing and experiencing, but it could, can, and should be a whole lot more. I am here.

—⟋⟍—

A few days later, we visit an Australian doctor, Dr. H., because Beth's nerves are frayed and the aching pain in her leg will not abate. Dr. H. is a decent, white-haired man in his seventies who meets us under a large picture of Jesus Christ. Although not the warmest guy in the world, he immediately puts us both at ease. Shuddering at the Chinese method of pouring iodine onto an open burn wound and covering it with gauze, he gives Beth ointment and non-stick bandages. Non-stick bandages. Now there's an invention.

186

As the countdown to Beth and I heading off for winter break continues ticking down, Alex and I take a Sunday trip to a frozen Forbidden City. Beth is just as happy to stay warm inside back on campus. The Forbidden City is the epicenter of the Imperial China of folklore, an expansive, high-walled enclave that was both the home and governmental offices of the Ming and Qing Emperors and their Courts during the last two Dynasties. The scale of the architecture is mind boggling. Tourists are not allowed to see much inside the buildings themselves—a peek through a window, a glance into a dark interior across a rope line. Much, much more is closed off than open for viewing.

We enter from the north and walk briskly south via the central axis. Frost rises from the stone ground in the frigid air. The Gobi wind is ferocious. My Mao cap keeps flying off my head. I lose feeling in my hands and feet. We pass a shivering African delegation on a VIP tour. An impressive, squat snow sculpture of Lenin watches us. Money changers accost us in one of the inner squares.

Leaving through the southern Tiananmen Gate of Heavenly Peace, Alex and I make our way over to the nearby Beijing Hotel to get food and warm up. We decide to taxi back to Beida because we cannot bear the thought of waiting outside for the buses. Arriving at Shao Yuan, our cab driver informs us that she wants *waihui*, foreign exchange certificates.

"Sorry. We are students. We do not have any." We say this calmly.

This does not sit well with the driver, and her tone changes in a flash. "Tough. Give me *waihui*." She is bossy and demanding.

"We do not have any." We repeat this again as calmly as possible.

Click—she locks us in and glares at us angrily in the rearview mirror. We are at a stalemate.

Communicating with our eyes and moving in tandem, Alex drops seventeen yuan RMB over the front seat as we unlock our respective side doors and jump out before she can relock them or take off with us hanging out.

We bolt inside. A glance back shows the driver throwing metaphorical daggers in our direction.

—⚉—

Our trip south is mere days away. I head to the Cathay Pacific office at the Jianguo Hotel to get the airplane tickets.

The agent informs me, "Next Tuesday's flight to Hong Kong is sold out. I can put you on the waiting list."

I stare dumbfounded at her for a moment. "No, this is not possible. We have reservations and must get to Hong Kong next Tuesday. We have to see a doctor. There must be something." I am in full imploring mode.

She holds her ground. "There is not. Every seat is sold out. Do you want to be on the waiting list?"

"No. I do not want the waiting list. I need tickets." I struggle to keep control of my voice. Then, I have a brainstorm. "What if I pay cash today?" I ask politely.

Dramatic pause. She looks at me and then at her computer. I swear I see a knowing smirk in her eyes. *Clickety-clack* on the keyboard. "I found two seats, confirmed for next Tuesday morning."

Now isn't that a surprise?

This is fortunate not only for Beth and me, but also for the girl at the ticket counter. If I had not been able to get confirmed tickets out of Beijing, I might have hurt her. I'm fed up. I'm tired. Physically. Mentally. We need to leave. To recover. Beth's healing is slow, but progressing with the non-stick bandages. Her leg is itchy, and new skin is forming around the outside of the burn. The center is still raw, but the new layers are getting ever closer.

For once, we have booked a place to stay ahead of time. A few weeks ago, I planned to write the YMCA in Kowloon for reservations when Alex suggested I telex instead. I'd never done that before. The telex went out and a reply came back within thirty minutes. I would have been pleased with a week's response. I now telex the YMCA again and ask to change our reservations to match our flight. A return telex from the YMCA confirms our room. They are getting better on my name. I am no longer "Andrew Chook." I'm now listed as "Sndrew Singer."

—๛—

My posse shrinks before we leave, and I lose another friend. A small group of us sends Alex off this morning with a sweet breakfast of toasted crescents with real black raspberry jelly from Harbin. He is not staying the full academic year. No more travels with my good-natured buddy. It was only that one time in Xi'an that he lost it. Once he leaves Shao Yuan, we pilfer everything that he left, including his room. Beth and I immediately move in temporarily. Toshiro has returned to my room, and we need space. This week is ours; Peter and Kate get it next week. Alex's room is rechristened "The Brothel."

I was down again last night. Everything got to me: A roiling mix of bad adjectives twisting my gut, my head, my life. It builds up and then I drop. It might usually pass in a few hours, but why can't I get off this ride? This time it was agonizing over how much Beth means to me and fear of losing her. I care for her more than I've ever cared for anybody else. She makes me feel better when I'm down and even happier when I'm up. She's knowledgeable, intelligent, and a great conversationalist. So many hours are spent talking in China. We are the best of friends, the best of lovers, the best of companions. Her presence in my life fills me with an all-consuming feeling of joy. The feeling is mutual, so what is the problem, Andrew? This is irrational. Yet, I am incapable of purging such thoughts from my mind. I keep searching unsuccessfully for an exit from this circular railway.

I feel foolish at having told Ms. Brennan that the Western press is giving the China protests too much hype. Even as we were speaking, the purge had started. We had been hearing rumors that Hu Yaobang, the popular, reformist General Secretary of the Communist Party, the favored successor to Deng Xiaoping, has or is about to resign and have now learned that the rumors are true. Hu resigned Friday night. He is officially "overworked." The conservatives wield more power than I'd given them credit for. So much for the reformers. Long live the Chen Yun clique!

I can't wait to get back to history class at Vassar and tell the prof, "Hey, I was there when Hu got canned, and I knew less about it than you." According to what I have now heard, Hu resigned as Party General Secretary, but retains his position in the Politburo and Standing Committee (where the real power lies). He is being replaced temporarily by his contemporary, Zhao Ziyang. I was under the impression that Hu Qili and Li Peng were being groomed for Deng's and Hu's spots (although in which order, I do not know). Because the liberals have faced a serious setback, those two will likely be kept down longer. Another rumor has it that the mayor of Tianjin is going to assume Zhao's former position of Premier (prime minister). All I get from the Chinese press, and that's limited to hearsay of the Chinese stuff that I do not read and the English versions, is the standard communist rhetoric—engage in self-criticism, promote re-education, uphold the four basic principles, and on and on and on. I do not seem to know much.

—⁓—

The weather moderates for our last two days in Beijing. One last visit to Dr. H. and a crutch-aided walk to our usual haunts—the Friendship Store, the Jianguo Hotel, the Alley, and Wangfujing. We study a menu liberated from the Friendship Hotel to learn Chinese vocab words for food. We wrap up the last afternoon hand washing our clothes.

We're packed.

We're ready to go.

We are so ready to go.

CHAPTER 25

ESCAPE TO HONG KONG

THE COMMUNISTS HAVE one last laugh at our expense on the way out. We board the plane at Capital Airport in Beijing, the plane pulls away from the terminal, and then the plane stops. It just stops on the tarmac. No message from the cockpit. No apparent issues that we can see. We wait for an hour with no news and no movement, bottled up in a locked cylindrical tube. Beth sits without comment. I, on the other hand, am close to the edge. If I hear one more "*mei you*," one more "no can do," I will lose it. This is unbelievable. Well, not really. This is China.

I am still on the edge when we finally land at Kai Tak Airport and flow through the crush of people at passport control and the taxicab line. The taxi drops us at the YMCA International House in Kowloon, our haven a couple of kilometers north of the Star Ferry terminal on the waters of Victoria Harbour. Kowloon is part of the British Colony of Hong Kong. We are no longer in China.

Though we have booked one room (and they do have the reservation), the front desk staff hands each of us a separate registration card. We hand them back as the two young Chinese look at us, a Caucasian male and a Chinese (American) female. It is Chengde in the mountains of Northeast China all over again.

"Are you a couple?

"Yes, we are."

They hesitate for a moment, exchanging unsure, but inquisitive glances from Beth to me and back. Then, somewhat reluctantly, they hand us the keys to a cozy triangle of a room with a double bed, television, phone, and private bathroom that would make an excellent dorm room. We settle in. No one rattles the door.

—⚬⚬⚬—

We go for a walk up Nathan Road, the main drag, into the Mongkok shopping district. Neon signs. Shiny storefronts. It is clean and modern and loud. The hustle of business in every direction. People. People. People. *Guangdonghua*, Cantonese, rules the day. My self-confidence in Chinese, in Mandarin, which had grown steadily over the past several months, is severely shot down with so much ease. They do not understand me here. I do not understand them. Their spoken Chinese is different, how they phrase things, their accents. In addition, the signs are all in *fantizi*, complex Chinese characters, where everything on the mainland for the last semester has been in *jiantizi*, simplified Chinese characters. Communication is once again a concern.

Hong Kong is not China. The choice of Western fast food is expansive—Burger King, McDonalds, Colonel Sanders, and Pizza Hut. There is 7-11, Benetton, and more banks than I can count. Stores are stocked with cameras and dual-cassette decks, rugs, and snuff bottles. The merchandise we see in a large China Arts and Crafts Center leaves me scratching my head. Quality luggage sets and leather briefcases fill the shelves. China makes these? It's got to be a sick joke. China has a market system after all, but they export the best in order to earn the most green and leave the scraps for their own people. Rolls Royce and Mercedes limos wait grandly in front of the Peninsula Hotel.

We cross the harbour to Central. Tiny Hong Kong has a clean, fast, and efficient subway system; Beijing has a subway line. We enter a Bank of America branch to change money. The guard at the front entrance is an older Chinese man overpowered by a massive shotgun. I feel like I am in Mayberry with Andy and Barney or maybe Bolivia with Butch and Sundance.

We walk past an alley that is a long, narrow corridor crammed with birds and grasshoppers. We stroll down a colorful alley bursting with fish, fruit, meat, vegetables, and chocolate sellers. We savor two fresh Sunkist oranges. The chocolate seller and her friend show us with their own money how much we owe as we complete a happy purchase. They want to know where we are from, particularly Beth. They speak Mandarin, but with a heavy accent.

Beth and I enter a dim sum restaurant and are seated at a large table with other diners. The pot of tea placed before us tastes like seaweed-flavored chlorine water. I am the sole Caucasian in this cavernous room. A bottle bobbing in the sea. The sounds of Cantonese fill the air. How are we going to order? A lady at our table notices our quandary and leans over to tell us that she also speaks Mandarin. With her help, as each *Ama* rolls her cart of steaming little dishes and plates past us, we flag her down and ask her to show us everything. We do not know names; we go by sight. A head nod and show of fingers for this plate or that.

Beth and I want *chashao bao* (steamed buns with barbequed roast pork inside) as our last plate. Our Mandarin-speaking friend, her companion, and every *Ama* in the place know we want them too. Our desire spreads like wildfire throughout the restaurant. Everyone wants to know if any more will be made. As we are beginning to accept that we will be disappointed, the door to the kitchen swings open and a new steaming batch comes streaming out. Three round white doughy bread buns, cracked open at the top revealing a hint of the red barbecue pork nestled inside, lie majestically on each plate. We are giddy as we snag an order and gobble them down with satisfied smiles.

We rest and snuggle on a bench in a small park on a warm and windy day that is refreshing and relaxing. There is a sense of liberation here. It is open, leisurely. Life is on our own terms. Beth and I hold hands, link arms, flirt in public. We have not experienced *mafan*. We are not faced with an onslaught of hardship. This society seems more accepting of Beth, of us. No relatives hover over us for face. There is no unseen, omnipresent political machine, or if there is, we do not feel it.

—〰—

On the way back to our oasis at the YMCA, however, we get lost in the maze of streets exiting the massive Ocean Centre shopping complex down by the harbour. For the first time since leaving China, I get frustrated, frightened, and not just a little claustrophobic. Being lost in a foreign rabbit warren is disconcerting. I feel like a trapped rat and am still hyper when we reach our room.

Thank you, food. Food is the universal antidote to anxiety. Soon after returning, the remains of our sedative lie among us on the bed: an empty bag of pastries, a hollow can of Pringles, a small pile of cherry pits and stems, empty soda cans. Moving a now mostly empty See's chocolate box to the floor, I become introspective, melancholy even. Maybe I am decompressing from the earlier stress of getting lost or possibly from the more entrenched tension of the last several months, or it might be that I am on a sugar-high crash.

I think about my parents and siblings, about my interactions with them. I occasionally do feel guilty about the way I treat my family. More amazing than thinking this, which itself is uncharacteristic, I go a step further and say so to Beth, who is lying on her back next to me as she stares contentedly up at the ceiling. She is ready to drift off, but gently asks me how. She knows that things are not always smooth, especially between me and my mom. She has witnessed my tirades.

"The whole 'huggy, kissy, I-love-you' scene. It's not me. It doesn't feel right, but I sometimes wonder why not." Is it wrong to not show much affection or warmth? Is it just that every person demonstrates feelings in a different way? If so, then my method is apparently impatience, questioning, and conflict. Probably not the top three qualities Dear Abby would recommend.

I recall a scene at the dinner table growing up. My father had a lot of evening meetings, but he would come home most nights for a family dinner before heading out again. One night, we three kids were bickering. I remember watching my dad at the head of the table. His face turned red and a vein began thumping feverishly on his forehead. He so wanted to snap, but he did not. Somehow he controlled it. I know what would have happened if I was sitting in his seat.

I have been known to beat up my brother and sister to get my way. I know I shouldn't, but I do. I have even less tolerance with my mother and her inability to respond to a simple question with a simple answer. I want a sentence, not a paragraph or worse, a chapter. Am I incapable of changing or is it a lack of willpower? Beth asks why I do not apologize to them and try to change. It is a good question. I do not have a strong answer other than I have trouble envisioning me having such a conversation with them. It feels so...against the grain.

I feel the warmth of Beth next to me. Her love. It is time for us to take a nap. But then my paranoia rears its head. I have lost all internal filtering because I now confess to Beth that I cannot shake a fear that I am going to lose her. I feel like crying and cannot. I descend into complete emotional disarray and ask her if she remembers the stuffed chimpanzee we saw at Ocean Centre. She looks at me with half-closed eyes.

When I first saw him, I choked up. I actually choked up. I have always wanted a stuffed animal. I have always wanted to receive one as a gift. I give them, but I'm not the type of person you'd think to give one to. This chimpanzee was special. I knew it the moment we entered the store. About two feet tall with the sweetest lifelike face, he was sitting on a shelf, his two legs hanging over the edge, and his two arms, with opposable thumbs on each hand, sitting comfortably in his furry lap. There was a soulfulness in his eyes that melted me.

Beth told me not to get him. How could I argue? She was right. It was not a practical purchase. Beyond the money, we are traveling. What are we going to do with a stuffed animal that would fill one of our small bags all by himself? She was eminently pragmatic as usual; I was crushed. Lying here now on our hotel bed, I leave my heartache on my sleeve. I have offered this tale of woe and am done. Out of words. Unsure of anything. Beth pulls me close, wraps her arms around me, gives me a kiss, and whispers, "If you want him, let's go get him." The next morning we return first thing to Ocean Centre for the third time in as many days. The stuffed animal again calls me when we enter the store. I head straight to his shelf and pick him up. There is no more question. He leaves with us. Cheetah is my friend. Beth, and Beth alone, calls him Chim-Chim. I own a stuffed animal.

—※—

In the days leading up to the three-day Chinese New Year celebration, we venture out to the market at Stanley on the far side of Central. Riding in the upper level of a double-decker bus, we swing around cliffy curves, bounce over speed humps, and view sheltered coves and bays as we travel through Mid-Levels, up and over the Peak, and down through Aberdeen, Deep Water Bay, and Repulse Bay. The large homes of the wealthy sit high in the hills. A spectacular yacht is anchored in the middle of Repulse Bay. A shepherd puppy sleeps in a beached row boat in a tranquil Stanley. I am reminded of Cape Cod—listening to the waves roll ashore, soaking in the warmth and the taste of the sea.

On the day before New Year's, the waters of Hong Kong sparkle as the afternoon sun beams down. We ride the Peak Tram on Central and look out to the mountains of the New Territories (the northern separation with China) visible in the distance through the sunny haze. We walk back down through the Zoological and Botanical Gardens to the city center. Other than one couple ahead of us, we are alone. The only sounds are the water running down a creek and the leaves rustling in the wind. Lushness. In the middle of winter. I take several deep breaths.

Chunjie, the Spring Festival, the Lunar New Year, is here. January 28, 1987. The traditional Chinese saying at this time of year is "Congratulations and May You Get Rich." In other words, "Happy New Year!" In Cantonese, this is pronounced, *Kung Hei Fat Choy*. In Mandarin, it is *Gongxi Facai*. Same characters. Same meaning. Completely different oral traditions. With its arrival, the entire, jam-packed British Colony screeches to a halt.

The traditional fireworks celebration dominates HK. The waters of Victoria Harbour and the high rises on Central light up in multihued splendor. The gunpowder explosions reverberate above and below us. We spectators, a throbbing mass of sardines in lower Kowloon, flicker in sequenced shadow. After the almost thirty-minute show, it is a long, mad, slow tussle to get out and back to the hotel, but no one complains. Everyone is happy.

It feels like ages since I was in China. Yet, it has only been a little over a week! It all seems so foreign. Before, I was there, a part of the Chinese lunacy. My world was circumscribed by its limits. Now, I dread going back to all the *mafan*. Our experiences here in HK are the polar opposite. We are not hassled by the authorities. We are doing what we want, when we want. I am blown away by the service of the local sales staffs. They are interested in us as customers, foreign visitors, students in Beijing. They are pleasant to deal with, helpful, and go the extra mile. When buying a patchwork baby-blue-and-white sweater for Beth, one of the ladies heads off looking for a box and packages it up. I purchase a card, ribbon, and wrapping paper at a nearby shop, and the girl there wraps the box for me even though the gift is from elsewhere. Such simple courtesy. Do I have to go back to the PRC?

CHAPTER 26

REFUGE IN THAILAND

AIR LANKA TO Bangkok. No checked bags. Hong Kong security is strict on this flight that continues on to Colombo, the capital of the civil war torn island nation of Sri Lanka. The agents search our camera bags and even remove the lens caps. The sign above my head is clear: "The X-ray equipment used is NOT camera safe."

Down at the gate, the surging mass bunches up again as they re-check everyone's passports and reopen a few passengers' bags. It is like riding a rush-hour Beijing bus with armed guards. I am nervous and now add edgy and a little hyper to my litany of mental state issues. Beth touches my arm in reassurance as we creep towards the boarding door. She has said it before and will almost certainly say it again: I do not travel well.

Descending into the Thai capital, my left ear does not pop. The sharp, persistent throbbing accompanies me into the airport. The heavy presence of soldiers and police adds to the tension. We change money at a Thai Military Exchange and catch a government taxi into town. I am in pain. This same thing happened during my freshman year in high school on a school trip to Spain. I wish it had not come back.

I chew gum. It doesn't help.

We walk over to a nearby luxury hotel to get a drink, thinking alcohol will relax me. Beth and I raise a glass in salute to our continuing adventures outside China. It doesn't help.

My first experience of Thailand is through a fish bowl, a cloudy, achy fish bowl.

Yet, even through this haze, I feel the friendliness of the Thai people. The taxi driver. Our waitress at the bar. The YMCA hotel staff most particular. The front desk staff smile in warm greeting and treat Beth and I like royalty. We are some of the first guests in a new wing. We are also some of the only guests in this more remote hotel. We saunter up to our room as the bellhop carries our one garment bag and knapsack with pride. Our princely room is pristine. Beth runs and leaps onto the plush bed while I slump into an overstuffed chair.

Bangkok is massive, and the noise is deafening. I cannot hear Beth as we walk down the street the next morning. Motorcycles and tuk-tuks clog the roads. Tuk-tuks (I like saying the word) are noisy, pollution-belching, three-wheeled motor bikes with open-in-the-back-seating that are used as taxis and resemble the Chinese auto-rickshaw. Tuk-tuks offer a convenient, white-knuckle perspective on the city—look around, see what is passing, and fervently hope your crazy driver does not hit it. The heat is overbearing. My ear has opened after a good night's sleep, but I feel the beginnings of a sun headache, and Beth is getting dizzy.

We retreat to our spotless, air-conditioned oasis at the YMCA. Our maids have a sense of humor. I positioned Cheetah (I could not leave him alone in HK and did stuff him into our carry-on bag) reading the Thailand Guidebook in a chair. Upon our return he now wears Beth's glasses while he reads. We feast on fresh pineapple, juicy oranges and grapefruit, scrumptious barbecued beef spears and fried chicken legs dipped in sweet-and-sour hot sauce, rice squares with a flaky topping, and *chashao bao* (the same sweet roast pork buns we ate at dim sum in Hong Kong). This is a picnic fit for a king and queen in a royal room.

—※—

Leaving an eerily quiet YMCA at 6:45 a.m., we head out to the Floating Market past Nakhon Pathom more than a hundred kilometers outside Bangkok. The thick, urban landscape quickly transforms into a green canvas of palm trees, coconut trees, and sugar plantations. Our bus parallels canals, rivers, and marshes. The weather is hot, but the sun is not as piercing, the humidity not as oppressive. Chopped-up coconut shells drying in the sun line the side of the road. We pass a salt factory with dozens of low cylindrical salt cones and workers harvesting the mineral in the distant fields. We visit a brown sugar factory nestled in a shaded grove of coconut trees along a river. A lady grinding meat out of a fresh coconut at a main entrance bursting with brilliant flowers offers us a taste.

Arriving at the boat landing, we embark in a covered, high-prow, long-tail boat with a long rudder pole. Sitting in the back of the eight-passenger boat, Beth and I get sprayed as we zip through the canals. The watery thoroughfare funnels down to ever-so-tight-a-squeeze and then blossoms out as quickly into a broad hourglass. We speed by people washing their clothes, their hair, and their children and fixing fishing nets in the canal. Thai houses set up on stilts creep up to both sides of the canal. Today, these homes perch high in the sunny air waiting in peace for the monsoon floodwaters that will rise higher and higher, closer and closer to the families. A couple of sculls with older women paddle back with their market purchases. A young guy on another boat grins wide as he drops down into a semi-squat and pretends to jerk off as we tourists slide by.

The Floating Market swells landward on either side of the canal. The complex includes large, open-sided wooden buildings, boardwalks, piers, and boat upon boat upon boat jostling in the confines of the narrow canal. Local entrepreneurs vie to sell us fruits, vegetables, eggs, candy, popcorn, dry goods, and touristy junk. Natives sit one by one in their slender craft reaching up to the foreign visitors above. One boat rides low with bunches of green bananas. Another is chock-a-block with small, round, dark green watermelons. A lady, floating up with a parasol over her head to ward off the late morning sun, sells hot food and soup. Another lady sells conical straw hats. Other boats overflow with peppers, vegetables, and fruits. We eat oily, fried bananas and leisurely boat shop in this isolated, rural center of commerce deep in Southeast Asia.

—∽∽—

Thailand is so nice, and so not China, that we decide to extend our stay. Koh Samui (Samui Island) is an overnight bus and boat ride away in Southern Thailand. The journey to the bus from the YMCA is complicated, involving a minivan, a long wait in Thonburi City across the river from Bangkok, a sketchy dinner from a street vendor, and a converted pick-up ride on crowded benches under an open cover rear bed. And then the bus. The on-board television blares, the air conditioning is frigid, and the seat in front of Beth is broken and lies back onto her legs. I hope our destination is worth this ordeal. Deep in the night, the bus loses power, limps to the side of the road, and then limps further on to a gas station. A group of us stand outside in the humid dark waiting for repairs. Once rolling again, we travel until 5:30 a.m., when we pull into another gas station. Wasted hours multiply while people eat at the restaurant next door. We miss the first boat out to the island from the coastal city of Surat Thani.

Entering a travel office to purchase tickets with two couples we befriend on the way down (one is British-Thai and the other is Malay-American), I notice four bright-red mosquito bites on my leg. These weren't there before we left Bangkok. The bus had to break down, didn't it? In a cold sweat, I take a malaria pill. My brain reminds me that I was supposed to begin this regimen a week or so before the trip. I have to chew the medicine because I still cannot swallow pills. The soda does nothing to get the sharply bitter taste out of my mouth. The rice soup we buy nearby does. We stock up on mosquito repellent. Even if it is too late, the purchase makes me feel better.

At long last we board a high-speed ferry and cast off into the Gulf of

Thailand. We relax up on deck as the boat whizzes by small islands and spits of the Thai mainland before cruising through wide expanses of open water. The sun blazes in all its Thai glory, but this does not bother me as the cool, rushing wind lulls me into a semi-conscious state of bliss. Beth and I sit next to each other and the two-hour ride passes in a blur. When we dock and I stand up, however, I realize that sitting out on the open deck in shorts was a really, really bad idea. My legs look like two Maine lobsters fresh out of the pot. There will be a price to pay, of this I am instantly sure. Beth covered her healing lower leg. Our time in Hong Kong and Thailand has done wonders for the recovery process, and she is back to normal.

Lamai Beach is a breathtaking sweep of soft sand on the southeast part of this rustic island. The fresh wind rustles the tops of the spiny coconut trees. Ocean waves crash ashore with a pronounced cadence. Every few hundred yards along the isolated beach, bungalow lots sprout up beckoning visitors. Down a long narrow dirt road we come upon a grouping of about a dozen secluded bungalows nestled among the coconut trees and sandwiched between the forest and the ocean. This enclave is so new that it is not even named yet. The smiling guy running the place opens the door to a building, and it is ours. Mere steps from the water, we are in paradise. Beth and I spread out towels on the beach and play in the warm Thai water. Swim. Dry. Rest. Repeat. There is not a soul nearby. Cambodia and Vietnam lie hidden beyond the horizon. The surf is strong. The scenery's delicious. A leaning coconut tree hanging over the top of our tropical beach captivates me. Beth soaks in the sounds of nature, and I am tickled that she is happy and at peace. I mold my own Great Wall at our beach out of sand with dirt ramparts and coconut guard towers. My sunburn aches. Heat pours out of my arms, my neck, the top of my feet. It is so hot here. But I cannot and do not complain. It is that tranquil. We get up in the morning when we want, we lounge about reading and writing, and we hang out all afternoon on the beach. We do a great deal of nothing and love every minute. The locals are friendly and easy-going. A late-day breeze is a staple, and the setting sun signals that it is time to eat. A local family runs a small restaurant next to our bungalows. Oh, the food! Fried rice topped with chicken, fresh whole fish topped with sweet-and-sour hot sauce, and fluffy omelets with vegetables. Fruit shakes and juice. Even the water we drink is delicate and sweet.

There is no world to bother us because we are in our own world on this secluded part of a secluded island deep in Southeast Asia. The bug bites on my leg are fading, and I feel fine. Yes, there are tiny, pesty ants that get into everything, but I am still so relaxed that I find I cannot muster the resolve to write in my daily journal and turn this afternoon over to Beth.

> *These two young guys came up to us on the beach today selling hammocks publicly and gems on the side. Rubies. This one punk tells us that his father is from Burma and made them there. Andrew and I are both very leery of buying these two small rubies, but after some onerous testing, we both decide that they must be real. First, our seller friend pounded the ruby between a piece of wood and a coin. Then he set the bloody thing on fire. I found the whole thing very funny. In the end, we bought the two small rubies for US$50.00 and took a picture of the two guys. And then, one of them takes out the good stuff—two small diamonds. He is willing to trade one diamond for a Walkman or camera, but we are not willing to trade our new cameras for two little diamonds. The beach has been wonderful. Tomorrow we leave this little haven and go back to Bangkok.*

—ᗰᗰ—

The noon ferry from Koh Samui to Surat Thani deposits us in the city several hours before the night bus is to depart. We find a hotel with an air-conditioned coffee shop to get out of the murderous sun. At the Lignite Travel Place, they charge us an additional twenty baht each for some obscure reason. I argue. I lose. The guy manning the office is having fun messing with me. The smile on his face. The glimmer in his eyes. I never have a chance. He knows I have lost. Others in the office know that I have lost. I am the only one not in on the joke.

Beth and I eventually head back out for a walk and stumble onto color and life—a market selling a starburst of cut flowers; vegetable stalls with mounds of red and green chili peppers; cabbages; cauliflowers; piles and piles of fresh fruits; some meats as well. A pick-up truck overflows with fresh, ripe pineapples. Down an alley, hidden from view by apartment buildings, we discover a secluded temple, golden yellow with oranges and blues. Five statue acolytes sit at the foot of the central Buddha receiving his teachings. Two enormous, three-story-tall Buddhas flank the temple. The more elaborate statue has long, narrow elongated ears, black hair with a top knowledge knot, and an immense headdress of seven snakes rearing up and over the side and top of his head. This Buddha's hands lay gently in his lap in the Dhyana meditation position. Looking down at us, he smiles ever so slightly in welcome.

Arriving early in the Bangkok morning a day before they expect us, the staff at the YMCA handles the situation with aplomb. Our princely accommodations are upgraded to a kingly suite this time. Beth comments on the sweet aroma of the roses at the front desk. Later in the day, roses appear in our room. After so many days on the beach with only the ocean breeze and crashing waves as accompaniment, we have difficulty tolerating the heat and noise and sheer everything that is the megacity of Bangkok. We buy a watermelon freeze and an orange freeze to hydrate and a blueberry sundae to savor. We stock our hotel fridge with six assorted pieces of cake from a nearby bakery, chocolate milk, gruyere cheese, fresh fruit, meat skewers from a roadside stand. With a tinge of alarm (but not remorse), we realize how much of our parents' recently wired money we have spent during our four-week vacation.

Arising early on a Thursday, what turns out to be the Buddhist holiday of Makha Bucha, we tuk-tuk way over to the western edge of the city—a graceful area of museums, temples, palaces, and historic monuments. The decibel level among the luxury is practically sane. Unfortunately, we are both near collapse from the suffocating heat. We enter the beckoning Wat Phra Keo (Temple of the Emerald Buddha), which is connected to the Grand Palace. The Wat and the Palace make everything I have seen in China pale by comparison. They take my breath away. Gold and an intricate rainbow of stones decorate every statue, corridor, building, wall, spire, and gate. It is blinding in the sunlight.

The palace, now government offices, used to be the home of the king. From the inner courtyard of the Grand Palace a simple field of grass leads to the high roofed outer wall of the Temple complex, a white wall with a large green and brick red roof. Everything is alive with color. A striking golden yellow stupa and vibrant layered, peaked, and gabled roofs of grand temple buildings erupt high above the protective outer wall. They are beauty that cannot be contained. Sculpted trees, walkways, roads, stone elephants, stone lions, golden mythical sentries, and throngs of tourists and worshipers co-exist within the walls. An old stone man sits atop a raised pedestal at the entrance to a large exterior prayer nook of the main temple building. Wrapped in a plain white cloth, one arm draped over a raised knee, he surveys the grounds and throngs. I spy a bemused look on his upturned mouth.

—⁓—

Flipping through an old newspaper later, my favorite movie buff, Beth, sees that *The Color Purple* is playing. Coming out of the movie, I begin to feel woozy. My stomach aches, and I do not think it was the popcorn. I lean on Beth as she hails a cab home.

Back in our suite, I get progressively worse. Beth feels my forehead and tells me I am a bit warm. Soon, I become hot. My head explodes, my throat is raw, and I am nauseated. Moaning in bed becomes my main preoccupation. I survive the night, but am not in good shape as the new day dawns. Beth takes charge and drags me to the Bangkok Nursing Home Hospital. An English-speaking, Chinese-trained, female Malaysian-Chinese doctor gives me a thorough probing. Remembering through my agonized fog the now partially faded mosquito bites from the bus ride south, I show them to her and ask for a blood test. She agrees.

She returns shortly and informs me, "You do not have malaria."

Well that is good news.

"You do have a virus, possibly also with bacterial strep." *Uh-oh.* "Most likely, you have dengue fever." *What the hell is dengue fever?* She asks me where we have been traveling, and we tell her. Her response is direct: "Dengue is transmitted by mosquitos and is common in southern Thailand. The incubation period is usually from a few days to up to two weeks." *So I was right to be worried about those early morning bug bites. Score one for hypochondria. I never should have left the broken bus.*

She prescribes penicillin and sends me back to the YMCA for bedrest.

When we return to our suite, I fall into bed and am quickly soaked with fevered perspiration. I keep reading and reading because whenever I stop, whenever my mind is not concentrating on that specific task, the pain is excruciating. The pressure in my head alternately squeezes like a vise and then explodes outward. The spasms travel down my neck and into my torso seeking a release. Forget sleeping. Forget speaking. I am sure Beth is nearby watching and caring for me, she is an angel, but I can only mechanically focus on the words in front of my eyes. The next twenty-four hours crawl by in an agonizing blur.

A day later, my head is not as volcanic. I am more aware of my surroundings and can put a coherent thought or two together. I see the relief in Beth's face as we realize that my fever has incredibly broken on the short end of the doctor's prognosis. I am so thankful for the Bangkok Nursing Home Hospital and Beth for finding it and getting me there. I am weak, but I can function. This is important because, ill or not, we are returning to Hong Kong.

—⚍—

Air Lanka check-in is once again a nightmare. Massed inside the airport doors is an angry mob stewing while its bags are hand searched before being allowed into the Air Lanka ticket booths to check the bags. We shove. We sweat. On the best of days, I have little patience. Today, I feel like shit. The language coming out of my mouth would make my proper mother blanch. So much for our Eden on Koh Samui and the pampering in Bangkok. The world waits to take us back in, and I apparently still do not travel well.

After what seems like an eternity, we make it onto the plane and back to Hong Kong. Arriving at the Fragrant Harbour is eye opening. The weather is bearable—I can breathe! There are only cars on the roads. They are so quiet. We get our old room back at the YMCA and spend Valentine's Day with rubies (now set as earrings in fourteen-karat Bangkok gold) and roses. When alone together, Beth and I are great. It is outside society that causes trouble. During our whirlwind of last minute activities in the British Colony, I am shattered to see how quickly my paranoia, my suspicion, my lack of control, come roaring back to the fore. It is not always, but it is not infrequent either. In just one instance, I have to get my garment bag fixed because the zippers got ripped out on the return flight. The store proprietors were nice and did a good job, but I did not trust them until the bag was back in my hands. I knew that something bad was going to happen (it did not). Where did the relaxed guy in Thailand go? Why did he disappear?

And what will returning to China be like? I dread the *mafan* I know is coming. I fear what I will be like and how it might impact my relationships. Beth looks ahead contemplatively, but I know that she is thinking of the hardship, of her relatives, of being Chinese in China. We enter the express train to Guangzhou, and the doors close.

CHAPTER 27

A TIANANMEN WEDDING

T HE STICKY WARM of Bangkok has become the uncomfortable chill of mid-February Beijing. Beth wakes and scolds me for forgetting the soap and her new soap dish in HK. First, I break my Cleocin, now no soap. This sums up our trip home.

—⁓—

I breezed through the green foreigner line at customs in Guangzhou; Beth got held up in the red Overseas Chinese line because she had to declare a television set we brought back as a favor for a friend we bumped into in Hong Kong. Transferring from the HK–Guangzhou tracks to the northern lines was hellish. We were overloaded with six pieces of luggage. My jersey dripped with sweat streaming from my scalp, my neck, my armpits, my entire body. My still-weakened muscles ached. My mood was anxious. Finding that our berth-mates for the next two nights in an antique soft sleeper car were two sketchy-looking Chinese men did not help. Two Japanese guys one compartment over generously agreed to switch with us, and we joined two female Beida instructors for the nearly three-day ride back. I pulled out Carl Sagan's *Contact* and the hours began to slip by.

The days back now tick by. A handful. Then a week. Then a few more. Leaving the country has given me fresh perspective on my resumed life here in China. I am not enjoying it. I am existing. At Vassar I looked forward to daily classes, dove into the course materials and readings, and eagerly anticipated the discussions I knew we would have. My friends and I would hang out shooting the breeze and having easy fun. My mornings began with a warm shower and anticipation of a good day. Chinese classes at Shao Yuan by contrast are rote, scripted, predictable. Eighteen hours of stultifying classes per week. Up early each day to avoid a cold shower and then freezing in the halls. It still amazes me that it is colder inside than outside. There's nothing to do at night. Friends are fewer and fewer. The *mafan* has returned as has my inability to deal with it. Is it all necessary? Our time out of the country already seems a dream. Was I fine then only because I had no responsibilities? China is dreary. I hope my folks are not wasting their money coming to visit in the spring.

I may be in the process of pondering my future, but at times I question if my brain's shut down from lack of use. I bounce around from thought to thought. I'm disillusioned with China, so what's keeping my interest? The question drives me nuts. Maybe my interest lies in what China was? I've always liked history. But do I want to teach? Can I write? How about running a book store? Yeah, living simply, reading, and running a little store. I wonder if there is money in that?

In the midst of my life turmoil, Gaoshan comes over and drops the news that he got married on January 23. What! I didn't know he had a girlfriend, let alone a fiancée. Two hundred or so people came to his father's home in shifts of forty for the reception. It must have been some shindig. His bride remains at home, while he has returned to Beijing to finish his studies. He really wants me to come home with him for a visit and lets me know that the trip would now be legal. No more special permission is required. Xingtai opened to foreign travelers on *Chunjie*, the Spring Festival. I agree to go.

As happy as I am for Gaoshan, I am even happier that Toshiro moved out this morning. I do not know where he is going, and I was too excited to inquire. I immediately ask Beth to be my unofficial roommate, and before the morning is out, the room no longer resembles a double. We push the beds together and lay a quality mat on the floor, and over the next couple of days we add posters, pictures, and plants. The room is clean and homey. The arrangement is unofficial because Beth has been re-assigned a new roommate on the fifth floor and us living together officially as a boy-girl-sharing-a-room is verboten. The Dragon Lady, Teacher Chen, squeezes me for extra FEC per month to keep my room officially a single. She graciously offers to give me another roommate if I cannot pay, but I really want to choose my own roommate.

—m—

We have updated our living arrangements, and I continue getting back on my feet after being laid up in bed for four days right before Toshiro left. Still weak from dengue, I overdid it and caught strep and a bad cold, probably from not taking all of my penicillin. I did not move. I did not eat. I have lost buckets of weight. I avoid mirrors because I do not want to see what I look like. Most ominously, however, after being some-what distant from Beth since we returned two weeks ago, I close down completely. I am not a good boyfriend or friend. I was not perfect before vacation, but now I do not talk or share at all.

Beth is not pleased. We've gone through the motions of joining our rooms, but she has had it with my being inattentive and poor company. She was already frowning on the fact that I agreed to take Gaoshan up on his offer to visit Xingtai. My shutting her out tears it. She does not stew for long. Pouting quietly is not her style. She tells me straight up that she has an issue with me. We argue.

"You keep talking with your other friends. Why not me?" She asks me pointedly.

"I don't know," I say with a shrug.

"That's not an answer," She retorts, crossing her arms. "Why won't you still be open with me?"

I do not give her a straight answer, but I know the answer. I'm repeating a pattern. When I date someone, I have this great fear of losing touch with my friends. It is always something with me. First, I fear I'm losing the girl. Then, I fear I'm losing my friends. And what do I do in these situations? I overcompensate, veering too much in the other direction. It is a recipe for disharmony and distress. This current incarnation comes to a head as we are supposed to leave for a wedding celebration.

Peter and Kate were legally married a few days ago. The marriage license was issued authorizing Kate to marry a foreigner, a government official read them the marriage laws, and presto, they are husband and wife. The formal process was anticlimactic. They couldn't even spend their wedding night together. Their friends decide that they need a proper wedding. Today, March 6, 1987, is the day. In Tiananmen Square.

Beth, however, is not sure if she wants to go with me to the ceremony, and that is not the only thing on her mind: "If you do not want to be with me, then why should we live together?"

I stare at her, mouth agape, like I was slapped upside the head with a frozen fish. A cold panic floods my chest, but for one of the few times in my life, I take a deep breath. As I slowly exhale, the blinders fall away, and it hits me that this is no way to treat the woman I love.

I take Beth's hand in mine. We sit on the edge of our bed. We talk. The details escape me (they often do), but not the emotional reality that I cannot lose her. This sears my memory. Beth is the jade I discovered in China. More precious than gold. More precious than diamonds. Jade is beauty. Jade must be held onto dearly. Jade needs to be caressed and treasured.

Putting aside, compartmentalizing really, the fleeting thought that it may be equilibrium and the lack of controversy that I cherish most, other tumblers begin falling into place. Again, my mind constantly shifts from thought to thought. Why China? I'm hooked by its culture, its history, its language. The present China is bad, but the "it" of what "it" was and may still be or could be is seductive. China captures my heart, and Beth is my China.

Holding each other in love, we decide at the last minute to join the wedding festivities. Rushing outside, we merge into the large group of more than a dozen as they commandeer Toyota taxicabs to caravan to Tiananmen Square. The overcast and gray afternoon does nothing to dampen the excitement in the group. Making good time, we are soon assembled in this most official of communist gathering places at the base of the Monument to the People's Heroes. Though it is cold, padded winter coats are shed in a pile, and the wedding party gathers in front of priest John.

John is an American exchange student from Shao Yuan Building 4 who sent in US$200 to the *Rolling Stone* "Become-a-Priest" offer. He is all Eastern wanderer this afternoon—flat-soled, black cotton Chinese shoes; white pants; long, flowing light brown top; large brown beaded necklace looped twice around his neck; and a long white scarf. With his back to the ten-story marble and granite obelisk commemorating Chinese revolutionary martyrs, John begins the service in a by and large empty Tiananmen Square.

Before him stands Kate, elegant in a sleek black dress and bright red belt, her long black hair cascading down her back framing a wide smile. Peter is debonair with his hands crossed low in front of him and a mischievous gleam on his face. Kate's younger sister, a stylish maid of honor, accompanies the bride. Sam has returned and flanks Peter as his best man. It is good to see Sam with a twinkle in his eyes and at ease. The four of them stand tall, a happy quartet gathered for a happy occasion, the only evidence of the cold being their closed hands as they try to keep their fingers warm.

The rest of us form an uneven semicircle around them. Our dress ranges from modestly formal to college casual. We are an intimate grouping occupying a cavernous open space. Two months ago, Tiananmen Square was thronged with protesters calling for democratic freedoms. We stand at the base of the monument where the masses spontaneously mourned for Zhou Enlai near the end of the Cultural Revolution in 1976. It is all too surreal. The English vows Sam wrote are thick with sarcasm. They are caustic enough to result in our expulsions if anyone but us understood.

As the ceremony concludes and Peter and Kate are now properly as well as legally wed, we grab our coats, spread congratulations all around, and hurriedly head to the nearby Beijing Hotel to warm up. The group of Chinese, including a cop, who gathered to watch our Western spectacle breaks apart and moves on with their respective lives. Once we stop shaking, we jump into a new set of cabs and go to the Lido Hotel for a curry dinner and bowling.

—⁓—

As if their union is a signal, the weather in Beijing soon breaks. It gets warmer and warmer day by slow day as the city emerges from the depths of winter. Fresh produce fills the bins at the Friendship Store and in the markets. The Alley has been spruced up with a few permanent wooden stalls and better quality products. A light breeze brings a refreshing clarity as it blows away the dreary doldrums.

The right frame of mind can make all the difference. I feel revived. I feel like studying, like learning. My Chinese is improving. The curriculum is more challenging in class, and we delve deeper into the nuances of the language. On the relationship front, Beth and I return to Shao Yuan one night after splurging on a fancy dinner of sweet-and-sour pork, Chinese greens, prawns, pudding, and wine in the Chinese restaurant at the newly opened, luxury Shangri-La Hotel and fall into each other's arms dancing around the room. On the personal front, at twenty-one years of age, I am embarrassed to admit that I have finally done something that has always eluded me. By the end of my erythromycin treatment (a supplemental course that I obtained from Dr. H. in Beijing after not listening to the doctor in Bangkok and finishing the first course), I swallow the pill whole. I first do it with applesauce and then with only water. I actually swallowed a pill! No more crushing it up into a disgusting granular mess. No more gagging as the pill would stop at the back of my mouth and not go down. It does not rank up there with scaling the Great Wall, but I am proud nonetheless.

I try to step back and appreciate this time of conflicting emotions. Living abroad, here in this place, is an assault of differentness, newness, weirdness. Change is not easy. I have to remember that this applies to the Chinese as well. I recently read that the "Chinese have been beaten into submission by the stability of socialist life." Before that, it was the rigidity of imperial life. The 1949 Communist liberation was itself a mask for a new imperial-like dynasty. New clothes. Same Emperor.

I try to remember and appreciate this, but it is hard. The disinterest of salespeople continues to exasperate me. When they say, *mei you*, it means much more to me than "I don't have any." I hear "I may or may not have any, but I am not going to check and wouldn't give you any even if I had them." It is the Chinese masses way of figuratively flipping us the bird. It makes me feel impotent. And cabbies? Don't get me started. It is always a fight with them. Their sense of entitlement is astounding. This so-called egalitarian socialist society is crammed full of division, distinction, and separation.

During a Scrabble game one night, two Chinese students from Bei Shida, Beijing Normal University, tell us that they are once again being encouraged at weekly political meetings to inform on friends and acquaintances who might have said or done anything in the last two years that is "counter to Chinese society." They tell a story of long Chinese memory. A few years back, two students wrote a play critical of the government. They received a mild reprimand, and the whole affair blew over. When they graduated, however, they were both assigned, banished really, to the hinterlands of Xinjiang. Beth also heard a complex tale of two musicians, a love affair, a jealous wife, a sister, and a *danwei* (work unit) leader bent on revenge. The end result of that soap opera is that a talented girl's musical dreams are being suppressed as she has been assigned the job of practicing and only practicing.

How can the government not recognize that placing people in dead-end careers with little to no responsibility results in an excess of free time, which leads to boredom, which causes frustration, which spawns agitation and unrest? How can the government not recognize this, particularly where agitation and unrest are exactly what an insecure leadership wants to avoid at all costs?

—⁓—

Beth is depressed and does not want me traveling to Xingtai. She asks me to stay with her. This is the third time the trip has been planned. We fight each time it approaches. I do not want to argue, but I do want to visit Gaoshan's home. It is a unique opportunity. Beth will be leaving again for Hong Kong the morning after I return. I see her point, yet still explain that I need to take this trip and promise that we will be together again soon. I'm dancing on a needle, and her vibe tells me what she wants to do with that needle. It figures that I for once make a decision and again hurt Beth.

All in all, I am in a disagreeable mood. The roller coaster of emotional wellbeing rises and dips with no end. Getting on the bus today, I force my body inside the door and punch my way up. I am a beast. It feels so good to let go and inflict my power on others. Karma, though, is a bitch.

Riding my bike later on campus, I enter a crowd of other bicyclists and see a Chinese student riding her bike off to the side coming towards the group. She stares ahead blankly as she pedals. We are on an intercept course. How can she not see me, us? I know she is coming, but I cannot stop and cannot get out of the way. I am hemmed in by bikes on all sides. She gets closer and closer.

I seem to be the only one aware of what is about to happen. Since I cannot avoid the imminent accident and since fate apparently does not want me to, I prepare as best I can.

The scene unfolds as if in a movie. Time slows. I marvel that she remains oblivious to my presence. I am not a small target. The mass of bikes I am in rolls onward. She approaches. As if scripted by a Hollywood director, an opening appears on that side at exactly the right moment leaving me open to attack.

Seconds before impact, I raise myself up off my seat and brace my legs on the pedals.

BOOM!

The student slams into me and jolts over her handlebars into my side. We both go tumbling down in an awkward heap. I am dazed, but my last second maneuver saves me from serious injury. She looks up at me for the first time with a look of incomprehension. The two bicycles are a tangled mess.

CHAPTER 28

FETED IN XINGTAI

GAOSHAN PULLS FOUR duck eggs out his bag and hands me two. They are larger than chicken eggs with salty yolks. I pull out my favorite *Dabaitu*, White Rabbit Candy, that Beth threw in my bag and think of her as I unwrap one of the small, off-white chewy pieces of creamy sugar and pop it into my mouth. She was not thrilled with me leaving, but still thought of me and my sweet tooth. A few hours south of Beijing, a guy traveling from Xinjiang Province in the far west learns that the express train we are on will not stop at his destination of Zhengzhou in Henan Province. He looks so lost and confused. I feel his alarm. I've been there. I'm often there. I silently watch a gray-haired peasant wearing a Mao cap and glasses sitting across the aisle. With his thin mustache, mini goatee, and years etched on his wrinkled face, this man could have been born during the late Qing Dynasty. Or maybe he is my father's age.

The Xingtai train station bustles even as the clock ticks towards 11:00 p.m. Taxi drivers hustle. The stench of stale urine hangs heavy in the air. Gaoshan's eldest brother and the driver assigned to the family by their work unit pick us up. Away from the train station, Xingtai is deserted on the six-minute ride to their family home. We carry several bags and boxes of food from Beijing for Gaoshan's mother. Gaoshan totes a fourteen-inch, color Mudan television he bought with my *waihui*, FEC. The television is one of the four new "must haves." In the 1970s, everyone wanted radios, bicycles, sewing machines, and watches. Now, it is color televisions, refrigerators, washing machines, and tape decks.

It is late, but the first obligatory stop is to meet Gaoshan's parents. Mom, dad, and all three of his brothers are waiting to meet me in the parents' portion of the family's courtyard compound. Spouses must be nearby. I can feel hidden eyes on me.

I am the nervous center of attention. While I met them when they visited their relative in Beijing, I am now in their home, in their city, on their turf. It is the moment of my second first impression. As my first order of business, I present Gaoshan's parents with the bottle of Dynasty wine and box of Cadbury chocolates I purchased specifically for them. In rehearsed Chinese, I say, "Thank you for inviting me to Xingtai. It is an honor to see all of you again."

Gaoshan's father accepts the gifts with a poker face that could cause a statue to blink and diplomatically says, "But I already have so much liquor." I hear this statement the same as when a Chinese person declines something three times out of polite etiquette before accepting. So far, so good. After examining the bottle, dad asks, "Is this American wine?"

"No, it is a Chinese brand." I say this quickly and immediately regret my words. A disappointed shadow flickers ever-so faintly across his dignified face. I shrink inwardly. My first faux pas certainly didn't take long. "It is for export only." I tell him in an attempt to right my wrong.

Gaoshan's father is too much the gentlemen to press the matter.

Five bowls of piping-hot *jiaozi*, dumplings, are laid out in front of each of us. We eat and drink tea. I ask Gaoshan where his wife is. I have seen their wedding photos, a happy couple comfortable in each other's arms. Gaoshan calls in Song Mei. She must have been watching and enters immediately. The face in the photographs is smiling and framed by silky black hair hanging at most a foot from the floor. The face I see now is somber. It might be nerves at meeting a foreigner. It might be that she has been at her in-laws' house alone the past several weeks. She has not seen her new husband since we arrived. She approaches, and Gaoshan introduces us. We say hello, and he then dismisses her with a curt "*ah, zou,*" "OK, leave now." She has been in the room for less than two minutes. Gaoshan hardly acknowledges her. Song Mei leaves. I am at a loss at this treatment, but wisely keep my mouth shut.

By Chinese standards, mom and dad's house is large and well appointed. There are five rooms plus a small private bathroom. The latter is a treat. The living room doubles as dad's study with a large desk as well as a refrigerator, washing machine, and small television set (three of the new "must haves"). The room is filled with numerous books and hanging calligraphy scrolls. I learn that Gaoshan's dad is accomplished at the art of *shufa,* calligraphy. Some of the scrolls are poems. Others depict flowers and animals. Hanging in the back corner of the room are two brushes, one large and one medium with thick, tapered black handles leading to even thicker grayish bristles. In another room, I notice several acupuncture diagrams hanging on the wall depicting details of the human body.

Well past midnight, I am on Gaoshan and Song Mei's side of the family's compound. More specifically, I am lying in the bride and groom's new double bed in their bedroom. The large room is plastered with Double Happiness emblems, the traditional symbol of good fortune and blessings for Chinese weddings. The furniture, including two tall armoires, is new. I've managed to kick the bride and groom out of their own place on their first visit together since the two-week marriage period. This is so not right. I should not be here. I protest. This is their home. Let them have their privacy. I protest more. I do not need this much space. There is, however, nothing that I can do, and at some level I know it is useless from the start. But still I try, right up until the point when I sense I am becoming impolite.

—\\\\\—

There is a knock on the door at 6:50 a.m. later that morning. I am the last one to rise. Jumping onto the cold floor, I quickly get dressed, and we head across the courtyard. Gaoshan's parents are having another *guizi*, closet, built. Three guys are already at work. Mom is busy taking measurements and instructing the workers. She loves to laugh, but I'd hate to screw up a job for her. She is definitely the master inside this home.

Leaving them in the courtyard, Gaoshan makes us a late breakfast at 7:30 a.m., a tasty and simple meal of *fangbian mian* (instant noodles), cooked eggs, and vegetables in a soup broth, and then we go out for a walk. The trees have budded, and it is green. There is a breeze. It is already hot in the sun. Xingtai pales in scope to Beijing, but dwarfs Qufu. The atmosphere is relaxed, the people open. We wander about, in and out of the few stores that are open early. Merchants are setting up their roadside stalls. The main streets are heavy with bicyclists; the side streets are quiet.

Lunch is with Gaoshan's father at the house of *da ge* (Gaoshan's eldest brother). Gu, the family's regular driver, joins us. *Da ge's* wife stays out of sight. The big, one-room home is U-shaped surrounding a courtyard. Gaoshan's brother and sister-in-law beat the implementation of the one-child policy in 1979 and have two children, a boy and a girl. After much gorging and when it appears that the meal is finally, welcomingly over, huge steaming bowls of rice and vegetables appear. My heart sinks. I drink more beer at this one meal than I have in my whole life. No matter how much I protest, they pour. Each time someone calls, "*lai*," I have to drink. Am I ever stuffed.

A driver brings an army jeep to take us around. Gaoshan's father is the retired head of the *danwei*, work unit, and has the benefit of a reserved vehicle. It's amazing how quickly I acclimate to the privilege of a free vehicle and driver available at our beck and call. No one ever said that life is tough for China's leaders.

The driver stays with the jeep when we reach the Xingtai Park and Zoo because he doesn't want any of the hordes of children fiddling with it. The green entrance to the park gives way to a bare concrete path bordered by dirt. People mob us and stare at me with open wonder. I was a rarer sight in Inner Mongolia and the more offbeat parts of Datong, but I am a brand new experience in recently-opened Xingtai. The kids all seem to speak one word of English: "Hello." It is a constant echo as we walk. I hear the murmured voices commenting and laughing over the American in their midst.

Xingtai used to be called Ox City, and a towering concrete statue of a cow rises proudly from its pedestal in the center of town. Each time we visit it, a group of twenty to thirty people closes in around us. My pulse quickens, and I begin to sweat, but not excessively. The first time someone inexplicably asked if Gaoshan is also from the United States. Dad could not be so mistaken in his austere, blue Mao suit, blue Mao hat, and black Chinese sandals. I wear jeans, sneakers, shirt, and beige sweater. Driver Gu looks at me with a short, disapproving shake of his head and mutters, "*Nide yifu tai suibian le.*" "Your clothing is too casual."

Later, we head to Dahuoquan Park to visit the most famous native son of Xingtai, Guo Shoujing. Guo was a Yuan Dynasty astronomer, scientist, engineer, and inventor. A statue of Guo stands prominently in front of a full-size gnomon. Back in the day of Kublai Khan, some seven hundred years ago, Guo's engineering and astronomical enhancements to the gnomon allowed him to calculate the length of a year at 365.2425 days. An astronomical screen, about the length of a large three-dragon screen, sits in front of the newly-opened Guoshou Memorial Hall. Decorated with celestial blue and white tiles depicting the sky, Guo is pictured at his drafting table, book-ended by many of his inventions.

A model in the Memorial Hall depicts the extent of this scientific complex during the Yuan Dynasty. What is left today is but a meager remnant. I am saddened to see how little still remains, and all at once, even though this particular situation is unrelated, I am angered by the wanton destruction of the Cultural Revolution. The Chinese spent a decade blindly and methodically destroying their history, their culture, themselves. Such a waste. It is regrettable when natural causes and time lead to loss of the past; it is another story entirely when such loss is premeditated. Guo Shoujing is an example of the historical Chinese triumphs of that past. A child prodigy, he grew up to create an accurate calendar and helped design and build dozens of observatories. He revolutionized water delivery to Beijing, in part by creating a reservoir and a series of canals to get the precious liquid from the mountains into the center of the Imperial Capital. The reservoir, now known as Kunming Lake, is the heart of the Summer Palace in Beijing.

—⁓—

I feast on food in Xingtai. After another large dinner at home, Gaoshan and I bike to visit a friend. Perched precariously on the rat trap on the back of Gaoshan's bicycle, it is a painful, twenty-minute ride over seven sets of railroad tracks. His friend's family is of course finishing dinner, and the extended family welcomes me into their home.

Dad begins with standard disclaimers dictated by innate Confucian modesty: "My home is not worthy." "My food is simple and bad." Grandma is charm and stereotype—short, white hair, incredibly wrinkled, quiet yet all knowing. I cannot understand a single word she utters. Dad, the head of the Education Department for their *danwei*, is a character, a proud intelligent man with no hair and a pleasing mien. They force feed us and make us drink two bottles of the beer-soda mix I first had in Qufu.

"Drink. Eat."

"No, no, no. We are fine."

"Drink. Eat."

"No, no, no. We are fine."

"Drink. Eat."

"No, no, no. We are fine."

The triumvirate of Chinese etiquette complete, we eat and drink. To refuse their hospitality would have been a loss of face. A visit with the foreigner gives great face to their family as well as to Gaoshan. I am beyond ready to burst.

"How old do you think I am?" Dad asks. I think he must be proud of how he looks for his age, whatever it is. I, however, am in a real bind. I don't want to insult him by aiming too high or too low, and I am a bad guesser of ages. This has danger written all over it. Just in time, Gaoshan bails me out, explaining that in America we do not ask others' ages. Dad lets it go. I am off the hook.

After this reprieve, I proceed to step right back into my own fire. Dad's drinking *baijiu*, Chinese moonshine. He presses me to drink. Thinking he means the *baijiu* and not willing to drink it, I do decline. Repeatedly (and pretty forcefully since I am in a bit of a panic).

The situation is uncomfortable. Gaoshan again bails me out. Speaking English, he says, "Andrew, please drink your drink, not the baijiu, or it will be an insult." I finally get it and drink my beer-soda mix. Dad smiles and drinks another shot.

When Gaoshan and I return to his home, we join Song Mei and watch the end of a *wushu, kung fu,* movie on their new television set. I sense that Song Mei is disappointed that the television is only fourteen inches and Chinese.

Gaoshan's parents have a twenty-inch Toshiba television (bigger, foreign).

Da ge has a twenty-inch Chinese, color television (bigger).

Sister has an eighteen-inch color Sharp television (bigger, foreign).

The family we visited tonight owns a twenty-inch foreign television (bigger, foreign).

Another friend has only a twelve-inch Chinese black-and-white set (smaller, local, no color).

Size and make matter in television sets.

—ᴍ—

This trip has been revealing. I am visiting Chinese homes, interacting with Chinese people, and immersing myself in spoken Chinese. Gaoshan and his family show me their hometown and their hospitality. Albeit as a special guest, I escape from bureaucratic hassles. I hold my own in conversation. I have not become angry or irritated in a few days. I like the relaxed atmosphere, the welcoming people, and the fine weather and simple scenery of Xingtai. The dichotomy leads to internal dilemma. How can I be pissed off at China, at the *mafan* we face, when everyone in private settings is so nice and down-to-earth? Can life really be so compartmentalized that individuals and society as a whole take on two discrete and mutually exclusive identities inside and outside the home?

—m—

We venture off road into the rural countryside to climb nearby *Zhang Guo Lao Shan*, the Mountain of Elder Zhang Guo. The mountain is a sacred Daoist pilgrimage site that is one of the "eight famous mountains named after angels," if I understood correctly. In this arid area of tractors, bicycles, and farmers wearing towels wrapped around their heads, *waihua,* the world outside of China, seems mystical, much like the American "Gold Mountain" of the 1800s.

After a steep, harrowing hike up past a scattering of temples, older ladies dancing to Buddha (it is a multi-purpose pilgrimage site), worshippers burning incense and paper offerings, and legions of day trippers, we make it to the rocky summit. Squat evergreens peak out of several crags. The three of us, Gaoshan, Driver Gu, and I, take in the hazy countryside. We stand at an intersection between heaven and earth. The top of the mountain, its slopes, and the land leading off in all directions are predominantly light brown, the color of rock and dirt. The green is dull. The hard-packed dirt road cuts through the valley and towards the mountain. This area is primitive. This area is poor. Are the two the same? The people here do not seem so much deprived, as not developed. Would modernization help or hurt these people?

—m—

Gastronomical overload remains an overarching theme of my visit. It is classic Chinese, but even I have a limit. (Who knew?) Large breakfast, large lunch, large dinner, three times per day, every day. Most at homes; some at restaurants. The company is great. The food is delicious. To even compare it with what we choke down at Shao Yuan is cruel. My various hosts spend significant quantities of scarce *kuai* and tremendous effort on my behalf. Much face is being offered and received all around.

Finally, during the last dinner at Gaoshan's parents' house with Brothers Nos. 2 and 3 (Dad is away at a meeting in the provincial capital), it is my turn to offer the best face I can provide. The family has been pressing me since I got here to try *baijiu*, Chinese white lightening. Avoiding it brought me close to social disaster earlier in my visit. Tonight, though, either out of a desire to be courteous or being beaten into submission, I relent. I accept the shot glass, only a quarter full. My hand shakes as I raise it to my lips. With a hearty *ganbei*, bottoms up, I throw my head back with the family. The clear liquid goes down quickly. My throat spasms. A searing heat erupts inside me. If I were a dragon, I could breathe fire at this moment. My eyes bug out, and I can only imagine the tortured look on my face. Gaoshan's two older brothers repeatedly drain full shots with practiced ease. All of the Chinese in the room are smiling, but everyone in the room is satisfied.

—m—

Gaoshan and I arrive breathless at the Xingtai train station ten minutes before departure to discover that the train has been rescheduled to leave an hour later. By the time it arrives one-and-one-half-hours later, the platform is jammed with a sea of humanity. The train pulls in. The mass surges forward. I flow along and then start to rise with the tide. I ride the wave up, and then ride it back down, my feet kissing the platform before the next breath launches me anew. I feel like a pulsing jellyfish—out...in, out...in, out...in. Three times do I unsuccessfully get on the train. I have no control over the situation. It is bedlam. I am frustrated. I am nervous. I get angry. It is my default coping mechanism now that I am no longer special. I shout to Gaoshan who is himself hemmed in out of sight near me, in English that he probably does not understand, "These motherfuckers are animals!" I am soon to become one myself.

On the fourth surge, I manage to get my foot down solid past the second step. At that moment I use this purchase to lay into the guy in front of me and send him flying a good three feet. Boy, does it feel good. I purposely stumble to make it look like it wasn't my fault. Then someone rams into me. *"Ta ma da!"* "Fuck You!" I am screaming. "These fucking *dongwu*'s (animals)!!" I get stares at both expressions, the Chinese and the Chinglish. I am out of emotional control, that quickly beyond caring.

I drag myself up and on. People cram into every seat, jam the aisles, press up against the windows and doors. The food cart people are stuck. Gaoshan and I grab a piece of a seat, which we share for two hours until arriving at the provincial capital, Shijiazhuang. There, we each manage to get a whole seat. The train car is hot, smoky, and noisy. I give away a seat twice during the return to Beijing because I have to stand in order to breathe.

My pleasant experience in Xingtai is a fleeting memory as the crush of public life in China returns. Have I become compartmentalized like Chinese society? Is this a rationalization for my lack of control? Although it releases tension, I do not like sinking to their level and acting like an animal. It both upsets and amazes me that the Chinese laugh at it all. Arguing and fighting is a game to them. We are trapped and crushed in this hard seat section of the train and cannot do a thing about it. Maybe laughing is the only way to keep from crying. From going insane. Maybe it's a sign of resignation to the backward state of their existence. Maybe it's any number of things.

No matter what I know or understand or think I understand about this China, I am unable to either accept or deal with it. I bury myself in Theodore White's *Thunder Out of China*, trying to blot out the chaos as the train rolls on. In 1945, White felt that the Chinese were beginning to start the process of developing beyond feudal incivility. More than forty years later, I am not so sure they have made the jump.

CHAPTER 29

ONLY IN CHINA

ARRIVING AT BEIDA two hours later than anticipated, I walk in as
Beth walks out. We hug and kiss, and I accompany her down to the
waiting cab. She seems relieved to see me before she flees China and
is looking forward to being in Hong Kong to rest and visit a doctor. Her
sweet scent lingers from our brief embrace as I wave goodbye.

For days after, walking into our room and expecting to see her, I
deflate upon realizing that no one is there. I see her in the decorations
of our room. I fall asleep holding Cheetah. When Beth calls Wednesday
morning, I am handwashing clothes in the wash room basin across the
hall. She is bored in rainy Hong Kong with no one to play with. My heart
tears.

"I'll meet you in Shanghai Sunday morning," I spontaneously blurt
out. And with that, I immediately set off for the train station to buy
tickets. I am so eager that I gladly pay in FEC instead of coming back the
next day to wait in a long line to pay RMB.

As I sit at my desk tonight looking with anticipation at the train
tickets, Zhou, a North Korean friend, knocks on my door. I do not have
much contact with the North Koreans even though they live across the
hall. They remain aloof. This being said, Zhou is one of a couple who have

reached out and with whom I have made an effort to cross the invisible partition that politics has erected. We are each, after all, young human beings learning the ways of the world while sharing the same space. It is not our fault that we were born on different sides of a dividing line.

"I want to speak confidentially with you," he begins calmly in English. There is nervous anticipation on his face.

"Sure. Come in." I put the train tickets down on my desk.

He enters and fidgets self-consciously standing next to my bed, the only other place to sit in the room. He clearly wants to ask me something. Is he having a problem with the words or is it something else?

He sits tentatively and takes a quick breath. "Do you have any sex books?"

"What?" I am surprised and want to make sure I did not misunderstand his heavy accent.

"Do you have any sex books?" Having said it once, he is more confident this time. *I did hear him correctly.* He does not wait for an answer. "I am interested in sex books because I have not got fucked yet." He says this matter-of-factly as if he is asking for an entrée in the cafeteria. I'd like the noodles please.

"No. No, I do not have any sex books," I reply, shaking my head and giving him a too-quick, honest answer to his serious question.

His face drops. His body sags. He took a shot and came up empty.

I feel for the guy. I understand what horny is. Dating and sex do not appear high on the North Korean activity list here. I have no idea what it is like for him back home.

I want to do something for him if I can. I offer to try to find girlie magazines to loan him. How, I have no idea. *Do I dare ask my parents to bring a couple over for him when they visit? I wonder what their response would be to that request!*

"Where is Beth? You are living with her." I am not sure if this is a question or a statement, but the answer is obvious since he lives nearby.

"She is in Hong Kong right now."

"Do you two have sexual intercourse?"

I look at him trying to decide how far down this road I want to travel. This is already the longest and most consequential exchange I have had with a North Korean. I take a deep breath and answer, "Yes."

"How often?"

At this point, I am committed to the conversation. "Most every day."

He looks more closely at me, a mix of interest and envy in his eyes. "How old are you?"

"I am twenty-one."

"So am I." This stops him cold for several thick seconds as he leans back on my bed against the wall and looks at me. "I am only interested in reading about sex because I have not done it yet," he repeats. "I cannot go to hookers because I do not have money." I have now become used to his accent in English, which is good because he has more questions. "What do you do so Beth does not get pregnant?"

Hopefully something better than we have done in our recent past, I think to myself. Out loud, I explain a few different birth control methods, but dodge answering his question. He listens intently. I cannot determine how much he truly understands.

"Do you two have to get married when you get back to America?"

I pause to reflect on the deeper implications of this question. "No, we do not. Western couples often go through a series of relationships before getting married. Having sex outside of marriage is not against the law in America."

He again stares at me pensively for several more heavy seconds. I cannot believe that I am having this conversation.

"It is illegal in China for unmarried couples to have sexual relations, and couples would be severely reprimanded for it in North Korea," he shares. This is his first statement that refers back to his home country.

Talking about Beth and sex this way seems so cold, so clinical. I try explaining the difference between "having sex" and "making love." He seems incredulous when I say that Beth and I love each other.

How do I describe love? That all-encompassing feeling of caring so much for another person? In his mind, at this point, which I appreciate, it is physical. It is lust. He wants a woman. He wants to experience sexual pleasure. How can I possibly convey how sex with someone you love brings you to another level of joy, something more than just a physical release?

Instead, I come out with, "Can I ask you a political question?" I want to ask him what he thinks about South Korea. My direct attempt at changing the subject (and expanding the conversation) flops.

"I do not like talking about politics, even with other North Koreans. And you would not understand anyway, coming from a capitalist country." He says this with finality and a twinge of confident contempt in the last phrase. There is a young person's lifetime of weight to his response.

I like to think that I can look at situations from a number of points of view, but this conversation is not to be. Thirty minutes of further non-political talk later, he leaves to go running. There is a sports meet coming up, and he's playing football. The Beida North Koreans are all practicing and training daily and want to win badly. It is a matter of national pride, maybe more.

Once alone again, I pick up the temporarily forgotten tickets and marvel at what just happened. I cannot wait to tell Beth.

—⁓—

The next day the weather flips. That's April for you. Two days before leaving for Shanghai and Beth, I am trapped inside by a steady, driving rain. I am bored and go upstairs with crescents to visit my friend, Mark. Mark is a Chinese-American foreign-exchange student from Texas. It is surprising that I have not traveled with him since we spend so much time together. He is part of so many Beida memories—our Thanksgiving dinner, our nightly bull sessions and parties, shopping at the Zhongguancun market, Pete and Kate's wedding. Today, we eat the crescents by his window overlooking the front courtyard and beyond to the nearby campus intersection north of Shao Yuan.

New pipes were laid across the road last week. Rather than use asphalt or concrete to fill the wide channels now crossing the roads in an "L" shape, the Chinese workers filled them with sand and tamped it down. As it rains and rains and rains today, the sand turns to mud and the channels transform into gaping, water-filled, squishy trenches.

A bicycle rider approaches the channels and goes down on the far side of the intersection. A couple of seconds later, a mother and son crash in the same spot. Neither knew what was waiting for them. Mark and I cannot help ourselves. We are soon doubled over in hysterics. Now, it is a spectator sport. In all, more than two dozen bike riders are waylaid in the treacherous intersection and six vehicles get stuck. The crunch of car chassis' scraping bottom. The *kerplunk* of bikes and riders as they tumble down. It is music to our sadistic ears. Tears flow down our cheeks. We should know this is mean and wrong, but it is so damn funny. We can't tear our eyes away.

A taxi driver thinks he can make it and guns it angled across the gap. Not. The front end of his cab slams down to the frame. He unsuccessfully tries to power his way through and slices his back right tire. With the rear shredded, he backs up and then drives into the middle of the trench. His car wedges hard at a painful angle. He changes the ruined tire spinning in the air and begins jacking up his car on each side and stuffing bricks under the tires. Thirty minutes later, he succeeds and limps back the way he came. Not less than five seconds later while he is still in reverse pulling back, another car passes him and crashes into the same spot.

One lady crashes particularly hard and does not get up, her damaged bike covering her. Others pull the bike off of her. She eventually rises and does not appear injured. In fact, no one seems to get seriously hurt. One person limps and another guy must have lost his balls, but they all eventually peddle away. The best bike crash is awarded to the smart lady who decides to let go. All of the others hold onto their handlebars and slam down hard. This lady releases her grip as her front tire begins dropping into the channel and flies in a graceful arc over the handlebars more than five feet past the trench before smashing down onto the pavement. If bike crashing were an Olympic sport, she would qualify for the National Team.

A cab with four semester-at-sea foreign students gets stuck on the near side of the intersection. We head out onto the balcony for a better view. This is by now a banner afternoon. Three Americans and a Turk crawl out of the cab. We strike up a conversation. They are in Beijing for five days. One of them shouts up, "This is the last place I'd ever expect to find Americans. What are you doing here?" After sitting in the trunk of the stuck, half-sunk car, pushing, and even letting one of the Americans drive, they give up the fight. The driver comes inside, and the students join us upstairs. One of them begins filming with his video camera. A busload of Chinese arrives. A large group of Chinese men lift the two cars then blocking the road and get them out of the way.

No one, including the drivers, seems to be upset. The Chinese are fatalistically good-natured about it all. While the six of us watch stuck cabs, stupid construction, and crashing bikes, the Turk turns and asks if this is typical of Chinese life.

"YES!" Mark and I shout simultaneously. This is China today.

CHAPTER 30

SHANGHAI RENDEZVOUS

"**W**HERE IS BETH?**" Shanghai is a big place to search.

After arriving in the city and securing a dorm room at the Pujiang Hotel, I spend much of the morning visiting the major hotels looking for my love. She is not at the Peace, Huaqiao (Overseas Chinese), Park or Shanghai Mansions. I waited at the Peace Hotel for an hour. Did she forget about the time change and show up fifteen minutes after I left? I kick myself. I should've waited a little longer. I left notes for her at both the Peace and Huaqiao Hotels. Where can she be?

Shanghai shocks me. My Sony mini-speakers and shortwave radio are displayed for sale in a store window. Local shops carry bottles of Coke and Pepsi and Nescafe that I have seen only at foreigners-only Friendship Stores elsewhere. The architecture on my walkabout today is predominantly early twentieth-century European. The streets themselves are narrower than the wide, cosmopolitan thoroughfares of Beijing. English is more common here. And the numbers of people are astonishing. The bike lanes along the sides of the roads transform into dense pedestrian sidewalks. Yet, but for the occasional crush of large buses and smaller minibuses, the roads themselves are generally quiet.

With no Beth in sight, I run into Dietrich, a German backpacker I met on the train down from Beijing. Since we are both alone and wandering, we hook up for the rest of the day. We visit the Shanghai Library. We climb a pedestrian overpass to witness the bedlam of a Sunday in Shanghai. The entire population must be out today. All the while, my stomach is in knots. The hours tick by.

As the sun sets, I head back alone to the Shanghai Train Station. I am out of options. Beth does not know where I have a room, and I have no way to contact her if she did not discover one of my notes. Maybe she caught a later train. I buy a *jin* of my favorite *chashaorou,* roast pork, and a can of coke and sit on a wall watching the exiting passengers as I eat. I scan each face in the crowd. This is the only door. If she is here, she will have to go by me.

Having long finished my dinner and when I am about to give up and return to my dorm room, a vision walks into the darkness. A mountain lifts from my chest. She sees me. Two young faces light the night. I jump off the wall, and we run into each other's arms and kiss, not concerned that the Chinese frown on public displays of affection.

The remainder of our time is spent together. I do not get to introduce Beth to Dietrich because like so many encounters here, he melted away after our day canvassing part of the city, likely never to be seen again. Beth and I talk about our respective trips to Xingtai and Hong Kong. We discover a street vendor selling heavenly *guotie,* fried dumplings. We stride hand-in-hand along the Bund, the former center of European Shanghai. For all the people, Shanghai has a small city atmosphere. Dietrich called it "profile," a character through its architecture. This developed Shanghai stops with the Bund at the west side of the Huangpu River. Looking east across the water and over the commercial boat traffic, the skyline is sky. The land appears to be mostly farmland.

Beth and I amble down to the old Chinese City, a Chinatown in the middle of a Chinese city in China. This is a holdover from when foreign nations sectioned up Shanghai for their International Settlements during the late nineteenth and early twentieth centuries. We enter the Shanghai

Foreign Language Bookstore. Something calls to me, and deep in a used book section on the second floor, I find a half-century-old, English translation of Lin Yutang's *Moment in Peking*. The fragile book has a faded red cover and yellowed pages, and I could not be happier to add it to my library.

Later, we meet an old man on the street near a stamp vendor. He approaches gingerly, sizes us up, and confides that he has a stamp collection back at his house.

"Would you like to see my stamps? Many are quite old," he says with pride.

Beth's eyes gleam. The collector in her sees an extraordinary opportunity. *How did this man save stamps through the Cultural Revolution? His collection must be amazing.*

"We would love to," says Beth excitedly without hesitation.

"Um." I clear my throat and look Beth's way. "I am not so sure." *What's the catch? Why would he be so friendly and offering to strangers?* Beth sees opportunity; I feel suspicion.

"What? Andrew, why not?" Beth looks at me stunned and questioning. "This will be fantastic."

"What do we know about this guy?" I whisper to her. "It could be a scam."

Beth stares at me. I can see that she does not believe that this is happening. She wants to plead her case, but she has seen this show before. My uptight, reactive, defensive self has taken over. I brook no argument.

"No, we should not go." I shake as I say this. My nerves are jumbled, and my fight or flight instinct has crashed onto flight. Beth wilts and tells the man that we cannot go with him. He looks sad and walks slowly away. Beth is distraught.

—⁂—

A few days on, I sit alone on Train No. 120 from Hangzhou to Beijing with a lot of time to think about my action. Beth got lucky when passing through Shanghai and moved up to a hard sleeper berth for the bulk of the twenty-seven-hour trip. I remain in hard seat. It is appropriate. I know Beth is disappointed that we did not go to see the old man's stamps. She is probably angry as well, and who would blame her? She wanted to go and had no say in the decision because of me. Why did I get irrationally nervous and shut down the possibility? There was no good reason not to take advantage of such an opportunity.

As I ponder my continued failings, and close in on twenty-four hours on this board bench, the tight quarters and strain of multiple, confusing and heavy dialects of my constantly changing companions are overwhelming. I have a window seat at the beginning of the car at the first table. In addition to three of us on either side of the table, three other people sit on top of the table, and there is one person under the table. The guy underneath presses against my legs. The only solace, such that it is, is that this ride is nowhere near the level of the horror of my trip with Alex from Xi'an to Chengdu.

I doze overnight, but do not sleep. People keep coming and going, the lights are on round the clock, and the car gets steamy at each stop and cold in between. The night is constant activity with haggling and steady quarrels and fights for seats and people asking me the same questions over and over. I finally retreat into myself and focus on finishing *Thunder Out of China* until the morning arrives. I look up at the geezer sitting on the table, practically in my lap. While eating, I found a piece of his chewed meat and rice on my jacket. My stomach turns now when he gobs from four feet up. *Please don't sway. Please don't sway.* I will the train to stay true as gravity grabs his ancient spittle. I close my eyes and force myself to be grateful that I even have a seat.

CHAPTER 31

QUESTIONING THE FUTURE

BEIJING. EARLY SPRING. We are late. Again. I guess we did not learn from our first trip down this road. The later Beth becomes, the more worried we are. I have a bad feeling this time. The tight, tangled knot deep in my gut grows heavier each day.

Beth and I talk about money, jobs, life, getting help. I'm scared. Beth is scared. My parents are due to visit the end of next week. I cannot get the Beatles out of my head: "Now my life has changed in oh so many ways...."

The unknown is agonizing. We spend one night crying in each other's arms, shaking with fear. We hold onto each other because we may have nothing else to cling to. We are alone. A negative pregnancy test at the Haidian Hospital the next day does not relieve the tension because, let's be honest, Chinese hospitals are, well, Chinese hospitals.

We try to banish disquieting thoughts by hitting the roads. We are on a roll. We've biked downtown to visit Beth's relatives (we need money); to CITIC (to eat); to the Overseas Chinese School, *Huaqiao Buxiao* (Beth's old school to visit friends); to the Shangri-La Hotel (to snack); and the Lido (to bowl and shop). These are long excursions in good weather and bad, into and out of biting head winds bringing stinging dust from the Gobi Desert. We return grimy and parched, exhausted and sodden.

It is easier to distract ourselves while burning calories and feasting on juicy Hunan chicken sautéed in a sumptuous brown sauce with hot peppers, bamboo, and water chestnuts, and glistening spinach conpoy (dried scallops) in an egg white sauce over Southern Chinese broccoli. Lentil soup, salad, and a potato generously stuffed with pork and chicken is comfort food to us. Cheesecake washed down with iced tea and soda and juice can always make one forget one's troubles, even if ever so briefly.

Meanwhile, the uncertainty persists. At times I weigh what the weather is trying to tell us. Take Saturday for example. We bike down to Jingshan Coal Park north of the Forbidden City for a picnic on a brilliant spring morning. Sanlihe Road breathes with colorful flowers, green trees, and an allure unbeknownst to the usually dusty metropolis. Thousands of roses grace the landscape. Beijing is beautiful. This is a sentence rarely on the lips. Later, however, as we return to Beida, the sky turns black, the temperature plummets, and a fierce gale blows away the brilliant spring day. Our short-sleeve shirts and light vests are no match for the tempest. Beth and I arrive winded and battered at the Friendship Hotel as it stops raining. After a short rest, we ride back the final leg to campus in bright sunshine.

We each manifest our frustration in our own way. Usually mild-mannered Beth gets into a fight with a vendor at the Zhongguancun bus stop when he overcharges her on a watermelon. Beth turns to the crowd (there's always a crowd in China) and complains that the guy is ripping her off. If she were native Chinese, they would have supported her. But she isn't. The vendor insults her and all Overseas Chinese as stupid pains-in-the-asses. Beth descends to my level and tells him to fuck off in Chinese, twice in fact, and storms off with the melon.

How does this rumpus over a piece of fruit at a bus stop fit into the historical precedent of foreign-native interaction in China? We attend a lecture given by the eminent Chinese history professor, Jonathon Spence. Professor Spence uses the context of creative writing to eloquently share with us how, where, and to what extent foreigners have dealt with China over the centuries as a nation, as a people, as a part of world history. The 1987 Zhongguancun Melon Incident is most assuredly at the lowbrow end of this long, storied spectrum.

I in turn break character and get into debates with my teachers over the bullshit we hear in class. In the grand socialist realism tradition, we keep reading of the selfless efforts of a worker/peasant/common person (take your pick) to dedicate his or her all for the benefit of the people, the country, and the glorious future of the Party. *Yay. Rah. Go team.* We are indoctrinated that "Marriage Centers must try to change the misguided thoughts of people in order to have correct thoughts and lead a proper life." *Do it my way or die.* The rote recitation of manipulated reality makes me want to puke. Teacher Zhang looks me in the eye at one point and tells me in an honest monotone, "You Americans certainly have a different attitude, and we Chinese must look at the criticism to see how to improve our texts for students." I want to slap back at this banal chaff. I want to release my pent-up dissatisfaction. I want to sound like other than a juvenile. But I do not. I cannot. I continue to be hamstrung by my linguistic chains and stew in silence.

The dichotomies of Chinese society are clear and strengthening. On the train back from Shanghai, two of my tablemates did not purchase the 1.50 Yuan (fifteen U.S. cents) boxed lunch because it was too expensive. The thirty-something aerospace engineer I chatted with shared that he secretly listens to Voice of America on his radio because it "gives me a broader picture on life."

And then there are the cab drivers. The other night we could not get a taxi to the Fragrant Hills Hotel Restaurant for dinner with Sam and his parents. Why? Because none of the six cabs idling in front of Shao Yuan would take us. You see, we wanted to go northwest, away from the city center. They wanted to go south toward their homes and the ends of their shifts. We beg each driver. We force the taxi manager stationed at Shao Yuan to call one up from the Friendship Hotel. During all of this time, the manager and six cab drivers sit on the stoop of Building 3 and watch us flutter in the wind. Sam's mom believes that the drivers are merely flexing their muscles since they now have a little independence. Maybe she's right. They can now make more money, and they do have a bit more control of their lives, but still they spite themselves by not taking the opportunity when it requires a little effort.

I discuss these frustrations with Teacher Guo. My relationship with her is different than with my other teachers. She opens up and even relates that she is not happy with aspects of traditional Chinese culture. "If one person races ahead, the masses chastise him—he should wait for them. If a person falls way behind, the masses wait for him to catch up. This is why China has developed so slowly." I tried recently to express my thoughts on the changes and lack of changes I see in modern Chinese society in an essay. The grip of ancient Chinese thinking—about family customs, about male-female relationships, about children—persist in my opinion in part because the large majority of the *laobaixing*, the Old Hundred Names, the common people, are afraid of change, of Western society. Outside of a minority of young city people, the thinking of the masses is locked in the past. But we need to learn from our past history if we want to improve the present and the future.

My essay is superficial. My thoughts are expressed in overly simplistic terms and phrases. I am thinking in English, not in Chinese. It is a hump I cannot seem to overcome. The helplessness in the face of the complexity of the language and the enigma of the thought processes that underpin it are captured in my inability to sound like a college student. I attached a note at the end apologizing for the generality and promising to write more on the topic next time. In a further demonstration of my pseudo-literacy, I forgot the characters for "general" and "topic" and had to write them in pinyin. In correcting my essay, Teacher Guo used such elegant vocabulary and phrases to express what I was attempting to say. It is not that what I wrote was wrong so much as it was weak. This only adds to my feelings of inadequacy with the recognition that my prose remains the murmurings of a man-toddler. After further more poignant edits on a subsequent assignment, Teacher Guo gives me a glimmer of hope with a personal Chinese note at the end: "To be a modern Chinese person, one has a duty to analyze traditional Chinese customs and bring forth the good ones in order to improve society." Teacher Zhang said something similar as a communist functionary. I believe Teacher Guo.

Her encouraging thoughts are not the only thing that is welcome. A few mornings later, Beth comes back from the bathroom radiating relief. She is not pregnant. That night as we watch a videotape of the movie, *Amadeus*, thanks to Sam, Beth and I hold hands listening to Mozart's melodies, our anxious hearts quiet for now.

CHAPTER 32

CAMPING ON THE GREAT WALL

THE SKY DARKENS. Thunder rumbles in the distance, the low base thrum echoing off the horseshoe-shaped walls of Shao Yuan. Peter and I have planned an overnight trip to the Great Wall tomorrow. If this is an omen, it is not a good one. Clouds shimmer with flashes of lightning. Thunder claps merge into a continuous pounding, getting closer and closer. The heavens open up.

Staring out my window at the torrent, I hope the weather is better for my parents. They are in China, making their way north to Beijing. I find myself looking forward to their visit. I want to show them some of my favorite places after their tour ends. This anticipation strikes me. I did not expect this feeling. Hopefully, mom and I will not clash too much, or at all, when reunited. I will need more patience than I have traditionally shown, especially when with their tour group. Mom likes to introduce everyone to each other with backstory and relationship detail. Doing so must be comforting to her, but it is generally more than I need to hear or care to wade through.

According to her aerogramme, their trip began well. She was delighted when they arrived at the Peninsula Hotel in Hong Kong. They were greeted with fresh fruit, flowers, chocolate, and smiles. Dinner their first full day was live shrimp soaked and quick steamed in wine, Peking duck, a whole fish, sweet-and-sour pork, fried rice, steamed rice, Chinese greens, dim sum, mango pudding, birds nest in coconut milk, and jasmine tea. Five people serve them breakfast, with china on silver service. It sounds like they are getting real royal treatment.

Attendants take their clothes to the laundry, replenish the room every time they leave, open the door, handle the elevator, bring the newspaper, fill water bottles, change towels and linens, clean without end, and arrange for any needs, no matter how strange. I asked them to bring me popcorn, which turns out to be scarce in the Crown Colony. A young man who sold them two rosewood chairs located some, and a white uniformed hotel page went out to pick it up so mom and dad can bring it to their eldest child (who wants to share it with his horny North Korean friend who has developed a taste for it).

As I reread her aerogramme, the downpour ends as quickly as it began, and our part of Beijing already looks brighter and smells sweeter.

—◌◌◌—

Camping on the Great Wall of China is prohibited. Yeah, but this is China. Peter and I ride the train to Badaling early on the morning of May 16, arriving at 10:00 a.m. on a sunny, blustery day. I lose my sunglasses getting on the train at Qing Hua Yuan. One minute, I have them. The next, they are gone. Mounting the wall, we head northeast towards Manchuria. We climb up and down, and up and up, and up some more. It is a wondrous hike, a labor of love and a journey away. We eat a picnic lunch on a particularly steep set of concrete stairs within the quiet North China wilderness.

The village of Badaling has dropped away far behind. We pass the last workers installing metal handrails and are, for China, alone. The isolated Chinese person keeps showing up though, intruding on our solitude, and it is only later that we discover an earthen path leading up the side of the mountain from the country road paralleling this part of the wall. Wide open expanses or not, it is fundamentally difficult to be completely alone in China.

After several exhilarating, arduous hours, we arrive at a restored guard house far from the tourist masses and decide to make camp. A shoddy wooden ladder leads up to a square opening in the middle of the ceiling above. Peter and I scramble up to the second level and store our sleeping bags and knapsacks. We want to leave the ladder up high so that no one can reach our bags, but we still need to be able to get back up later. A heavy wire lies anchored on the second level. After I climb down, Peter brings up the ladder, drapes the wire over the edge of the hole in the ceiling, and uses it to lower himself down. Only someone fit will be able to grab the cable and haul himself up to get the ladder and our stuff. I am not such a person. Peter is. I wish I had that type of upper arm strength and fortitude.

We continue hiking along the unrestored ruins until it becomes too treacherous. The timeworn vestiges of this mighty wall rise and fall off into the distance, past the horizon. A light Mongolian breeze brushes us as we crunch back down over broken rocks, stones, and loose sand. Returning to our campsite, we meet a group of kids who have used the path to get on the wall. The oldest is maybe fourteen, although they insist they are eighteen. We share some of their *guazi*, melon seeds, before going our separate ways.

Standing in our concrete loft (because Peter stretched up to the wire and climbed through the air to reach the stored ladder for me), I look out to see black clouds roll in, bringing thunder and lightning. Anyone left on this section of wall scampers to get down and away. The window holes in the watchtower are open and the wind howls. A chill descends, but we are well protected. Civilized China is to our south. The former barbarian lands lie to the north. The Great Wall of China looks majestic against the backdrop of threatening weather.

Yet, the afternoon drags a little after that. You can only stare at majesty, awesome though it may be, for so long. Trapped by the storm, neither Peter nor I are great conversationalists. We play cards for a long while.

A book would have been a good thing to pack. I add this to my mental to-do list for the next time I illegally camp on the Great Wall of China.

After eating a picnic dinner of ham, sourdough bread, hard-boiled eggs, cookies, candy, bananas, apples, and water, we decide to venture down the locals' path and along the road towards Badaling to explore. Clear, bright sunshine has returned. The wall is empty as far as the eye can see. We have beaten the crowds. We are, for once, completely alone in China. I again feel a sense of connection to old China. I need to work at keeping this flame alive when the other China intrudes.

Peter and I soon realize, though not until after we descend the path and begin the hike along the road, that the sunshine was an illusion. We were in the eye of the storm and are exposed when a furious deluge of cold, wind-whipped rain plunges from the sky. My poncho stays dry tucked safely in my knapsack back on the wall. We are drenched in a heartbeat. Arriving at a deserted Badaling dripping like sodden rats, we grab temporary shelter under the front overhang of the ticket office building.

"Good evening. Do you need help?" The Mandarin voice comes from the ether and scares the daylights out of us. Peter and I lurch away from the building, spinning around in startled confusion.

An old man stares at us from behind the milky window of the ticket office. He asks again if he can help us. By now convinced that he is real and not a ghost, we nod yes, and he invites us in.

This is how we meet Peng, the grandfatherly, overnight security guard at Badaling. Normally, I would question what could possibly happen after hours that would require an on-site security man. However, the fact that we are here and speaking with him answers the question. As we drip dry on his concrete floor, Peng offers to go into the closed restaurant next door to get us a beer and a coke. We gratefully accept. Peng tells us that he has six children and many grandchildren and that this job allows him to get out of the house. The tourists are gone, the bustle of a busy family is removed, and he can think. Even Chinese people need alone time. In the darkness of this part of China, Peter and I and Peng enjoy a quiet evening.

We do not want to tell Peng that we are spending the night (it is after all against regulations), so we tell him that our driver is coming back to get us down the road a ways at 9:00 p.m. We leave a bit before then to make it look good. The rain has stopped, but our clothes are still waterlogged, and it is cold. We make it safely back up to the wall and our watchtower. Once the rain passes, so too do the clouds. Thousands of brilliant, tiny specks of light twinkle in the jet-black sky. The landscape falls away, and the night is utterly silent. The effect is tremendously peaceful and not a little terrifying. I am glad for Peter's company. I wrap myself in my warm sleeping bag and even the cement floor is comfortable.

Awaking the next morning musty and chilled, I stroll outside onto the narrow veranda of our renovated imperial campsite. Peter sleeps. I wanted to see the sun rise from the Great Wall of China, but I slept through it. Standing here before a clear blue sky and the muted stirrings of a new day, I see a shadowy Qin Dynasty peasant conscript laboring to build his emperor's northern defense barrier. I see a ghostly Ming Dynasty border warrior standing guard duty for his emperor against the threat of a barbarian attack. I see an emaciated mid-twentieth-century peasant scavenging bricks during his emperor's tumultuous 1960s. I am a young Massachusetts man halfway around the globe, content for another moment in China.

CHAPTER 33

MOM AND DAD VISIT

THREE DAYS LATER, Mom and Dad arrive in Beijing. More than seven months after we said goodbye, I bicycle down to the swanky Shangri-La Hotel to see them. I give them each a hug. My mom captures our reunion in her journal: "Andrew arrived - it's Great!" My father and I have both lost a lot of weight. He looks good, having shed forty pounds before the trip. I am still down at a buck forty after my bout with dengue fever.

I immediately become an adopted member of their tour group. Mom does her introductions. Their first stop is the Great Wall at Badaling. This is my fourth trip and, I cannot believe I am saying this, hopefully the last. There is nothing left for me to see at this particular location. Heck, I camped here less than a week ago! A new restored section at Mutianyu has recently opened. I would like to get out there. Today, though, I join my parents as we head a little way up the left side in bright sunshine. I regale them with my previous adventures. I show them my wall. The hike is steep and mom and dad aren't up to going too far or too fast. The allotted hour is soon gone, but they seem happy and excited to be here.

Lunch is at the ubiquitous foreigner's restaurant located near each tourist site. As I shovel plate loads of standard Chinese banquet faire into my mouth, most of the twenty-two tour members pick lightly at the mounds of food arrayed before us. They have eaten similar feasts repeat-edly for the past two weeks. They may be at saturation, but after so long on a tight budget, I am not. The Lazy Susan swings by with bountiful plates of fried noodles, braised beef, chicken with cashews, sautéed cab-bage. My bottomless, little bowl of white rice raised near my chin, my chopsticks pick this and that and more this and more that. Of the ten people at our table, I eat as much as the rest of them combined, and even then, we barely scratch the surface.

When the tour bus pulls into the Ming Tombs, I am not only pleas-antly stuffed, but also in no need to re-enter the underground palace or walk the Sacred Way. I break from the group and head alone down a cir-cular cement walkway running around the mountain. Arriving back at the bus early, I strike up a conversation with the driver. He likes the perks of his job—FEC tips and access to foreigner-only stores, but he is not a fan of the two-currency system. "The development of socialist countries like the USSR, China, and Romania is stunted by having two currencies. I am not sure if China will ever shake off her backwardness at this rate. We need to modernize." I did not expect a socio-political conversation, let alone a forward-thinking one, with a bus driver. Here is another young Chinese, like Teacher Guo, who seems sincere in discussing China's short-comings and developmental challenges.

I am with the group when they visit the Mao Zedong Memorial Hall, Tiananmen Square, and the Forbidden City. Theirs is a whirlwind experience of the major Beijing area tourist sites. As a Western group, we are whisked to the front of the gigantic line waiting to see the Great Helmsman. This preferential treatment makes me uncomfortable. One of our guides confides that she too thinks the waxy body in the open sar-cophagus is a fake. Exiting back into the sunshine with no time to spare, I take my folks to the Monument to the People's Heroes and tell them about Peter and Kate's wedding. An honor guard of red-kerchiefed middle school students holding flowers stands proudly at attention commemo-rating those who've fallen in the name of the revolution.

Luxury touring is the life. Dim sum at the Jianguo Hotel. Spicy fried noodles at the Chinese restaurant in the CITIC building. A formal dinner at Maxims for which I finally wear the suit and dress shoes I toted all the way to China. And best of all, dinner at La Brasserie, the Shangri-La's French restaurant. I do like being pampered. I base myself at the sweet Shangri-La Hotel as my home-away-from-campus. My parents' room is clean, plush, and oh-so comfortable. One evening, Beth and I snuggle and make out while my parents attend a birthday celebration. Room service wheels in dinner, I sign my dad's name, and the tour company picks up the tab. No *mafan.*

These last few days have been an ego boost. The tour members treat me like a resident-expert. My conversations with the Chinese guides are substantive. At times, I almost feel like I am thinking in Chinese. Could it be possible? I am comfortable, and for once I enjoy being the center of attention and answering questions. My mother notices this and more, and I am left to consider that she might actually be aware of some of the tumult with which I live:

> *It is fun for us to hear [Andrew] chatting in Chinese and to hear his dialogue with people. He speaks Chinese very ably, though he denies it. When he and Beth are together, they lapse into Chinese without thinking. Their insights into China and the life of the people are different than ours. Andrew is ready to come home...he's a bit jaded now, and not always gracious to the Chinese. He feels he must protect his interests at all times and makes it a point not to be taken advantage of by cabbies, clerks, etc. People are enterprising and fiercely competitive for money. Neither he nor Beth shares our feelings that the average Chinese is very poor. Their opinion is that while the Chinese earn little, things cost pennies for them, and their union ensures them multiple benefits re: housing, transportation, food and medical care. I feel the people have a long way to go, and I can't see how they can stay content for long once Western fever really hits.*

After their tour ends, my parents stay on in Beijing for several days. I show them some of my favorite haunts—the Lama Temple at Yonghegong, the arts and antique district at Liulichang, Beida, the Alley—sites that are not standard on the foreign tour itineraries. The three of us get along well. My annoying habits lurk in the background, but I have not lost my patience with mom. Beth still sees these tendencies and has told me on more than one occasion recently that I'd better reign myself in and cut out the worry over the smallest thing or else. She is particularly miffed when I rush her. I am mostly successful in this during my parents' visit.

When we explore campus, the grounds are lush, all green, and glistening with water droplets after a morning rain. I am once again in awe as to how a little water transforms my surroundings. We begin at the new Cervantes statue nestled in the woods north of Shao Yuan. The City of Madrid presented this to the university last fall. We walk around Weiminghu, still the Lake with No Name, past the library and the giant Mao statue out front, and down the main road. My mother, the nurse, is not impressed with the campus hospital.

Since mom and dad missed their tour's trip to the Summer Palace, we jump on a double bus with the accordion center for the short ride. After seeing the crowded highlights, we break away from the throng and head up the steep path through the middle forest to the top of Longevity Hill. It involves lots of sweat, but the view from the top out over the Temple and Kunming Lake towards Beijing proper is worth the effort. I am glad that they can experience these parts of Beijing that so many foreigners miss.

The day turns warm. We're hot, and dad labors with the exertion. We stop partway down, and my father does something that puts a smile on my face. While I dab my forehead, he pulls out a bag of balloons. I knew he had them because he and I blew up several to give to their tour mates when they left. I did not realize he was also using them for other purposes. As I watch, he blows up a solitary red balloon, ties off the end, and leans over to offer it with two hands to a little Chinese girl standing nearby with her parents. While the girl's mom and dad look on with smiles of their own, their daughter reaches out with a sparkle in her eyes, takes hold of the gift, and says "*Xiexie, Aiyi, Shushu.*" "Thank you, Auntie and Uncle." The balloon is bright and cheery. It matches the color of her dress. My father has found such a simple way to communicate across a deep language barrier. It does not involve words or characters or complex thoughts. It is straightforward and effective. I hope the little girl remembers the foreign couple that gave her a bright red balloon long into her future.

There is so much I want to show my parents, but there isn't enough time. On the way to Zhongguancun market near campus, we walk past the Uighur men from far west Xinjiang Province who operate mobile food carts selling grilled lamb skewers. Customers bustle as usual, bicycle bells tinkle in cadence, and the wafting smoke from the vendors' efforts carries all the exotic spices of their seasoning. I relish that aroma and do not often pass by without stopping for a snack.

I take mom and dad on another bus ride. We are hunting for a simple, white, Chinese cotton shirt for my grandfather. Somebody told him that they are the best cotton shirts anywhere. We find a nearby shirt factory, but they are sold out. On a cab ride downtown to visit the commercial hub at Wangfujing Street, my mother is thrilled that our taxi driver is a woman:

It is great fun to hear Andrew speak with the Chinese. Our cab-driver was a lady! She was delighted that Andrew could speak, couldn't believe he was our son and didn't believe my age. Funny, many Chinese women have commented on my age, or call me pretty. Chinese women age quickly with their hard lives. She was thirty-one, looked forty-one, and has a five-year-old daughter. When asked why there aren't more female cabbies, she said it isn't seemly for a woman to drive. She has to pay eighty-four kuai (yuan) per day for her cab rental, but can work as long as she wants. She said more than twelve hours in a row makes her sick. She makes ten kuai/kilometer and can keep what she makes over her rental. She pays for gasoline and prefers payment in FEC because it is worth more to her than kuai. She can only buy in the Friendship Store with FEC. She was delightful and spontaneous. Not like many of the independent cabbies who won't take you where you want to go because it isn't far enough, or they won't get a fare back, or they don't feel like it....Andrew's frustration with China's lethargy shows up when he deals with cabbies!

My attitudes toward society are apparently clear. It seems that mom does understand me more than I give her credit for. I am not sure how I should feel about this.

—m—

The visit with my folks is at its end. They are returning to America. Most of me is staying here. Our room at Shao Yuan is a wreck, and I am a mess as I frantically pack to give them several bags to bring home for me. I spend their last night with them at the Shangri-La, a few more hours of luxury before they leave.

A dense fog blankets the hotel as we depart early the next morning for Capital Airport. I sit in the cab glad that each of us has had a good time and feeling satisfied about where our relationship stands. I still feel awkward hugging and saying "I love you" and all that mushy stuff, but who knows where things will go.

I wave goodbye at passport control as mom and dad head down the jetway, beginning their odyssey back home.

CHAPTER 34

LEAVING BEIJING

THE COUNTDOWN TO the end of the school year has begun. This means that the end of our time in China, the end of Beth and I living together as one, draws closer. Amidst the tumult of packing and shipping box upon box back to the States, there is disruption. We both feel it. I am uneasy, like when traveling with no definitive plans, but on a grander scale. Where do we go from here? What awaits us back in the real world? Everything we do takes on new import because it may be the last of this and the last of that.

One bright Sunday afternoon, after being cooped up by morning rain, Beth and I grab our bicycles and head to the Zizhuyuan, the Purple Bamboo Park. I cannot believe we have not been here before. This expansive park is the type of place where one inhales a deep breath and instantly relaxes, the weight of life and the surrounding urban jungle disappearing even if only for a short time. It would be a great place to practice *qigong*, if I had not long been negligent in such practice. The air is fresh. Trees are in full bloom. Young couples row quietly across the main lake through open channels cleared of thick colonies of glistening lily pads. Other couples, including us, walk arm-in-arm and hand-in-hand along lush, secluded paths. Will this be my last visit to a Chinese park?

One week later, on a sweltering summer day, Beth and I bike to Wutasi, the Five Pagoda Temple, a small complex hidden in a surprisingly rural section of the city a stone's throw north of the zoo. When my folks and I tried to get here during their visit, the cab bogged down in the mud, and we never realized how close we were. The dilapidated gardens are under renovation. Broken and toppled statues and steles lie scattered. Scrub growth in the rear courtyard strangles what must have once been elaborate carved animals, turtles, and scrolls. A horse has no ear. A ram no face. A beast no front legs. One of the two lions guarding the entrance is being repaired by several workers who look like they are crafting with plaster and papier-mâché.

The temple itself is small and distinctively un-Chinese in design. A dark corridor leads around the inside of the square building, which has four Buddhas set in alcoves along the inner core, one per side. Five pagodas (hence the name) rise from the flat roof to the sky. Along the outside of the individual pagodas and tiered in multi-levels up the outer walls of the temple are hundreds, no, thousands of carved Buddhas, attendants, fruit trees, elephants, horses, and many other animals. They are worn, but not destroyed. Wutasi is peaceful in the hot sun. I get a thrill discovering a new piece of history off the beaten path. It feels so intimate. Will this be my last visit to a Buddhist temple?

Sweat oozes out of us on the ride back to campus. The sun and suffocating heat beat us without mercy. Sneaking our bikes through the side entrance of the Friendship Hotel compound, Beth and I stop for a dunk in its enormous fifty-meter swimming pool. The bottom of the pool is coated in a gross green slime. We keep our heads above the refreshingly cold water and try not to look down.

—⁂—

Exam days creep closer. The packing intensifies, and the clutter in our room gets to us again. Beth and I steal away to Yuanmingyuan after class on Tuesday. This remains my favorite escape. Intoxicating weather, no crowds, and history that soaks into your skin. Like the Five Pagoda Temple, it is so close, yet so far away. Today we discover a large lake in a location new to us. Walkways ring the shore; bridges span a number of canals; and a causeway leads out to a central island. The lake shimmers with the intricate simplicity and harmony that at one time spread throughout this imperial garden. Will this be my last visit to the Old Summer Palace?

The next day, we head to the Alley to change money, and I spy a blue-white porcelain snuff bottle with hints of reddish-brown sitting on a table. The bottom is marked, *"Daqing Daoguang Nianzhi."* This translates as "Made during the Qing Dynasty for the Emperor Daoguang (1821-1850)." This is an imperial mark, the stamp of quality and provenance. It is a fake. Even I can tell that. And this little piece of art violates my personal rule about buying bottles without either a stopper or spoon. Still. I cannot walk away. But I also have no stomach or skill at hard-nose negotiation. Beth steps in and works her magic. Back and forth, cajoling, sighing. A head shake, a hand flip. I get antsy just watching. Beth is good. She is better than good. She prevails. As we walk away triumphant, I clutch the tiny vase-shaped bottle showing a man leading three camels out of the vast desert into a welcoming oasis behind a high city wall. Will this be my last snuff bottle purchase?

Life in China has been smooth of late. Our trips to the International Post Office have been hassle free. The clerks have been pleasant. Shops have accepted the White Card Billy left me so that we can pay for most things at the state subsidized price. Even the cab we recently caught from the Friendship Store to the U.S. Embassy and back to Beida to escape sudden rains went without a hitch. The cabbie beguiled us with his travels and stories. He made us laugh. I want to accept when things go well, not fret that the other shoe must be about to drop. More importantly, I want to accept when things do not go well, or at least to deal with them better. Is it possible to live in China without *mafan*? Is it possible for me to live without non-stop internal angst?

—⚏—

Exam days are here. All I care about is passing. A general academic apathy settled over me early on that I, the good student, could never shake. Thus, once exams are over, I expect relief, a sense of completion if nothing else. But I do not. I do not feel anything. I cannot even say that it is anticlimactic. It just is. I attend a meeting of the foreign-exchange students who recently sat for the *Hanyu Shuiping Ceshi,* Chinese Language Proficiency Test. This was a comprehensive test covering listening comprehension, grammar, Chinese written characters, reading comprehension, and more. I scored a middling 106/170, but it shows improvement. I am more confident in sitting down to take the test than the nervous wreck who blanked on everything during the diagnostic tests at the beginning of the year. I know more what I know and more what I do not.

My time as a student in China is over, and a significant question remains: Have I learned, grown from this experience? If knowing one's weaknesses is growth, then I have. If growth, however, is facing one's issues head on and attacking them, striving to improve and break free of their limitations and negativity, then not so much. My proclivity is to get defensive, to bury, to run. I did not make the full effort. Is it hubris, or a cop out, to say that I can sort-of understand now how the Chinese who are battered day in and day out, year after year, become less and less angry and more and more resigned? Chinese society is ostensibly trying to change; it's all the rage to allow public criticism to appear. Articles have critical topics. A previously censored movie was shown last night. But for all the "criticism," everything still ends up sounding socialist rosy. And there is no doubt as to who is in charge. A cabbie told me that *"Zhongguoren bu pa sile."* "Chinese people are not afraid to die." If that is the case, why try? Or might there be another interpretation?

I've been eating a lot and still losing weight. I have a cold. I am run-down. The smooth patch before exams has naturally (in my life anyway) transitioned to the opposite end of the spectrum. I've been sweaty, sticky, and hot for days. I am not a good companion. Again. Echoing my feelings, the weather turns. A blackness slides over Shao Yuan Lou, and a squall whips up. Trees sway. Dust swirls. People flee the front courtyard. Thunder claps, and lightning splashes the black day in an eerie shadow of light. Yet off to the east I can see clear sky. The rain begins quietly, yet in a complete sheet, bouncing and swaying like a dancer. The road is instantly submerged. I am fascinated by the display and sit, part of the time with a sullen Beth, transfixed by what is going on outside our open window. I feel a tingling inside. I cannot tell if it is meteorological or emotional. The whole sky is now an even, dark grey. The rain slackens. The wind still blows, lightning still flashes, and thunder continues to rumble.

—⁂—

We are done here. It is time to settle up and leave Beijing. The North Korean diagonally across the hall gives me six 3-D postcards of Pyongyang scenes. Zhou, my sex-seeking, North Korean friend, gives me Korean dried fish. I was unfortunately never able to get him his magazines. I leave him my floor mat. My trusty bicycle, my first significant purchase in China, is with Beth's relatives.

Gaoshan comes by with a scroll his father painted for my parents. With all the hubbub since we returned from Xingtai, I have not seen him much. I look at his father's calligraphy. It is elegant with cultured black strokes mounted on silk with a cream-colored border. We give him a bottle of imported Japanese Suntory Royal whiskey for his father to thank him for his generosity. It is not American, but it is foreign.

Gaoshan has a request. "Andrew, would you sell me your camera?" He is still on the Chinese prowl, and it comes across so innocently that he catches me off guard. I wish he had not asked. I decline because I need it. He offers me an old, crappy camera to tide me over.

I decline.

"Would you trade me FEC so that I can buy my father a present?"

I am bothered by his requests. I shouldn't be, but I am. His asking is natural. He grasps at opportunities. Why do I get upset by this? Am I any different? Shouldn't I instead commend his gumption? He and his family have been nothing but generous toward me. I have so much. He is seeking to get ahead. I am leaving. He is not. I get defensive, though, trying to ferret out the angle. This is so much more about me than him.

I do agree to change the money and give him a discount. It is awkward because I make it awkward. And what happens? As usual, once he leaves, I feel deflated and embarrassed at my thoughts, my actions. This was not the proper way to end our relationship. Beth and I decide to give Gaoshan the last box of chocolates. It is a token, but it is what we have. We rush over to his place and present this gift to him. A few final moments of conversation, and we take our leave. We feel better, I feel less the fool, and I sense that Gaoshan is relieved too. After close to a year in Beijing, we have closure.

CHAPTER 35

HEADING SOUTH

THE PORT CITY of Qingdao faces the Yellow Sea in Eastern Shandong Province. Reminders of its German occupation at the turn of the twentieth century are written in the architecture. Solid stone, brick, and masonry buildings fill the lower reaches of the historic city. Red-clay, tiled hip roofs stretch as far as the eye can see. Towers thrust into the sky. It is not a classic Chinese city. A European train station stands sentinel with a looming clock tower. Twin spires on a Romanesque Catholic church climb toward the clouds. Elsewhere, another imposing former church has been commandeered by the Public Security Bureau.

Beth and I are looking for peace, for things to go our way, as we travel south towards the border crossing into Hong Kong. An auto rickshaw couple helps us with our four overstuffed bags when we first arrive and head off hotel hunting. Foggy mornings give way to cooler days that are a break from the oven that was Beijing. I take a deep breath. The Chinese flock to the No. 1 Bathing Beach and play in the waters of Huiquan Bay. The native pagoda and pavilions in Xiaoyushan, Little Fish Hill Park, contrast with the German vista dotting the landscape down to the shore. The curved sands of the beach give way to rocky crags farther up the coast. And. We receive word that a room is waiting for us at the end of the rainbow in HK. It is a private apartment, and the owners have offered to pick us up at the train station. Overall, not a bad start.

Graceful faces of well-aged Chinese glance our way as we roam the side streets of the old town. We bump into the friendly auto rickshaw couple and again express our gratitude for their efforts when we emerged from the jostling crowds at the train station straining under the weight of our luggage. While devouring mouthwatering *bing*, fried round cakes filled with meat, vegetables, and onions, hot and fresh from the vendor's cart, we look up and a medieval castle beckons. We have to investigate.

Located in the *Badaguan* section of Qingdao, a serene area of immense German, Japanese, and Russian mansions along tree-lined streets hidden by high protective walls, Huashi Lou is now a dilapidated hulk of a structure that yet exudes a strong charm. The door is open. Model wooden boats fill the dens. Early twentieth-century switches, chandeliers, and furniture are a snapshot of another time. Padded staircases lead to haunted-house hallways. An antique billiard table on the third floor sits waiting for someone, anyone, to play. The building appears to be deserted. Feeling like Fred and Daphne trying to solve a mystery with Scooby-Doo, I half expect to find hidden eyes staring at us from paintings and secret passageways. It's too spooky. We retreat.

―∿―

We have one problem. Our money is almost gone, and we need train tickets for our continuing journey. We serendipitously bump into friends from Beida who are staying at a rental house in *Badaguan*. They not only let us shower at their place and help us find accommodations in Shanghai, but one of them loans us 150 *renminbi* to get us there. Now for tickets. Arriving at the train station at 6:30 a.m. Monday as directed, the girl behind the glass wall tells us that the Shanghai tickets are sold out. "You should have been here when the window opened at 5:00 a.m. Come back at 3:00 p.m. this afternoon." I could recount our efforts to explain our situation, to seek assistance, to accomplish our simple goal. But, really, what would be the point? We leave the train station with no tickets.

It is early, and we now have eight hours to kill. I propose a day trip to the Daoist Mountain *Laoshan* to Beth. She looks at me with a significant amount of disinterest and tells me she would rather hang out near the hotel and rest. I want to go. I cajole. I push the prospect of fresh air, scenery, and native philosophy. I promise her that it will be fun. Beth grudgingly agrees to go, and we buy our tickets.

The trip I envision will be relaxing, a chance to replenish composure and experience harmony at a sacred site, an opportunity for Beth and me to keep sharing as our time together comes to an end. Alas, promise can be fleeting. The bus is full of petulant Chinese crammed in every nook and cranny. We are the only foreigners. The ride into the mountains is long and slow and anything but peaceful. The Chinese fight over seats. They bicker about the pettiest little thing. Their capacity to be obstinate is epic. The close air is redolent with their shrill whining.

Beth and I are trapped in this lunacy, and the petulance is contagious.

"Andrew, this has got to be the most boring thing we have done yet. Why did you make me come?" Beth scowls and sits rigid next to me on the crowded seat.

"I did not make you come. I asked you to come. I did not expect it to be like this." This comes out more strident than I intend because I am more than a little defensive. I did in fact make her come. I wouldn't listen when she suggested we take a rest day.

"You are always making us go to this, go to that, all the time." The tenor of her voice rises. She is about ready to explode. "Why can't we rest and stay put. I'm tired and don't want to be here." She spits out this last part. The accusation is heavy. The look I am getting would shrivel flowers.

I am embarrassed. And frustrated. The tension is suffocating. We are at each other most of the day. Eventually, I suggest a compromise. "How about if we occasionally split up and do our own thing? I also promise to rest more and not try to see so much." Arms crossed, a deep frown on her beautiful face, she agrees with my suggestion. But, for now, we are trapped.

The day slogs on, the several stops each more forgetful than the last. The *coup de grace* is lunch at a dive high in the mountains, a bad meal made horrifying when I realize what I have eaten. The script on the hand-written menu board on the wall is hard to read. I am uptight to begin with, my lack of patience not helping my Chinese comprehension. I recognize the character for pig and order it. I like pork. I eat my pork. In my giddiness at recognizing something on the menu, I missed the next character. *Xin*. Heart. A basic word. A meaning I know. It is all I can do not to gag.

Many hours later, the bus eventually, mercifully, returns to Qingdao.

At 3:00 p.m. we return to the train station and stand in a long, long line. A Chinese line. Beth radiates displeasure. People keep cutting in as usual. One more guy cuts rights in front of us, and I finally lose it. "Fuck you."

In what must have been his only English, he responds, "OK."

Another guy tries to cut in. I've had it and block him. "Go line up like the rest of us."

He pulls out a piece of paper and waves it in my face. "I have reserved tickets, see."

"It's because of people like you, using *guanxi,* that I cannot buy any tickets to leave here. I don't care if you have reservations, you are not cutting in." I actually feel the blood vessels straining in my forehead.

He doesn't leave, but I must look really angry because he waits for us to go ahead before cutting into the line behind us. When we finally make it to the window, the shift has changed, and the new clerk tells us, "There are no tickets."

Dumbfounded, we complain to another clerk.

"Where are you staying?"

"We're staying at the *blah blah* hotel. Why?"

"You have to buy tickets through CITS (China International Travel Service) at your hotel."

What! Foreigners cannot buy berths at the Qingdao Rail Station?

Arguing gets us nowhere. When we return to the hotel, the ticket desk is closed for the day.

It is the end of a long, deeply unsatisfying, failure of a day.

—⟋⟋⟍—

I wake early the next day and head alone to the CITS office at the *Huiquan* Hotel to try once again to get tickets out of here. After a forty-five-minute wait, I succeed in scoring tickets. Not just any tickets, mind you. But the most expensive soft sleeper tickets, complete with a service charge. They are costly, but what choice do we have? We are *guanxi*-less.

I walk up to our friends' rental to tell them the good news and see how they are faring. They also had trouble getting tickets, but they found a way into the system. They got *guanxi*. After waiting to buy boat tickets, they were told that the line began forming at 3:00 a.m. and tickets were no longer available. A friend of theirs at the station directed them to a friend of his and that friend of the friend disappeared upstairs. Shortly, he came back with a note authorizing three boat tickets. Returning to the same ticket girl who not fifteen minutes before had said there were no tickets, the note was handed over, and the girl gave them the tickets. The backdoor system is infuriating when you are on the outside looking in.

Shortly after leaving *Badaguan* on my walk back to the hotel, the heavens open up. Too stubborn to turn back, I keep going. I wait under one tree and then scramble down to another tree. The rain intensifies. I am soon sopping wet. I come upon an open vegetable and meat stand and cower under its makeshift cloth roof. One of the proprietors loans me a windbreaker to throw over my shivering shoulders. I stand on two rocks just above the muddy torrent flowing downhill. The truck from their *danwei*, work unit, arrives thirty-five minutes later to bring them back. They offer to give me a lift, and I gratefully climb into the cab for a ride back to the hotel. As I squish and seep into our room, Beth orders me to strip.

As so often happens, after the deluge, the sun comes out. Beth and I decide to spend our last afternoon at the beach. The sand at the No. 1 Bathing Beach isn't the smoothest or the cleanest, but it is a decent beach. An assortment of odd looking, outdated Chinese bathing suits, rafts, and inner tubes are for rent. Bath huts sit on the sand. The water is shallow and cold, though not as cold as Nauset Beach in Orleans. Out about two hundred feet from shore we are still only waist deep. When we enter the water, the Chinese move away from us, giving us wide berth. Amidst the crowds, we have all of this open water to play in. And play we do—spinning each other, racing after one another, jumping, making noise, splashing. We rent large inner tubes and make a ruckus (well, I make the ruckus and Beth laughs). We link up and float lazily in Huiquan Bay. We speak of the future.

—∞—

Qingdao to Shanghai. Shanghai to Guangzhou. When we finally found an office in Shanghai that would sell us train tickets to Guangzhou, the former Canton that is our jumping-off point for Hong Kong, they naturally were first-class, soft-sleeper tickets. The ticket agent said that these were all that were available. I called him a liar in so many words (which he was), and he got huffy. I quickly apologized for fear that he would not sell us anything. This reality of the PRC is unreal. But I shouldn't complain. He did us a favor. The exorbitant soft sleeper from Shanghai turned out to be more than twenty-four hours of air conditioned bliss while the scorching ninety-degree Southern China heat reflected off our sealed windows and baked the hard sleeper cars. I sat comfortably watching the mountains, the trees, and kilometers upon kilometers of cultivated rice paddies flow by in green splendor.

—∞—

After 309 days, today is the day. My last full day in China. It is apropos that we face one more day of *mafan*. The bad now outweighs the good. We are overcharged for train tickets to Hong Kong. Walking under the elevated highway being constructed above *Renmin Lu*, the People's Road, Beth and I get splattered with mud from cabs and bikes on the ground and dust and grime from above. We go to the Friendship Store to change money for our room and discover that my White Card is not accepted here in Southern China. After arguing with the salesgirl and her manager, I wave the former off with a nasty "*suanle*," "forget it," and storm away. Still seething, we line up to purchase a root beer and a package of my favorite White Rabbit candy in the downstairs supermarket. Same deal. I am shaking and come up to and cross the line. "*Nimen shi zhentamade zaogao!*" "You are all very fucked up!" Oops. I just yelled that in Chinese in a Chinese store in China. Now might be an appropriate time to get out, of the store and the country. There is a strong possibility that I have worn out my welcome.

CHAPTER 36

CHINA IN THE REARVIEW MIRROR

As THE TRAIN crosses the Hong Kong border at Lowu, I am scared. This is not the same fear I felt when first arriving in China alone. No. This is the fear of escaping Communist China. I sound as melodramatic as a Taiwanese television show, but I picture a hole opening in an unseen net that has totally ensnared and threatened us. We dive through and are free.

Do the Chinese feel suffocated like this? What would happen if the net lifted for them as well? As it is, each time there is a small tear, a possible opening, the Communist Party sews it up quickly and brutally. There used to be so much—culture, power, position, world stature. Now, it's gone. I've no doubts as to China's future—decades of stagnation await a country in her position of social, personal, and political degradation. Economics will change, maybe increase, become respectable. But money isn't everything for modernization to be successful. I hope that sometime during the change the suffering will climax in a positive social revolution that will encompass all aspects of Chinese society.

Why am I still interested? I have spent a great deal of time these last many months pondering this question. There is the analytical answer. The language is intricate and intriguing. The study of what China once was

271

is fascinating. Then there is the root answer. I find that many aspects of Chinese culture feel comfortable and right to me. The culture is in my blood. But this connection with China, the draw of my inner thread, does not necessarily mean returning to the source. The train chugs south into the British Colony waiting to welcome us, and I know I am content for now to keep following my path from afar.

—〰—

Hong Kong is once again sheer delight, freedom. That quickly, we are beyond the net, on the outside. This time it is for good. Beth and I each take a deep, cleansing breath. A quick phone call upon arrival in Kowloon and we are met by a refined Mr. Lin. We taxi back to his flat in Causeway Bay. He has four rooms to rent on the third floor of a building above a Daimaru Department Store. There are three movie theaters in sight, food, accessories, everything HK has to offer. Our room is small, yet clean and comfortable. It has the same type of thin, wall-mounted air conditioner we saw at the Shanghai Museum. There is a bathroom with shower across the hall. Mr. Lin, who obviously likes having Chinese-speaking guests, comes in a few times to chat.

Beth and I soon set out. Holding hands. In a number of days, less than a handful, Beth will leave. I will follow a day later. We pushed this impending reality aside as we made our way south from Beijing. Now there is no denying it. We stay close as we eat McDonalds for an early dinner and Kentucky Fried Chicken for a late night snack. We relax shoulder-to-shoulder for three-and-a-half air-conditioned hours watching *Gone With the Wind*. We walk the streets and together revel in what to us is an open society.

—〰—

We now confront a new type of fear—the fear of being separated. I see it in Beth's eyes. She reads it in mine. There is not much more than can be said. Our lives have been one in this intense, surreal setting. Beth made China bearable. She made me bearable. I hope I have done the same for her. What will it be like to not see her every day, to not be an integral piece of her daily life? I am not sure how I will cope with the three hundred miles that will separate us in America.

Taking Beth to the airport is crushing. A lump the size of my heart, I think it must be my heart, pounds mercilessly in my throat. I struggle to keep it together on the subway to Kai Tak Airport and then while we walk linked into the terminal. Beth is leaving. Right now. We kiss goodbye.

We share one long, last hug. Our mutual teardrops caress each other. Beth walks through the gate, and a part of me vanishes.

—✕—

I turn back and head downtown. I entered Asia alone, and I will leave Asia alone. I eat two solitary meals. I do not like eating by myself in restaurants. I am anonymous, yet self-conscious. I return from a screening of *A Little Shop of Horrors* to a seemingly different room. The stark emptiness is haunting. I finish reading *20,000 Leagues Under the Sea*. I wander weepingly around Tsimshatsui. I will have to relearn how to live on my own. I will have to see if I can do better in the future.

I pull out one of the last things Beth and I picked up together and stare at it. A T-shirt. A simple piece of cheap, white Chinese cloth. I involuntarily purse my lips, give a little snort, and bob my head with the wry appreciation of the initiated. On the front screams a crowded scene of the Great Wall: lazy workers, money changers, shoddy quality, a bus jammed with people punching and kicking, and a Party official quoting outdated policy. Arching over this madness, in English, it reads:

"I Survived China."

2009

I SHIVER ALONG THE shore of frozen Weiminghu, Beida's Lake with No Name. An old man practices *tai chi* on a stone dock. His rhythmic movements slice gracefully through the biting December winds. My path at long last has led me back to China. As I continue my walk around the lake, I begin to feel strange. I cannot get enough air into my lungs. My heart catches. My throat tightens. In the blink of an eye, heavy tears well up. I make my way to a waterside bench and drop down. Through a nervous fog, I know that I have sat on this bench before.

I need to gather myself. If he were here, my current *qigong* teacher would repeat his mantras: "Remember to breathe." "Take long, slow, deep breaths." "Empty your mind." "Remember to breathe." "Take long, slow, deep breaths." "Empty your mind." Good advice, but easier said than done with racing thoughts and a heaving chest gasping in frigid North China air.

These overpowering sensations leave me unsure and on edge. *What is my shen, my spirit, trying to tell me?* To say that I was disillusioned when I left China more than twenty-two years ago is an evocative understatement. Today, it feels right that I finally returned. *Am I any more capable of processing my emotions now than I was then? Have I grown beyond immature reactions to a complex existence?* Cocooned in wintry silence,

I am nonetheless deafened by the pounding of my heart, my blood, my body. *What did my being here mean?*

I force myself up and walk in a stupor south towards what should be my old dorm building, Shao Yuan Lou, the Spoon Garden Building, the foreign student enclave where I lived, studied, and loved. I am good with directions. This morning, though, I am turned all about. As with Beijing in general, Beida has expanded and morphed into something vaguely familiar, yet virtually unrecognizable. No longer located in a smaller sub-urban-like district far removed from the downtown urban scene, Beijing University is today hemmed in by high-rises and cityscape.

The campus is dotted with new buildings. Centennial Lecture Hall, an imposing, modernist structure, sits on the old center of the former campus proper, roughly where the post office and notice/news wall were located. The subtle, glass-lobbied Museum of Peking University nestles near the once-secluded Cervantes statue. I stand there for several minutes, the words to "The Impossible Dream" running through my head, and slowly turn in a silent circle, my frozen breath tracing an arc in the air. The weather is bright and sunny. No clouds and no pollution.

Crossing a now active roadway network winding through campus and dodging cars, bicycles, and pedestrians, I finally approach my old dorm. With a start I see a gigantic, three-story, glass and concrete twenty-first-century building, the Wa Luo Li Lou, the Edificio Valori, rising in place of the multiple tennis courts, stacked end on end, where I twisted my ankle and wound up without a "factory" in the Beida Hospital. I face Shao Yuan 2, the central building directly across the street, where I lived. The large, red characters for "spoon" and "garden" still hang prominently above the main entrance. This front courtyard is where my original qigong teacher, Li, practiced his sword-slashing, lurching, drunken *wushu*. I look up at the window of my former room. Shao Yuan was the center of my China universe. It was home.

The lobby guard ignores me as I enter and head straight for the third floor. Moments later, I stand in the dark corridor outside Room 2-323. I am transported through the closed door to what was then my life. It was there, a few feet away, that I spent the early days waging war on cockroaches. It was there where I worked with my Chinese friend, Gaoshan, on his English. It was there where I eventually drove my staid roommate, Toshiro, nuts with my relationship with Beth. Behind this door, I was stuck like an acupuncture pincushion; I partied with friends; I made love to my best friend. There was joy and sorrow and the seeds of growing. I think about knocking, but do not.

For the first time in many years, I think back to what became of Beth and me. Not every fairy tale has a happily ever after. We moved in together in an apartment building across from the National Zoo in Washington, DC after we graduated college. I got a job working the nightshift at a hotel while I waited for security clearances to come through on a government translation job. It should have been wonderful, a fantastic resumption of the life we began together in China. But there was tension. We were the two China friends and lovers, but the world around us, the inputs we received and responded to, were completely different. The perfect match did not, or could not, meld here as it did there. In truth, the stress had been building during our year apart, and only a few months into our one-year lease, Beth moved out.

A humming in the deserted hallway brings me back to the present, and I notice two mini-refrigerators outside my old room. I now also notice that boxes and assorted personal items are piled outside the doors of many other rooms. Visions of Toshiro and his Japanese compatriots come flooding back. Some things never change. I cannot remember if the North Koreans also stored their boxes this way. Probably not. They had so little.

I make my way out of Shao Yuan, and my mind drifts back to the regrets I have about my time in China. I do not mean my flashes of temper and occasional callous treatment of others, though these are related and strong and are a part of me that I battle to this day. No, I think of those opportunities that I wish I had taken when I had the chance. I wish I had pushed myself to attend regular Chinese classes with Chinese students. I wish I had put in the time to read and understand the posters and notices hung around campus during the student demonstrations. I wish I had agreed with Beth to visit the old man's house in Shanghai to see his stamp collection. Ah, the hindsight to realize that opportunities not taken are opportunities lost.

What I learned then about myself and about China was eye opening. Seeing myself stripped of all social and emotional human pretense was more than simply unsettling; it was downright alarming. The twenty-year-old me could not see the forest through the trees. I was unrooted, ripped from the security blanket of my early life. I fought to control my emotional and physical existence in a foreign environment. I was not prepared for facing my insecurities about the most minor of things, my nervous tics, my ability to drive those closest to me crazy. I was not prepared for the trauma of the comings and goings of friends, pregnancy scares, and guilt over actions taken and not. I was more than challenged by an intricate language, a complex culture, and a bizarre political and social ecosystem. There was more nightmare than I care to remember.

And what of China? China is a land of extremes. Everything in China has historically been big, outsized. The Great Wall. The Grand Canal. The Imperial System itself. So too the depths of its societal dysfunction. China had been in the throes of revolution and chaos since the Western interlopers first appeared in numbers off the Chinese coast in the early nineteenth century. The early growing pains of the 1980s, when I landed on her shores, were themselves full of extremes. There is no middle ground in the Middle Kingdom. The China I left was also struggling fitfully to find its place in the world. It was not then a China I wanted to return to.

With the passage of time, I realize the gift that this journey gave me. Besides following my passion for good and bad, I got to know myself. That is the lifelong takeaway. I am driven to seek the interesting and unknown, to take as many opportunities as possible, all the while appreciating that being in the right place at the right time never hurts. An integral part of this drive is the strong connection to China and Asia that pulses through me. At the same time, I know that I will rail and get anxious, that my blood pressure will redline, when things do not work out, when my vision goes awry, when the unexpected happens. I know it. This doesn't make it easier to deal with, but it is a start.

It is during these episodes that I try as best I can to "Remember to breathe." "Take long, slow, deep breaths." "Empty your mind."

And when this fails, as it frequently does, there is always Cheetah. My stuffed chimpanzee sits in an upstairs bedroom. Every now and then, I pick him up and hold him.

ACKNOWLEDGMENTS

I DEDICATE THIS MEMOIR to my parents, Elaine and Myer Singer, for allowing their first-born son to travel to the other side of the planet at a time before technology allowed frequent, and now instant, communication. It was a different, far less connected world, and they let me go explore it.

On Thanksgiving Day 2011, I traveled the short distance to my parents' house. My father called me downstairs and handed me a folder entitled, "Andrew in China." Opening the old manila cover I found my original acceptance letter from the Chinese Embassy in Washington, DC, the 1986 "Rules Governing Foreign Students in China," and receipts for all the money they wired me in Hong Kong. My parents kept every letter, card, and postcard I sent that they received (and there were some that we know never made it through). The rice-paper-thin Beida stationery crinkled to the touch as I scanned my statements home of long ago.

I offer sincerest thanks and gratitude to the members of the former Sands of Time Writing Group (Katrina Valenzuela, Anne Ierardi, Priscilla McCormick, Cynthia Neil, Dick Ottoway, and other memoirists who joined us) and to Debra Lawless, Arlene Kay, and Christine Merser, all of whom spent considerable time and effort reading and commenting on draft versions and selections of my manuscript and offering advice. I am grateful to the Cape Cod Writers Center and every person I have had the privilege to meet and work with there over the last ten years. And a special thank you to my editors, Cristina Schreil and Diane O'Connell, without whom the final manuscript would not be what it is or even in existence. The assistance of each of you has been instrumental in the long journey of crafting my story.

To the readers, thank you for spending time sharing in my life.

Finally, and most deservedly, I thank my family for their understanding when I frequently disappeared in full sight into my laptop and my journal, my photographs, and my old guidebooks—to my two boys, Adrian and Ethan, and to my wife of almost twenty-seven years, Fanny, a Chinese-Indonesian-American woman, who lost her valiant, eleven-year battle with breast cancer as *China Sings To Me* was going to print. I love you all.

ABOUT THE AUTHOR

ANDREW SINGER IS a traveler, history lover, and collector of books and Chinese snuff bottles who supports his family and interests working as a land use and environmental permitting lawyer on Cape Cod, Massachusetts. He has translated top secret documents professionally for the CIA somewhere near Washington, DC, driven across America on an epic road trip, skydived over Southeastern Massachusetts, and hiked the Salkantay Trail to Machu Picchu in Peru. He remains the only person (with no scientific evidence to back this up whatsoever) who has handled a zoning hearing for a client on Cape Cod in both Chinese and English.

To learn more about Andrew's travels and interests, please visit www.andrewsingerauthor.com and sign up for his mailing list and follow him on Facebook and Twitter (and other social media platforms that he will probably need to join).

CPSIA information can be obtained
at www.ICGtesting.com
Printed in the USA
BVHW08s0925110818
523889BV00001B/4/P